KU-766-489

Reading
Brokeback Mountain

ESSAYS ON THE
STORY AND THE FILM

Edited by Jim Stacy

McFarland & Company, Inc., Publishers
Jefferson, North Carolina, and London

LIBRARY OF CONGRESS CATALOGUING-IN-PUBLICATION DATA

Reading Brokeback Mountain : essays on the story and the film /
edited by Jim Stacy.
    p.   cm.
    Includes bibliographical references and index.

    ISBN-13: 978-0-7864-3044-4
    softcover : 50# alkaline paper ∞

    1. Brokeback Mountain (Motion picture)   2. Proulx, Annie.
Brokeback Mountain.   I. Stacy, James, 1936–
PN1997.2.B75R43   2007
813'.54 — dc22   2007022872

British Library cataloguing data are available

©2007 Jim Stacy. All rights reserved

No part of this book may be reproduced or transmitted in any form
or by any means, electronic or mechanical, including photocopying
or recording, or by any information storage and retrieval system,
without permission in writing from the publisher.

Cover photograph © 2007 Comstock

Manufactured in the United States of America

McFarland & Company, Inc., Publishers
  Box 611, Jefferson, North Carolina 28640
  www.mcfarlandpub.com

To my mother, Hazel Miriam Moss Stacy, whose death on March 14, 2005, left an open space between what I know and what I try to believe. *Brokeback Mountain* helped me both to grieve and to ground myself beyond that void.

Acknowledgments

I want to acknowledge the long-time support and friendship of my teacher Gresdna Doty and my colleague Jack Wann, whose professionalism and intellectual curiosity have set the standards for me in my own academic career. The three of us share the loss of our mutual friend and teacher Bill Harbin, another standard setter. The biggest fans of my writing, Charlotte Nordyke and Pam Smith, also merit my gratitude as do two other lifelong friends, Taylor Rock and Tom Rudolph — all great cheerleaders to have on one's side. Thanks also to my friend Johnny Peden for sharing a first viewing of *Brokeback Mountain* with me. A special thanks to Ginger Jones for ongoing nurturing.

I feel fortunate as well to have worked with intelligent, articulate, committed, responsive authors, who valued the collaborative process and welcomed reader feedback. Thanks, too, to our readers, whose insights and evaluations were invaluable both to our authors and to me: Brenda Allen, Professor of Communication Studies, University of Colorado at Denver; Gresdna Doty, Alumni Professor Emerita, Theatre, Louisiana State University; Roy Grundman, Assistant Professor of Film, Boston University; Valerie Holliday, Instructor of Film, Video Games Studies, Philosophy, and English, Baton Rouge Community College; Susan Kattwinkel, Associate Professor of Theatre History and Literature, College of Charleston; Rob Latham, Associate Professor of American Studies, English, and Sexuality Studies, The University of Iowa; Howard Miller, Associate Professor of Literacy Education, Mercy College; Scott Phillips, Associate Professor of Theatre, Auburn University; Marilyn Schultz, Assistant Professor of English, Delta State University; Jack Wann, Professor Emeritus of Theatre, Northwestern State University of Louisiana, and particularly, Annette Olsen-Fazi, Associate Professor of English and French, Texas A & M International University, for her support of this project.

A most sincere thank you to Annie Proulx for birthing Ennis del Mar and Jack Twist and to the film artists who brought them to life.

Finally, thanks to poet Dean Kostos for seeing the film six times as I did, for finding the words to express its visceral density, and for sharing it:

On Seeing Brokeback Mountain *for the Sixth Time*

by Dean Kostos

When Jack watches Ennis vanish
through his rearview mirror, that sphere

of disappearance becomes a tunnel, drawing
me back into the film.

Again the projector's beam
magnetizes dust into hands and mouths:

tongues taste tongues,
tasting the fractured crumbs

of words not spoken,
inhaled. Every cusp of red

nuance impels me like a fist pushing
living tissue through a sieve.

Perhaps the best that desire can offer
is to carve a phantom silhouette of the beloved —

outline of a murdered body.
But this crimson has no

consequence — flesh, act and lie
translated to ash.

Jack's bloody shirt no longer smells
of cigarettes, sweat, sweet hay;

even the ghost of scent has abandoned
Ennis. And as winds roil dust

past matchstick houses, searching
for codes lost

in the folds of remembering,
shirts embrace.

Table of Contents

Preface

Six blind sages were led to an elephant, a creature none of them had ever encountered. Each approached it from a different angle and made contact with a different part of the beast. One touched the side of the elephant and declared the animal to be like a wall. For other sages, touching the leg inspired the conclusion that the elephant was like a tree; the ear, like a fan; the tusk, like a spear; the tail, like a rope. The final sage, who touched the wriggling trunk, declared them all wrong: "The elephant is like a snake." Drawn from an Indian fable, this story has long been my favorite illustration of the role of perspective in perception.

Like the elephant in the fable, Annie Proulx's "Brokeback Mountain" and the movie it inspired are unassuming giants that cannot be fully perceived by a single touch. Like other literary and cinematic masterpieces, the prize-winning story and film invite multiple perspectives for critical analysis, even those that question how masterful the pieces really are or how the works have fallen short of someone else's expectations. The gay content throws the works into the middle of the social-political-cultural arena where the chief critical concern is polemics, not aesthetics: Did they get the message right? In this anthology, each author of our fifteen essays has found a path to explore the short story, the film, and/or the sociocultural phenomenon that followed the release of the movie in December 2005. In having two men (cowboys, at that) fall in lust and in love, the story spawned controversy and debate about many issues relevant to living itself, to living in service to traditional society, to living in the rural West, and to living with a same-sex preference. Answers of every ilk addressed whether the film can be viewed as a gay story, a gay love story, a gay lust story, or a universal love story, and whether Ennis and Jack should be labeled gay, queer, homosexual, heterosexual, or bisexual — or not labeled at all.

Moviegoers responded to the film in unpredictable ways. Some saw it as a groundbreaking, Zeitgeist event that would help reshape the nation's perception of homosexuality at a time when the issue of gay marriage had claimed significant political space. While anticipating a film that would move beyond the campy depiction of gays on network television (e.g., *Will and Grace, Queer Eye for the Straight Guy*), others saw it as a disappointing heteronormative cautionary tale, the all-too familiar "one dies, one lives" scenario of the past. Some gays were bored by the film; others wept. Many queer critics were angered by the low profile of "gay" in marketing the film and vexed by what they saw on screen. Some middle-aged and older heterosexual couples accepted the images of same-gender affection and sex (perhaps the first time they had seen a man kiss a man with such unbridled passion) and found themselves deeply moved. Others walked out as the kissing began. Some saw it as another sinful manifestation of the moral bankruptcy of Hollywood in service to a leftist agenda. Some women viewers saw it as one of their favorite "chick flicks," slang for action-light movies too emotional and too focused on character for the macho hubby. Some older homosexuals came unglued in recognizing their own lives in Ennis's and Jack's and recalling how much torment seethed in the closets of the '60s and '70s, particularly for rural gays.

For me personally, seeing the film and then reading the short story had a wrenching effect, one that possessed me for months. Now, I have been revitalized by my contact with *Brokeback Mountain* as written and as filmed. In processing its effect on me, I chose to think of the short story and the screenplay as complementary, as one story; critically one can make a good case against their being complementary, even for their being antipathetic. Feeling wiser now and better grounded, I believe the story and film helped me to complete the grieving process for my mother, to redeem the memory of a love long lost, and to find a new footing in the power of the written word and in a return to self. I had to write about *Brokeback* and my response to it. Surfing the Internet, I discovered in countless websites, blogs, and groups that thousands of other people had also had intense reactions, both positive and negative. By February 2006, the mania was in full swing; people wanted to communicate.

A call for academic papers drew submissions from scholars all over the world — Canada, Germany, Italy, Greece, Finland, Australia — and from twenty-one states in the U.S. A rich array of nearly sixty essays made several rounds to an editorial board of readers, and fifteen were finally chosen for inclusion. It was illuminating to read what several dozen writers had to say about Proulx's "Jack, I swear:...." or "There was some open space between what he knew and what he tried to believe, but nothing could be done about it, and if you can't fix it you've got to stand it." The spareness of Proulx's reverberating prose and the objectivity of Ang Lee's still filmic imagery seemed to invite diversity of response. The select bibliography at the end of the book demonstrates the expansive diversity of modern and postmodern perspectives that have served our authors, who draw from so many traditional academic disciplines to make their cases: American literature, communication studies, psychology, sociology, anthropology, geography, music, film studies, and philosophy as well as newer fields related to gender and sexuality.

The anthology begins with selections that take more traditional approaches, use classical or modern sources as primary critical groundings, and invoke philosophies that evolved in the mid-twentieth century. We move along to scholars whose perspectives have been heavily influenced by postmodernism and academic disciplines which brought independent status to newly developed criticisms in women's studies, gender studies, queer studies, sexuality studies, ethnic studies, and American studies. The focus then turns to essays that are primarily concerned with the film, its critical reception, its stars, its director, its soundtrack, and its cultural implications. (These essays do a great job of reporting on the critical honors and the controversies as well as the financial success of a movie which cost $13.9 million to make and has taken in over $83 million at U.S. theatres and $180 million worldwide.) Finally we end up with reflections from two authors who grew up in the 1950s as Ennis del Mar and Jack Twist did and who reflect on the lessons that can be learned from the film.

Reading our 58 essays on Brokeback Mountain, I think I now know the answers to all the questions in my mind about the story and film as well as to questions I had not thought of. Only one question remains unanswered: Why didn't they fish?

All references to the primary texts are taken from the combined collection Brokeback Mountain: *Story to Screenplay* (New York: Scribner, 2005). They will be indicated within the body of each essay as SS for the short story by Annie Proulx and SP for the screenplay by Larry McMurtry and Dianna Ossana, followed by the page number of reference. (Within the *Story to Screenplay* collection, each work begins with p. 1.) That collection also contains short essays by Proulx, McMurtry, and Ossana, which will be referenced in the notes.

1

Arcadia and the Passionate Shepherds of Brokeback Mountain

by Henry Alley

Both as a short story and film, *Brokeback Mountain* presents an alternative world to what Annie Proulx herself calls the "the destructive rural homophobia" of its American locales.[1] Of course there is Brokeback Mountain itself, where Jack Twist and Ennis del Mar can pursue their love and sexual desire for each other, but also we can find an idyllic refuge in the promised lands Jack envisions, as well as the additional Western landscapes Ang Lee, Larry McMurtry, and Diana Ossana add to their script. In fact, placing *Brokeback Mountain* in the context of a gay "Arcadia" can help to accentuate key differences between the story and film, between Proulx's heavily particularized naturalism and what McMurtry defines as "lyrical pastoralism" in Ang Lee's creation: "Since it is to the mountains that the two lovers go for their brief reunions, the landscape itself poeticizes their union."[2]

"Arcadia" is a term completely in accord with McMurtry's "lyrical pastoralism"; as defined by the Holman/Harmon *Handbook to Literature*, it is "the reputed home of pastoral poetry ... portrayed by pastoral poets as an ideal land of rural peace and contentment. *Arcadian* suggests rural withdrawal and simple happiness."[3] The mythic region, in relation to shepherds and a restful, charmed life, originally sprang from the Sicily of the *Idylls* of Theocritus, the Hellenistic Greek poet, and "the first great voice in the homoerotic pastoral tradition."[4] From the very start, the land was associated with gayness. As Gregory Woods writes in *A History of Gay Literature*, the idyllic world of Theocritus "is conducted in accordance with natural law. And everything includes love between men and boys."[5] Frontain adds that "Theocritus'

5

pastoral idylls figure the naturalness of homoerotic desire through nature itself."[6]

Virgil, Theocritus' Roman successor, reformulates the *Idylls* into his *Eclogues*, and it is in them that Arcadia emerges as a pastoral region that is not only homoerotically centered but also, according to Bruno Snell, more given to poets and visionaries.[7] In his article, "This Other Eden: Arcadia and the Homosexual Imagination," Byrne R. S. Fone tracks out a tradition from Virgil's celebrated Second Eclogue all the way through to Gore Vidal's *The City and the Pillar*. This Arcadia functions, Fone writes, as "a place where it is safe to be gay: where gay men can be free from the outlaw status society confers upon us, where homosexuality can be revealed and spoken of without reprisal, and where homosexual love can be consummated without concern for the punishment or scorn of the world."[8] He also mentions the aesthetic usefulness of this place as a means of making a non-explicit statement about gayness and as a way of launching the search for "the good and beautiful" and the "Ideal Friend."[9] Fone points out that this tradition runs deep through American literary tradition particularly in Whitman and his Calamus poems. When Proulx set forth to write her story of sexual desire between two men herding sheep in Wyoming, she was indeed launching into something quite uncharted in the genre of the Western. Of this event, McMurtry was, in fact, to say, "There the story was, all those years, waiting in patient distance for someone to write it."[10] On the other hand, however, the story had been already written, over and over again, in the landscape of Proulx's American literary forebears, as well as their ancestors who were writing in the homoerotic pastoral tradition that had not yet included two loving cowboys.[11]

Following out Fone's definition of the Arcadian experience, one does not have to look far to find "the outlaw status society confers upon us" in *Brokeback Mountain*. Death by tire iron is a horrifying end. With Ennis' launching of the anecdote of "these two old guys ranched together down home" (SS 14), a tale which foreshadows Jack's own gruesome demise, we have the outlining of "rural homophobia" from 1963 to 1983 in America. This picture also exposes the apparently more proper and certainly more frightening homophobes who, like Ennis's father, countenanced and/or participated in the bashing and then exposed their children to it as a moral lesson. Although neither Proulx nor McMurtry, Ossana, and Lee make an effort to allude to the changes in gay liberation over these two decades, no historically savvy spectator can witness the progress of Ennis and Jack's story without thinking about the growth of the Mattachine Society, the picketing of the White House, the rioting at Stonewall, the invasion of the American Psychiatric Association in San Francisco, and the ultimate removal of "homosexuality as an illness" from the APA's diagnostic manual within the same twenty-year period. The point, of course, is that while these sea changes occurred for fortunate gays in urban areas on either the West or East coasts, the sense of danger and threat remained constant in Ennis's and Jack's world. To an interviewer's question about whether the two protagonists could have survived in "a more urban or progressive setting," Lee answered, laughing, "Yeah if they'd moved out to San Francisco."[12]

A more subtle exploration of the "outlawing" of male-to-male relations occurs in the presentation of straight marriage in *Brokeback Mountain*. In speaking of "family and hearth" in the film, Stephen Hunter writes, "[T]hese venues are expressions of the impoverishment of the heterosexual family lifestyle. Ennis lives in a shabby apartment where he is regularly assailed by his doughy, clueless wife." He goes on to describe Jack's Lureen as a wife who "ages gracelessly into a chain-smoking harridan with big blond hair and bad teeth." [13] For Hunter, Jack Twist's family of origin is presented similarly — as "American Gothic."[14] While these impressions overstate the case, particularly in regard to a film whose actresses play their roles with remarkable subtlety and care, "the resistant world" is certainly prominent, summed up in Proulx's description of Ennis' post-child bedroom as one "full of the smell of old blood and milk and baby shit" (SS 9). Indeed throughout, the procreative world is at odds with the lovemaking that Ennis and Jack share. After her inflamed discussion with Ennis about condoms, Alma considers, "what you like to do don't make too many babies" (SS 16).

Arcadian Privacy: Insiders and Outsiders

The very nature of the Arcadia developed in the story and film is defined somewhat by those who exist outside it. In one of the masterstrokes of *Paradise Lost*, we do not get a full description of Eden until we enter into Satan's point of view. In similar fashion, very early on, Joe Aguirre watches Jack and Ennis' dalliance "through his 10×42 binoculars for ten minutes one day" (SS 7), later issuing the accusation, "you guys wasn't getting paid to leave the dogs baby-sit the sheep while you stemmed the rose" (SS 14) and refusing to hire Jack back. Here Joe becomes a kind of Satan, whose isolated nature and whose envy are clear — and whose complicity with rural homophobia casts a shadow across the Brokeback landscape and emphasizes its vulnerability. "Envy" does seem the right word and the right link to Satan, since if Joe were merely disgusted with the coupling, he would not have watched it for ten minutes and close-up at that. Like the arch-enemy of mankind, he cannot help lingering over what he has exiled himself from.

Similarly, Alma, in witnessing the reunion kiss and "looking out for a few seconds at Ennis's straining shoulders" (SS 10), immediately imposes the perspective of a jealous outsider, with a marked desire to retaliate. Although her feelings are understandable, she harbors her resentment and hurt until well after the divorce and her second marriage to Bill (Monroe in the film), as shown, ironically, at Thanksgiving and in her own kitchen, in her rehearsed detailing of her past detective work on Ennis' secret life. His ensuing abuse and rage show that he, as well as Jack, can participate in the homophobia that surrounds them. For a moment, Alma's phrase "Jack nasty" (SS 17) has become true for him.[15]

To answer what, in a positive sense, the Arcadia is for Jack and Ennis is to say that it above all lacks this exterior view; it is a place where, as Jack says, it is "Nobody's business but ours" (SS 7). In ruminating over what Joe Aguirre said to him, Jack says he fears "maybe somebody seen us that summer" (SS 13), as a means of articulating his dread but also of hiding, from his lover, what Joe more directly accused them of. The best plan for maintaining their sense of Arcadian privacy would be to head off future intruders while still remaining somewhat vague about the past shadow in the garden. After all, he does not want to scare the shyer Ennis off. In his chapter, "Arcadia: The Discovery of a Spiritual Landscape," Bruno Snell writes that this ideal world "is ruled by tender feeling."[16] He then adds, "[Virgil] allows no hope, not even any desire to do something about the suffering world, to lighten his sorrow and his despair."[17] Similarly for Jack Twist, the visionary of the story, certainly this ideal world would be free of all sorts of strife — domestic, political, spiritual — "if you and me had a little ranch together, little cow and calf operation, your horses, it'd be some sweet life" (SS 14). As Snell also points out, Arcadia would be a landscape delighting in the pathetic fallacy,[18] where nature is in accord with human feeling, including even sorrow and despair, as long as they are developed in the lovers themselves and not brought in by the world outside. Intensify by one more degree this sympathetic interchange between character and his surroundings, and we are in a world where gay lovemaking is natural, unlabeled, even if it sometimes brings pain and uncertainty to those involved. In Virgil's Second Eclogue, "the most famous poem on male love in Roman Literature,"[19] the unabashed premise is, "A shepherd, Corydon, burned with love for his master's favorite,/Handsome Alexis,"[20] with the couple becoming the great gay icon of love for millennia to come. It is also clear that Jack, in his desire to "twist" real life as he knows it, wants a sustained and protected place where he and Ennis can be sexually intimate and develop a life together, and where their agreed statement "I'm not no queer" (SS 7) still makes sense.

In a close examination of how the Arcadian life manifests itself for the two men, the story and the film, however, part company in very profound ways. The nature of gay lovemaking and of nature itself comes across quite differently in the two separate works. Consistent with the *Esquire* magazine tradition from which Proulx's fiction career bloomed,[21] her narrator is a hard-boiled one, and is frequently and sometimes greatly repelled by the stuff of human contact. Andrew Holleran has defined the style of the piece as "*faux-gruff*, stoic cowboy" sort, closely allied to the voice of Ennis himself.[22] We have, for example, not only the earlier reference to Ennis' bedroom smelling of "baby shit" but also the postcoital motel room stinking of "semen and smoke and sweat and whiskey, of old carpet and sour hay, saddle leather, shit and cheap soap" (SS 12). While the film shows the sexual encounter with softened faces and naked bodies in burnished light, in carefully posed closeness on the bed, the narrator in the story says, "Ennis lay spread-eagled, spent and wet, breathing deep, still half tumescent, Jack blowing forceful cigarette clouds like whale spouts" (SS 12).

Proulx's presentations of their sexual intimacy in nature are not any more grandiose or even attractive. "Ennis ran full-throttle on all roads whether fence mending or money spending, and he wanted none of it when Jack seized his left hand brought it to his erect cock" (SS 7). Later, the narrator sums up their unions — "One thing never changed: the brilliant charge of their infrequent couplings was darkened by the sense of time flying, never enough time, never enough" (SS 20). In speaking of creating sexual contact in fiction, novelist Edmund White has said, "I try to write sex scenes through character, by showing how the sexual experiences that I'm describing illustrated or come out of the character I'm dealing with."[23] Proulx's scenes, however, definitely do not follow this personal guideline for they are distinctly from the outside; they do not spring from one deep and clearly subjective point of view, but rather come from an exterior vantage. This approach seems troubling at first in a story whose design is to move us away from the attitude of critical observers like Alma and Joe Aguirre. The truth of the matter is, however, the hard-boiled narrator is put off by "the fecundity" of life in any of its forms, whether straight or gay, and will sometimes turn to being insinuating and even lewd when men and men, women and men, draw together — "[Ennis'] fingers [moved up] her ribs to the jelly breast, over the round belly and knee and up into the wet gap all the way to the north pole or the equator depending which way you thought you were sailing" (SS 9). Of Jack's outside exploits, the narrator observes, "[he] had been riding more than bulls, not rolling his own" (SS 13).

At one with Proulx's other forms of physicality, Arcadian sex in the story is, then, rushed, compensatory, and not necessarily sexy — it is, indeed, at one with the general messiness of life that her vision conveys. Proulx's idealistic Jack Twist coordinately envisions a domestic sphere quite distinct from the "high altitude fucks" (SS 21) of their mountain excursions, a sustaining of the summer memory of their leaning together by the fire, caught in "the moment of artless, charmed happiness in their separate and difficult lives" (SS 22). For Proulx, Arcadia for these men is more a product of the mind, more connected to fleeting vision than embodied in the natural settings of the Wyoming or "the infrequent couplings." Nature, being uncontainable, untrustworthy, and sometimes repellant, cannot supply an Arcadian manifestation of what Jack sees. The mountain of Brokeback is at best partly "broke," for in the short story text at least, even that first summer together was not charmed in any full sense. "But knowing Jack," Lureen says later, "it might be some pretend place where the bluebirds sing and there's a whiskey spring" (SS 23). This tragic lack of fruition, as accentuated by a receding dream, is also summed up by Jack's father, the man who blocks Ennis attempt to take Jack's ashes and perform his rite of personal apotheosis for his friend: "Then, this spring he's got another one's going a come up here with him and build a place and help run the ranch, some ranch neighbor a his from down in Texas. He's going a split up with his wife and come back here. So he says. But like most a Jack's ideas it never come to pass" (SS 25). For Proulx, Arcadia *would have* meant continued intimacy and gay marriage, as symbolized by the two shirts, one hanging within the other and consecrated by Ennis' own blood. The final note of the piece suggests *Romeo and Juliet* without the resolving speech from the Prince of Verona: "And if you can't fix it, you've got to stand it" (SS 28). Thus, for the story, the world of "rural homophobia" prevails, and Arcadia remains mostly a mindset briefly arrived at by Jack.

On Screen: The Discovery of the "Pure Place"

The film, however, changes, accentuates, idealizes, embodies. The Arcadia, both mental and actual, is transformed, perhaps without the cinematizers' full understanding of what they have done. To hear them say it, the writers of the script developed a direct translation of what the hard-boiled narrator saw. In an interview for the DVD version of the movie, Diana Ossana spoke of "The West ... [being] rich in character, in experience — it's ... real, gritty, raw — we like that — we like the reality of it."[24] In lumping the author and the screenplay writers together, James Schamus, one of the producers, said that "Larry McMurtry and Diana Ossana, and Annie Proulx are enormously dedicated to the idea of paying attention to the smallest piece of verisimilitude they can find to give the story the depth and the grain of reality that it needs."[25] Continuing this line of thought, Andrew Holleran, in his review for the *Gay and Lesbian Review*, writes, "The romance depicted in the first half-hour of *Brokeback Mountain* recalls the idylls of Theocritus — but here the shepherds' love erodes into the grim poverty, homophobia, and hardscrabble bleakness of life in the modern American West."[26] The film, however, is anything but consistently "hardscrabble" and grainy, and while it contains the frustrations of Jack's visions, it is not at all dedicated to the naturalistic reality of Proulx's story. To begin with, the major actors and actresses are quite beautiful. In his review for *Slate*, David Leavitt observes, "The big-eyed Jake Gyllenhaal is a far cry from Proulx's small, bucktoothed Jack Twist, just as the blond square-jawed Heath Ledger is nothing like her Ennis del Mar, 'scruffy and a little cave-chested.'"[27] Michael Rowell, writing for *Out Smart*, Houston's LGBT Magazine, exclaims, "Two cowboys falling in love — and not just any two cowboys, Heath Ledger and Jake Gyllenhaal — this is the stuff dreams are made of."[28] Combined with the breathtakingly idyllic natural landscapes, these somewhat larger-than-life-characters work to form a tale in what Northrup Frye would call the high-mimetic mode, as distinct from the low-mimetic, which includes "realistic fiction."[29]

Repeatedly in his interviews, Ang Lee, as distinct from McMurtry, Ossana, and Schamus, has made clear an attempt to transcend the down-home, stereotypical "cowboy": "The film is not a Western; it's a romantic love story."[30] He also names Jack in the film as "the all-American boy — dreamy and romantic, adventurous."[31] In many ways, this Jack fits the definition of what Frye maps out for the high mimetic hero of epic and tragedy: "He has authority, passions, and powers of expression far greater than ours, but what he does is subject to both social criticism and to the order of nature."[32]

That Lee is after epic or tragedy rather than realistic fiction is also asserted in his vision of the plot of *Brokeback Mountain,* which conforms to Frye's outline of the "general dialectic structure" of epic or what he would term "romance": "Characters tend to be either for or against the quest."[33] Coordinately, Lee in another interview has said, "I think great romance needs great obstacles and textures. Romance and love are abstract ideas, an illusion. How do you make that? I think, most of the time, obstacles help build the romance."[34] While some may balk at the idea that Jack has extraordinary powers of expression, his willingness to be "more adventurous"[35] than Ennis or than many of the rest of us helps to single him out.

Further, as suggested earlier, the film works painstakingly to illustrate the kind of life and lovemaking Jack and Ennis enjoy in the natural world. Of this Arcadian landscape, Jake Gyllenhaal has said, "Brokeback Mountain is that pure place you take someone that's free of judgment," and then, after speaking of the challenges of the external homophobia, has added, "I mean people's minds have been changed. That's amazing."[36] Lee, Ossana, and McMurtry have come, whether consciously or unconsciously, to posit a way of living, much realized on Brokeback or in other mountain landscapes, which is viable for the two men and which plays off of Jack's musings, which, in the

story, were seen as best feckless. One force, perhaps, behind this dramatic realization of a visionary life may be McMurtry's own stated lifelong admiration
for *Don Quixote*, "the first book I read that belonged indubitably to world literature."[37] As with the mission of the old knight, Jack's quest for a higher
world eventually captivates the audience and starts to imbue the narrative
itself.

Additionally, in the film, the director and the scenario writers carefully
build the growing intimacy between the two men so that at last a posed "better world" of family and "marriage" actually seems possible and even, in
another form, transferable. From the start, the filmmakers, in taking advantage of the larger canvas, develop much more psychological intimacy between
the protagonists before their first carnal moment together. The incident with
the bear is moved from 1983 back to 1963, so that Ennis and Jack can share
more in front of the fire as they are getting acquainted, with Jack acting as
tender nurse. "JACK removes the bandanna from around his neck, wads it
up, takes the whiskey from ENNIS, and pours some into the bandanna. Raises
the bandanna to ENNIS'S forehead" (SP 11). Lee's *AfterElton* interview discloses that through this homeward-returning-husband scene, Ennis and Jack
are, according to directions, deliberately mimicking a straight couple. "They
live together..." Lee said, laughing. "They're partners."[38] After this, we have
three more scenes where they sing, clown, laugh, and talk together. "Hell,"
Ennis says, "it's the most I've spoke in a year" (SP 15). These moments serve
as a bridge to the initially tender and ultimately violent sexual union in the
tent. By this point, however, the audience is responding to this reckless physical moment as something unusual, not because it is gay, but because it seems
out of keeping with their growing intimate concern for each other.

Totally nonexistent in the story is the second encounter, which is pre-
luded by glowing view of Ennis before the campfire, and characterized by a
decorum and tenderness consistent with Milton's vision of pre-fall sex in
Eden. "The next love scene I added," Lee has said, "because I wanted the characters to commit to each other. Ironically, they declare to each other that
they're not queer so they can put [the label] aside, and then commit to each
other and be tender, accepting, and sexy."[39] In the script, the scene reads:

JACK sits atop the bedroll, naked, his shirt draped over his lap. He looks up as
     Ennis enters.
ENNIS cautiously steps in. JACK raises his hand to him. ENNIS takes it.
     JACK, gentle, reassuring, takes ENNIS's face in his hands.
                                   JACK
                      It's all right ... It's all right.
JACK kisses him.
They lie back. Embrace. Kiss [SP 21].

Even more enlightening, however, are the softening changes which the finished film makes to the script. Actually, we start outside the tent, seeing Ennis work up his courage to go in, as though he were a frightened suitor. The scene then moves to Ennis lowering his body to meet a supine Jack, who, inside, is not naked but is more enticingly stripped to the waist. Very touchingly, Ennis is holding his hat in his hand (a close-up on the hat), before a bolder Jack takes him in an embrace.

In coordinate fashion, in the scene that follows, what Joe Aguirre sees through his binoculars is not the story's unceremonious coupling which requires "waiting until they'd buttoned up their jeans" (SS 7), but the idyllic "TWO MEN pulling off their clothes, out in the middle of nowhere ... play[ing], running, joking" 21). In the film, Joe's role as Satan is magnified by several degrees, since he is not witnessing lust but, as is true in the case of Milton's Adam and Eve, innocent happiness. He has a great deal more to envy as the demonic figure. His viewing of Ennis and Jack is much shorter here than in the story, but his pain, rather than disgust, is evident in Randy Quaid's performance, as indicated by his continuing to observe the two men with wounded curiosity, even after he has put the binoculars down. This event is a foreshadowing of their moment in 1967, where "the boys race to the cliff edge, taking off their clothes as they go. Jump off the cliff into the lake below" (SP 51). Stephen Hunter has called this "the happiest image in the film, and the most poignant" and sees the waters as "the great river of homosexuality, and safe and free immersion in it is utterly joyful to ... [Jack and Ennis]."[40] This idyll leads into a vision of the moon and, ultimately, the more realized development of the Arcadia Jack articulates in the story:

JACK
(earnest)

What if you and me had a little ranch together somewhere, little cow-and-calf operation, it'd be some sweet life. Hell, Lureen's old man, you bet he'd give me a downpayment if I'd get lost. Already more or less said it....

ENNIS
(tense now)

Told you, ain't going' to be that way.
JACK looks stricken [SP 52].

The Quest of the All-American Boy

We need to acknowledge, of course, that even in the film's Arcadian settings, there is much to disturb and discourage what Jack hopes for, as we hear in Ennis's "Told you, ain't going' to be that way." At an earlier point, back in 1963, the men allow their playfulness to disintegrate into an ugly, brawling dance of internalized homophobia, where in response to "JACK accidentally knee[ing] him in the nose," "ENNIS reflexively cold-cocks him hard in the jaw" (SP 26). In the later scene, Ennis is about to counter Jack's euphoric thoughts with the recollection of the gay older man who was bashed and murdered fifteen years earlier. However, as opposed to its counterpart in the story, Jack's Arcadia becomes a signal for the audience to be on the watch for other refuges, not only for him but for other characters as well. The sum effect of such mitigating "stops" along the cinematic path is to say that the ideal can be combined with the real, if only for a short time, as in the nude swimming, the bare-chested frolicking which Joe Aguirre observes, or the courtly lovemaking of their second encounter in the tent. What Jack wants is not so much a utopia as what Frederich von Schiller, one of the masters of the form, would call an idyll:

> Its character thus subsists in the complete reconciliation of *all opposition between actuality and the ideal* [emphasis his] which has supplied material for satirical and elegiac poetry and therewith ... all conflict in the feelings likewise. Calm would then be the predominant impression of such a poetic type, but calm of perfection, not of inertia: a calm that derives from the balance not the arresting of those powers that have spring from richness and not emptiness, and is accompanied by the feeling of an infinite capacity.[41]

In Proulx we get the stuff of "satirical and elegiac poetry"—for indeed Arcadia is consistently frustrated, but in the film, we are presented with landscapes which, while dominated by the harsher realm of workaday reality, still offer a combination of timeless beauty and dynamic sexual experience. Drawing on their times together, and perhaps imagining a combination, Jack proposes a ranch to Ennis rather than a fairyland. Toward the end of the cinematic version — that is, by 1978 — he suggests Texas. When Ennis roundly turns him down again, the Jack of the film tells him, "You want to live your miserable fuckin' life, go right ahead" (SP 72).

Based on hints in the story, the cinematic Jack Twist begins to change; he starts to diversify his quest and turn more defiant. Consistent with Fone's earlier definition, he comes to search more generally and more single-mindedly for the Ideal Friend. While the film has shown moments of breathtaking pastoral bliss for the two men, Jack wants more—he wants, in Schiller's terms, to link the ideal with the actual and have the experience on a sustained basis. His sense of direction is marked by his high-speed trip to visit Ennis in the aftermath of the divorce, his subsequent forays into Mexico and the world of male prostitutes, and, quite surprisingly, his standing up to his father-in-law in that remarkable scene at the Thanksgiving dinner table. Jack is coming to know more and more what he wants because he has experienced it from one brief moment to the next with Ennis over the past fifteen years. By 1978, he is open to the invitation of the ideally handsome Randall, whose mind is similarly Arcadian — "[Our boss has] got a little cabin down on Lake Kemp. Got a croppie house ... little boat. Said I can use it whenever I want. (pause) We ought to go down there some weekend" (SP 76). In keeping with the high mimetic or larger-than-life tragic hero which Northrup Frye outlines, Jack, in being disappointed in one partner in the quest, simply goes on to another. It is for this reason that neither the story nor film have the lovers return to the specific landscape of Brokeback Mountain — the quest for it has become a way of life and can be transplanted anywhere, a place which, as actor Jake Gyllenhaal defined in his earlier statement, is that "pure place you take someone that's free of judgment."

Jack's growing insistence on achieving a gay Arcadia and Ennis's increasing skepticism lend particular poignancy to their final scene together in the film. The beginning reminds us that their idyllic times have been held in tenuous balance, for right after Jack has admitted the night before, "I miss you so bad I can hardly stand it," they are shown "asleep in the tent, ENNIS curled around JACK" (SP 80), in just the sort of domestic intimacy Jack and presumably Ennis crave. The next morning Jack proposes they add heat to his ideal by going to Mexico, only to discover that the very name symbolizes the sort of sexual compensations Ennis will not allow him. The sentence in the script, lifted directly from the story, "Like vast clouds of steam from thermal springs in winter, the years of things unsaid and now unsayable — admissions, declarations, shames, guilts, fears — rise around them —" (SP 83), shows how the characters in both fiction and the film are linked in their bitterness. The flashback that follows also doubly demonstrates their desire to return to their intimacy of what they shared twenty years prior: "Nothing mars this moment for JACK, even though he knows that ENNIS does not embrace him face to face because he not want to see or feel that it is JACK he holds — because for now, they are wrapped in a closeness that satisfies some shared and sexless hunger, that is not really sleep but something else drowsy and tranced..." (SP 84).

The story itself achieves closure through its presentation of Ennis's private rituals. Between the publication of "Brokeback Mountain" in the *New Yorker* and its appearance in the collection *Close Range*, Proulx added an italicized prologue taking place in the mind of Ennis, suggesting that he has found some solace in his dreams of Jack and in his relationship to his married daughter.[42] This impression is accentuated by the ending where he hangs the combined shirts below the postcard of Brokeback. The film goes two steps further. First, it shows Alma Jr. searching for her own better world by asking Ennis if she could come live with him. Second, even in the wake of being turned down by her father, she is later shown asking him to her wedding, with him uncharacteristically articulating concern about her happiness and actually toasting the event while saying he will attend. In the script, she is said to be "luminous" (SP 96). Thus, Jack Twist's envisioned death by tire iron — presumably a direct result of his transferring his Arcadian quest to Randall — proves not to be in vain in the sense that Ennis has been softened in his reception to family, far from Arcadia though he may be. Ennis has finally learned enough to say "yes" to his daughter's request, so he does not live entirely in domestic deprivation and regret his whole life, and thus serves as the appropriate mourner of, or tragic choral figure to, a man who was willing to stake everything on a goal that turned on one-to-one intimacy. Quite significantly, however, Ennis ends as a Romeo ready to follow his lover into death, whereas Jack proves to be more like Lear, who went down fighting with his hand raised. Restated in Lee's words: "They're both gays but one chooses to be more adventurous. The other has to go through self-denial and only accepts it when it's too late, when he missed him. That is true. Eventually we surpass the obstacles and it's really a search for that obscure object of love."[43]

Gay cinema historian Vito Russo observed that gays "have cooperated for a very long time in the maintenance of our own invisibility."[44] Although none of the major creators of "Brokeback Mountain" the story or *Brokeback Mountain* the film have identified as gay, we can certainly assert that both in print and on the screen the gay Arcadia, whether suggested or boldly embodied, has become a visible milestone for our cultural imagination. It may be no more sustained or real than King Lear's vision of prison, where, in Act 5, he looks forward to a beatific life with his beloved Cordelia, but the sanctified broken Wyoming mountain like the mythic prison becomes, in story and film, a palpable goal, a luminous side to an ongoing tragedy and slow-plodding epic, and a way of life to be sought once the tale is over.

Notes

1. Annie Proulx, "Getting Movied," in *Brokeback Mountain: Story to Screenplay* (New York: Scribner, 2005), 130.

2. Larry McMurtry, "Adapting Brokeback Mountain," in *Brokeback Mountain: Story to Screenplay*, 141.

3. C. Hugh Holman and William Harmon, *A Handbook to Literature*, 5th ed. (New York: Macmillan, 1986), 36.

4. Raymond-Jean Frontain, "Theocritus," in *The Gay and Lesbian Literary Heritage*, ed. Claude J. Summers (New York: Henry Holt, 1995), 700. For a more in-depth look at Theocritus and "Brokeback Mountain," see the essay "Proulx's Pastoral: Brokeback Mountain as Sacred Space," beginning on p. 19 of this anthology.

5. Gregory Woods, *A History of Gay Literature: The Male Tradition* (New Haven: Yale University Press, 1998), 25.

6. Frontain, 700.

7. Bruno Snell, *The Discovery of the Mind in Greek Philosophy and Literature*, trans. T. G. Rosenmeyer (New York: Dover, 1982), 299.

8. Byrne R. S. Fone, "The Other Eden: Arcadia and the Homosexual Imagination," in

Essays on Gay Literature, ed. Stuart Kellogg (Binghamton, N.Y.: Harrington Park Press, 1985), 13.

9. Ibid.

10. McMurtry, "Adapting,"140.

11. The gay cowboy, however, has made earlier appearances. Andy Warhol, for example, presented homoeroticism in his film *Lonesome Cowboys*, and the painter Delmas Howe developed a combination of erotica and myth in his *Theseus and Perithous at the Chutes, Zeus and Gaymede*, and *Hercules Dressing for the Arena*. He places beautiful male nudes (all with cowboy hats) in a rich gay rodeo setting. See Edward Lucie-Smith, *The Male Nude: A Modern View* (London: Sarema Press, 1991), 52–54. The actual International Gay Rodeo Association has been in existence since the mid-1970s.

12. Gregg Shapiro, "Interview with *Brokeback Mountain* Director Ang Lee," <*AfterElton. Com*, Dec. 9, 2005, http://www.afterelton.com/movies/2005/12/anglee.html>, 2 (accessed June 16, 2006).

13. Stephen Hunter, "A Picture of Two Americas in 'Brokeback Mountain,'" *Washington-Post.Com*, Feb. 2, 2006, <http://www.washingtonpost.com/wp-dyn//content/article/2006/02/01/AR2006020102477.html>, 2 (accessed May 22, 2006).

14. Ibid.

15. Ang Lee has said, "To me Ennis stands for the conservative side of America. He's the biggest homophobe in the whole movie — culturally and psychologically — but by the time he admits his feelings, it's too late"; see Robert Ordona, "'Brokeback Mountain' — As Gay as It Gets: An Interview with Ang Lee," *Gay.Com*, <http://www.gay.com/entertainment/interview.html?oll=pno_entertainment&sernum=1139>, 2 (accessed June 15, 2006).

16. Snell, 288.

17. Ibid., 293.

18. Ibid., 291.

19. Louis Crompton, "Virgil," in *Gay and Lesbian Literary Heritage*, 719.

20. Virgil, *The Eclogues and Georgics of Virgil*, trans. C. Day Lewis (Garden City, N.Y.: Anchor Books, 1964), 14.

21. See Karen L. Rood, *Understanding Annie Proulx* (Columbia: University of South Carolina Press, 2001), 6.

22. Andrew Holleran, "The Magic Mountain," *Gay and Lesbian Review Worldwide*, May-June 2006, <http://glreview.com/13.2-holleran.php>, 1 (accessed July 16, 2006).

23. J. L. Deker-Lesaint, "An Interview with Edmund White," *Meridian* 12 (2003): 67.

24. Ossana, "Bonus Features: From Script to Screen," *Brokeback Mountain*, Universal Studios, 2005, DVD.

25. The association of grittiness and grimness with reality comes up again and again in the interviews in "From Script to Screen" and "Sharing the Story" as part of the special features section of the DVD version of the film. For a fuller discussion of the concept of "imitating reality" and what classical artists and philosophers actually meant when they talked of following a form that was in the mind, rather than the tangible world, see Henry Alley, *The Quest for Anonymity: The Novels of George Eliot* (Newark: University of Delaware Press, 1997), 31 and 156. Lee seems definitely in the league of those who idealize and transform what they observe; however, some members of the cast and crew, now on camera, praise him and the film for rendering reality as journalistic reality.

26. Holleran, "Magic Mountain," 1.

27. David Leavitt, "Is *Brokeback Mountain* A Gay Film?," *Slate*, Dec. 8, 2005, http://www.slate.com/id/2131865/, 1 (accessed May 10, 2006).

28. Michael Rowell, "Mountain High," *Out Smart Magazine* (Houston: Dec. 2005), 30.

29. Northrup Frye, *Anatomy of Criticism: Four Essays* (Princeton: Princeton University Press, 1957), 34.

30. Ordona, "As Gay as It Gets," 3.

31. Ibid., 2.

32. Frye, *Anatomy*, 34.

33. Ibid., 195.

34. Garth Franklin, "Interview: Ang Lee, 'Brokeback Mountain,'" *Dark Horizons* (Dec. 7, 2005), <http://www.darkhorizons.com/news05/brokeback2.php>, 4 (accessed June 15, 2006).
35. Ibid., 2.
36. "Cover Story: *Brokeback Mountain.*" *EW.Com*, Dec. 9, 2005, <http://www.ew.com//ew/report/0.6115, 1136042-2-7_11105582123361211_0_,00.html.>, 2 (accessed May 22, 2005); Larry McMurtry, *Walter Benjamin at the Dairy Queen: Reflections at Sixty and Beyond* (New York: Simon and Schuster, 1999), 113.
37. McMurtry, *Walter Benjamin at the Dairy Queen: Reflections at Sixty and Beyond* (New York: Simon & Schuster, 1999), 113.
38. Shapiro, "Interview," *AfterElton*, 1.
39. Ordona, "As Gay as It Gets," 4.
40. Hunter, "Picture of Two Americas," 2.
41. Frederich von Schiller, *Naïve and Sentimental Poetry and On the Sublime: Two Essays*, trans. Julius A. Elias (New York: Frederick Ungar, 1966), 153.
42. Originally published in the *New Yorker* in 1997, Proulx's short story was also part of her collection *Close Range: Wyoming Stories* (New York: Scribner, 1999), 255–285.
43. Franklin, "Interview: Ang Lee," *Dark Horizons*, 2.
44. Vito Russo, *GLAAD [Gay & Lesbian Alliance Against Defamation]*, <http://www.glaad.org/glaad/news/9603/vito-russo.html>, cited in Nikki Sullivan, *A Critical Introduction to Queer Theory* (New York: New York University Press, 2003), 192.

2

Proulx's Pastoral: Brokeback Mountain as Sacred Space

by Ginger Jones

The ancient Greek poet Theocritus is generally credited with creating the *pastoral*, a kind of literature that tells the story of shepherds who herd their sheep to a mountaintop where they live free from the difficulties and unpleasantness of city life. While Theocritus (c. 310–260 BCE) called his poetry "bucolic" (a word probably derived from the Greek word for *cowherd*),[1] he was the first to write poetry that has been identified as "pastoral" from the Latin word *pastoralis*, of or pertaining to shepherds. Critics often remark upon the homoeroticism found throughout several of Theocritus' idylls, noting that 12, 29, and 30 are specifically about men loving a young man. Critic Kathryn Gutzwiller defines Theocritus' art even further, writing that his "pastorals are *representations* of the speech acts of herdsmen, their conversations and songs"[2] [emphasis hers]. These idylls are what Aaron Copland might have called "fanfares for the common man." In the idyllic world of Theocritus, after the sheep quiet for the evening, shepherds, using simple language, talk and sing to each other about their experiences with love and death, or about the stories of heroes who shared the human emotion of love the same way shepherds do.

This classical tradition is revived in Annie Proulx's short story, "Brokeback Mountain." The popularity of her short story, especially its adaptation, is not just due to its notoriety in depicting he[men] in love out West, but to its familiar story of rustic men wh[o sing] about love and death, and learn even more while they he[rd the sheep] of a mountain, a tale that has been told in the Western t[radition for] 2300 years. The environment of a pastoral is usually pr[esented as a] mediate zone of contentment between the city and the [wilderness,] that is always temporary. The pastoral life is liminal, that is[...]

[handwritten marginal note: Brokeback as only temporary]

a place of license, a place of possibility that can lead to growth and transformation. Theocritus' shepherds come down from the mountain to attend religious holidays and city celebrations, and Proulx's characters take the job herding sheep only for the summer, the end of which will see them moving down the mountain with the sheep.

In "Brokeback Mountain," Jack Twist and Ennis del Mar withdraw from the world when they accept summer jobs as shepherds in a mountain's "great flowery meadows" where dawn appears as "glassy orange, stained from below by a gelatinous band of pale green" and where "lodgepole pines ... [are] massed in slabs of somber malachite" (SS 4). Most of the idylls of Theocritus begin by describing a mountain pasture or glade, or in the middle of conversation between shepherds (less commonly goatherds or cowherds) on their way down from these natural environments. Theocritus' first idyll describes two shepherds meeting under a pine tree near a mountain waterfall, where one shepherd invites the other to sit on a sloping knoll to sing or tell a story about a constant lover: "By the nymphs, goatherd, would it please you to sit down / On this sloping hillock here where the tamarisks grow / And play your pan-pipe...?"[3] In exchange for a song, one shepherd will give the other "a deep ivywood drinking cup coated with sweet-scented wax, two-handled and newly wrought."[4] Allusions and references to drinking, to wine, to grapes, to the god of wine, to drinking cups, vines, and wine-vats are made throughout the *Idylls*. Theocritus' emphasis shows how convivial drinking, singing, and conversation (a symposium) was of great importance to shepherds. As the narrator of Idyll 29 says, wine is the companion of truth.[5] In Proulx's story too alcohol seems to be a frequent companion of Jack and Ennis, when they are together and when they are alone. After they meet each other outside Joe Aguirre's trailer, Proulx's shepherds first "sing" in a bar, where Jack, who has been to the mountain pasture before, tells Ennis about the "need for plenty of whiskey up there," also boasting that he had shot an eagle, whose feather is still perched in the hatband of his hat (SS 3). The men share whiskey and beer at the end of their work days on Brokeback, and drinking whiskey is part of the way they spend time together in the years to come. When she tells Ennis about her husband's death, Lureen says she thought Brokeback Mountain was just a place to get drunk, a "pretend place where the bluebirds sing and there's a whiskey spring" because Jack, who "drank a lot" said it was "his place" (SS 23). In Proulx and Theocritus, as in countless other tales, alcohol creates a sense of well-being, relaxes socially acquired inhibitions, and stimulates unrestricted conversation and behavior.

By only briefly describing the setting of his *Idylls* Theocritus is illuminating the human situation. Theocritus gives readers the impression of men in repose, relaxed, *learning* about themselves. In Idyll 14, for example, one shepherd tells another "time creeps down the jaw, / frosting hair after hair. One must act while the knee is still limber."[6] Proulx also focuses on telling us how her shepherds interact with each other in their environment, more so than on the environment itself— for both writers seem to understand that a specific environment gains significance by provoking an encounter with the self. Theocritus and Proulx depict environments that become holy or sacred places because of the rituals practiced by those who are in that environment. The activities of shepherds in the pastoral tradition include caring for their animals, singing, playing music, telling stories, and making love,[7] all of which Jack and Ennis do during their summer on the mountain; moreover, they work to reenact these return-trip rituals during their twenty-year romance, turning Brokeback Mountain into a sacred symbol of their love — although they never actually revisit Brokeback itself.

Stewards in an Oasis of Contentment

The "ruling motive of the good shepherd," writes Leo Marx in *The Machine in the Garden*, "was to withdraw from the great world and begin a new life in a fresh, green landscape."[8] Marx's good shepherd lives in an oasis of contentment enjoying the spontaneity of nature, while being part of the order imposed by civilization, to which he always returns. This character contributes to what Marx identifies as a "pastoral strain" in American literature, representing "a delicate blend of myth and reality ... particularly relevant to American experience."[9]

Proulx's characters, "high school dropout country boys," before they reached age twenty, suffered from a lack of opportunity and from poverty; both men are accustomed, Proulx tells us, "to the stoic life" (SS 1–2). Jack Twist is described as "crazy to be somewhere, anywhere," while Ennis del Mar works to make enough to marry in December (SS 8). By herding sheep, by choosing to withdraw from the world for a summer, Jack and Ennis establish themselves in the world of men. They become stewards of the herd and accept a mantle of male power. Philosopher Paul Shepherd writes in *Man in the Landscape* that sheepherding is "a continuing lesson in the relationship between authority and lineage," an affirmation of the authority of patriarchy: a boy goes up the mountain, however a man comes down.[10] Jack carries the runt of a litter of puppies in his coat jacket up the long trail because, like a boy, he loves little dogs (SS 3), but by caring for the sheep and the dogs that herd them, Jack and Ennis show that they have the social maturity not only necessary for their own survival, but for the survival of the animals in their charge as well. Accepting his role as steward, Jack mentions that he spends "half the night jumpin up and checkin for coyotes (SS 4)," and during his first night as herder, Ennis shoots a coyote with "[b]alls on him the size of apples," who could have killed some of the lambs (SS 5).

As if newly secure in his emergent role as guardian and steward, Ennis bathes himself in view of Jack back at camp and that evening begins to talk. He and Jack engage in long conversations that make them "respectful of each other's opinions. Each glad to have a companion where none had been expected" (SS 6). The two men keep "tossing sticks on the fire to keep the talk going" (SS 5). The catalogue of topics includes their families, horses, rodeos, the draft, and how men might endure the last doomed moments of their lives (in reference to the sinking of the naval submarine *The Thresher*). Theocritus' shepherds talk about themselves and the lives of people they know, telling stories of the warriors Castor and Polydeuces in Idyll 22, and the drowning of young Hylas in Idyll 13. Theocritus' shepherds tell about their dogs ("he barks / and fixes his gaze on the sea"[11] and "the dog with the white patch is barking"[12]). Jack and Ennis also talk about dogs they have "owned and known" (SS 5). Theocritus' shepherds play panpipes and sing. Proulx writes that "Jack pulled a squalling burr out of the harmonica" (SS 6), an instrument whose sound and design echoes that of ancient Greek panpipes. The two men sing about animals ("Strawberry Roan," a horse that cannot be broken) and the gods ("Water-Walking Jesus," about the redemptive power of Christ). That first summer, the only subject the men do not discuss is women, but the talk and the songs make Ennis think "he'd never had such a good time," make him feel as if "he could paw the white out of the moon" (SS 6). Love-inspired images are also evident in Theocritus as when one shepherd sees his lover: "[T]o you I run / Like a wayfarer parched by the sun to the shade of the oak."[13] As their summer on the mountain lengthens, Jack and Ennis deepen "their intimacy considerably" (SS 7). Each has been given complete attention by the other, an attention that fosters trust, reliability, and finally a love that leads to sexual expression. After the first night of lovemaking, the men think of themselves as "suspended above ordinary affairs," so much so that "[t]hey never talked about the sex" except to declare that neither was simply queer (SS 7).

Like the story of a shepherd in Theocritus' Idyll 13 that tells of Herakles, who signed to sail with Jason on his ship *The Argo* and chose to abandon it in order to search for his male lover, Jack and Ennis abandon most of their responsibilities to the sheep in order to be together. After their first long talk, "the hours [Ennis] was away from the sheep stretched out and out" (SS 7). After making love, the men spend less and less time with the sheep at night. Their failure to do so undermines their stewardship and leaves them culpable. By choosing to shirk their responsibilities as shepherds, they expose themselves to Joe Aguirre, the critical, judgmental overseer who will ridicule them and their relationship. While their love brings them joy, they share culpability in abandoning the responsibilities of adults, responsibilities they have chosen to set aside because "both knew how it would go for the rest of the summer, sheep be damned" (SS 7). Again that summer, predator loss was great — the coyotes well fed.

At this point, the men have set aside their mantle of stewardship. Now the mountain becomes a playground for them. Jack and Ennis turn from the responsibilities of manhood and indulge in all the emotions that had been denied them as boys. When Ennis remembers the summer, he will recall it as the time "when they owned the world and nothing seemed wrong" (SS 1). Proulx writes: "There were only the two of them on the mountain flying in the euphoric, bitter air, looking down on the hawk's back, and the crawling lights of vehicles on the plain below ... distant from the tame ranch dogs barking in the dark hours. They believed themselves invisible" (SS 7). Not content with a shepherd's life, they cultivated the life of divine children at play, stalking, pursuing, wrestling and other harmless roughhousing. As each meets the other's emotional needs, the mountain itself becomes a place of nurture. The men behave as though the mountain protects them from the lives they had left behind for the summer. But Brokeback is not only a place of nurture and of protection; it also becomes a place of leisure. To experience leisure, according to Shepherd, is to experience "a form of silence prerequisite to the apprehension of reality"[14] or to appreciate the limits imposed by society, the self, and the environment. Leisure is not the opposite of work; rather it is a state necessary to the understanding of the limits of reality, and participating in it with another person allows an openness to loving that person.

While the men think they are invisible, they are at any time subject to the devouring gaze of the coyotes or of Joe Aguirre. The intrusion of Aguirre will make the men subject to the profane; the reality the men have created will become conditional and limited. Lulled by the sense of protection from their place on the mountain where they have after all created a home together, the men begin to express their love for each other in the open, "with the hot sun striking down, and at evening in the fire glow" (SS 7). They allow themselves to become vulnerable, to fall under the disapproving gaze of the city, that very place that had cost them so much in their childhood. In fact, Aguirre's message that Jack's Uncle Harold was deathly ill with pneumonia is meant to recall Jack to an awareness of conventional family ties and duties.

Failure to watch the sheep one night prevents Jack and Ennis from keeping their sheep mixing with those from another herd, and as the two men come down from the mountain with their mixed herd the mountain boils "with demonic energy," is "glazed with flickering broken-cloud light, the wind" combs the grass and draws "from the damaged krummholz and slit rock a bestial drone" (SS 8). Change is often manifested in the wind, what Shepherd calls "that invisible, bodiless presence."[15] Proulx makes the wind a literal wind of change, precipitating an emotional shift in the lives of her characters.[16] Descent from the mountain is descent into the world, the world the men had known before. Forced to leave the environment where he had loved and been loved, that intermediate zone of comfort between the city and the wild, Ennis feels he is "in a slow-motion, but headlong, irreversible fall" (SS 8). Even though he and Jack return with most of the sheep they took up the mountain, the sheep are mixed, contaminated by another herd. Ennis' emotions are mixed as well, not as unsullied as they had been when he was with Jack on the mountain.

Reunited and Longing to Return to the Mountain

Four years will pass before Ennis will feel as alive as he did that summer on Brokeback Mountain. Even though he will have married and lived in a bedroom "[f]ull of the smell of old blood and milk and baby shit, and the sounds ... of squalling and sucking, all reassuring of fecundity and life's continuance" (SS 9), it is only when he receives a general delivery letter from Jack that he recognizes "the first sign of life in all that time" (SS 10), not just from Jack but for himself. When they meet again, Ennis smells the "musky sweat and a faint sweetness like grass, and with it the rushing cold of the mountain" (SS 11) on Jack and leaves to spend the night with Jack in the Motel Siesta. In that motel room, Jack tells Ennis that "[o]ld Brokeback got us good and it sure ain't over" (SS 13). By naming the mountain and its impact on them, Jack establishes it as the center of their world. A sacred space, Shepherd reminds us, "is not a supernatural explanation of a natural phenomenon, such as a volcano." It is, "more precisely, endowing the world with order." Brokeback Mountain has become a home to Jack and Ennis, a sacred space, one which is "associated with events important to the mythos — to the legend and the ritual" of the men, or a space that can be "represented by a symbol" whose value is evoked when the symbol is at hand.[17]

The longing to return to the mountain is a longing to return to what was sacred to the men, a source of nurture and permanence. Geographer Yi-Fu Tuan explains that intimacy comes about "in moments of true awareness and exchange. Each intimate exchange has a locale which partakes in the quality of the human encounter. These places may be etched in the deep recesses of memory and yield intense satisfaction with each recall.... No one can deliberately design such places than one can plan, with any guarantee of success, the occasions of genuine human exchange."[18] When one witnesses or experiences a life-changing event, the place where the event occurs, the place where one happens to be at the time, becomes the symbol of the event since the experience itself cannot be replicated. People remember *where* they were when major and minor events occurred in their lives. The memory of a place is necessary to making the place sacred, in Shepherd's view, and ritual endows a place with permanence.[19] People rely on icons or symbols to remind them of what they hold in reverence (a crucifix, for example, symbolizes the Christian belief in sacrifice and redemption). The mountains, and Brokeback Mountain in particular, will be for Jack and Ennis a sacred symbol of their love. A picture postcard of Brokeback Mountain nailed to a wall will be Ennis's icon. The shirts hung underneath it will be relics of the only love that allowed Ennis to transcend the world in which he found himself.

During their reunion, however, Jack learns that Ennis has accepted the mantle of another stewardship when he tells him, "I built a life up in them years. Love my little girls. Alma? It ain't her fault. You got your baby and wife, that place in Texas" (SS 13). Ennis abandoned his responsibility as a shepherd before; he isn't about to suffer loss again. He now understands how to survive in the world away from the mountain, yet he also understands that he is in the grip of something he cannot control. The untamed has intruded upon Ennis's domesticated city life. He tells Jack, "There's no reins on this one. It scares the piss out a me" (SS 13). In his recollection of seeing the brutalized body of a murdered ranch owner who lived with another man, Ennis reveals his belief that living is more important than loving; he doesn't "want a be dead" (SS 14). At this point, the idea of returning to "the mountains" becomes imperative. Jack asks Ennis to "Get us out a here...." Their relationship "ain't no little thing that's happenin'" between them (SS 15).

While Ennis accepts his responsibility for Alma and his children, he resents it, perhaps as much as he resented the sheep for which he had to leave Jack at night all those years ago. He does not shirk his duty to her. Yet, when he and Alma divorce, Ennis is "glad enough to be around stock again, free to drop things, quit if he had to, and go into the mountains at short notice" (SS 16). Like Joe Aguirre, however, Alma has been watching Ennis carefully — another disapproving supervisor. After their divorce, when she finally confronts him, Ennis leaves her in the kitchen rather than admit to what she's told him she knows.

Over the years Jack and Ennis arrange to meet at series of mountain locations, "never returning to Brokeback" (SS 17). Ennis is divorced and Jack's marriage is meaningless. No longer stewards, the former shepherds can only escape the city to the wilderness, and then from time to time. Like the sheep that were mixed, and their marriages that were tainted, Jack and Ennis do not want Brokeback to become sullied. It is sacred, not the place for "high-altitude fucks" (SS 21). Jack emphatically states that everything was built on

LIVERPOOL JOHN MOORES UNIVERSITY
LEARNING SERVICES

Brokeback Mountain: "It's all we got, boy, fuckin all" (SS 21). What they have built together since Brokeback, is ephemeral; there is "never enough time, never enough" (SS 20).

Jack longs to return to the "single moment of artless, charmed happiness" (SS 22) he experienced on Brokeback Mountain. For him, that time on Brokeback was where he encountered himself and gained his identity. From Proulx's vivid description of Jack's sheer pleasure in love, we understand why the mountain is holy ground. It was the place where Jack's ideal life occurred: "Nothing marred it" (SS 22). If life mattered more than love for Ennis, for Jack, love was more important than life itself. It is these opposing perspectives that doom them as though they were characters in a Greek drama. Familiar with ancient Greek tragedy, in which characters who wish to achieve some goal inevitably encounter limits — usually those of their own human frailty, the gods, or nature — Theocritus based his idylls on the themes of ancient Greek epics, which told of the deeds of heroes.

In Theocritus, hero and shepherd have the same desires, and can suffer in the same way. Endowed with superhuman qualities, yet human passions, certain heroes in Theocritus' *Idylls* are shown reverence, perhaps because their stories assured the identity of his pastoral community. One of most famous heroes, Herakles (the Roman Hercules) was the protector of men who embodies pathos or suffering.[20] Jack is like Herakles. His father appears to be as detached as Zeus was from Herakles. A high school dropout, Jack fails at achieving his dream of becoming a rodeo champion. Also like Herakles, he kills an eagle but is not punished. Herakles and Hylas, a fellow sailor, are lovers, but Hylas disappears, perhaps by drowning, and leaves Herakles to search for him. Finally, like Herakles (who wears a shirt or robe given to him by a lover), Jack dies a painful death. Herakles will join the ranks of the gods, while Jack will be deified by Ennis at the shrine of two shirts and a postcard.[21] He will dream of Jack "sometimes in grief, sometimes with the old sense of joy and release; the pillow sometimes wet, sometimes the sheets" (SS 28).

As do the characters in classic Greek tragedy, Jack and Ennis each get what they want. One wants to live, the other wants to love, but the survivor doesn't pay enough attention to loving for he is "not the swearing kind" and the lover doesn't pay enough attention to the world in which he lives for "he had never asked [Ennis] to swear" (SS 27). Jack dies before he can regain that perfect moment on Brokeback Mountain. Ennis is condemned to live alone with a postcard, that icon of the sacred place where he learned how to love.

In her short story, Proulx resurrects Theocritus' aesthetic that the truth of the lives of men can be found in the humble language of shepherds. If Theocritus understood the nature of men, so does Annie Proulx. Like Theocritus, Proulx depicts shepherds and heroes, heterosexual and homosexual lovers alike as enjoying evanescent moments of pure happiness alongside rejection, frustration, and indelible memories. As he did, she tells of the simple and natural evolution of love between two people in an open landscape, a place of respite and beauty. This story is one we know. It is as old as the Sicilian hills that first inspired the original and not surprisingly ends as does the last idyll of Theocritus in which a shepherd, in the tale of a man whose lover has left him, sings that "memory lingers on..., and longing eats at his marrow, and dreams beset him by night...."²² One imagines that for this shepherd too, the pillow is sometimes wet, sometimes the sheets.

Notes

1. David M. Halperin, *Before Pastoral: Theocritus and the Ancient Tradition of Bucolic Poetry* (New Haven: Yale University Press, 1983), 8.
2. Kathryn J. Gutzwiller, *Theocritus' Pastoral Analogies: The Formation of a Genre* (Madison: University of Wisconsin Press, 1991), 5.
3. Theocritus, Idyll 1, "Song of Thyrsis," in *The Idylls of Theocritus*, trans. Thelma Sargent (New York: W.W. Norton, 1982), 1.
4. Ibid.
5. Theocritus, Idyll 29, "Aeolic Love Poem," in *Idylls*, 117.
6. Theocritus, Idyll 14, "Aischinas and Thyonichos," in *Idylls*, 55.
7. Halperin, *Before* Pastoral, 61.
8. Leo Marx, *The Machine in the Garden* (New York: Oxford University Press, 1964), 3.
9. Ibid., 19.
10. Paul Shepherd, *Man and Landscape: A Historic View of the Esthetics of Nature*, 2nd ed. (College Station: Texas A & M University Press, 1991), 51.
11. Theocritus, Idyll 6, "Pastoral Song," in *Idylls*, 26.
12. Theocritus, Idyll 8, "Second Pastoral Song," in *Idylls*, 36.
13. Theocritus, Idyll 12, "The Favorite," in *Idylls*, 47.
14. Shepherd, 36.
15. Shepherd, 51; the story is filled with references to the wind and the weather (always important to herders) — snow, hail, rain, thunder, and lightning.
16. Proulx makes thirteen references to wind in her story, all metaphorically rich, such as the booming wind in the opening scene that "strikes the trailer like a load of dirt coming off a dump truck" (1) or the "slippery wind" that they heard in their reunion motel (11).
17. Shepherd, 37–38.
18. Yi-Fu Tuan, *Space and Place: The Perspective of Experience* (Minneapolis: University of Minnesota Press, 1977), 141.
19. Shepherd, 37–38.
20. For further information about Herakles as passionate sufferer read *The Origin of the Gods: A Psychoanalytic Study of Greek Theogonic Myth* by Richard Caldwell (New York: Oxford University Press, 1993) and *Myth and Territory in the Spartan Mediterranean* by Irad Malkin (New York: Cambridge University Press, 1994). Both authors detail the trials of the innocent child hated by his stepmother Hera who was jealous of her husband's affair with Herakles' mother. Herakles was given his name to appease the goddess Hera, but rather than be happy, she tried to kill him. Herakles, after his death, is eventually flung into the heavens with the other immortals.
21. Ennis can be view as Prometheus, the god who was punished by Zeus for giving humankind the gift of fire. Proulx writes that the first time Jack sees Ennis he is "as night fire, a red spark on the huge black mass of mountain" (SS 4). Prometheus was chained to a moun-

3

Buried in the Family Plot: The Cost of Pattern Maintenance to Ennis and Jack

by Jim Stacy

On a larger-than-life movie screen, viewers watch two shepherds on horseback — aspiring cowboys — drive a herd of a thousand sheep to summer grazing lands up Brokeback Mountain. That river of mindless sheep follows where they are led as billions of their ancestors have done ever since humankind realized that their wool was desirably warm. When sheep stray, they are barked back into line by the dogs as the shepherds expect them to do. Ennis del Mar and Jack Twist ride the banks of this river of sheep. Forbidden passion lurks astride their saddles. That summer will challenge those men to decide what they really want to be: two more head among the sheep or equestrians apart. Graze or gallop?

Over thirty years before, on a Broadway stage in 1974, six actors in metallic, skeletal horse masks, stomp their cothurnus-like hooves on the floor as the "Equus Noise," an eerie humming, fills the theatre. A teenage boy, Alan Strang, who lives a secret life far outside the norm, acts out his ritualistic preparation of one of the "horses" for a clandestine midnight ride. Latin for "horse," *Equus* is the name the boy selects for his self-proclaimed god whom he passionately worships and rides, galloping across the misty field of nettles to sexual climax.[1] Like Ennis and Jack, Alan periodically indulges a nonconformity that seems in many ways more authentic and certainly more passionate than his quotidian existence.

For Ennis, Jack, and Alan, life in contemporary society offered few, narrow, and well-trodden paths — patterns proven safe, predictable, and rutted in the procreative instinct. When passions far afield called, these characters rose to the occasion — occasionally and temporarily — but patterns have a way of insisting adherence. So they adhered, or in Alan's case, broke down. Reflecting many of the same thematic existential concerns as *Brokeback Mountain*, Peter Shaffer's *Equus* tells the story of Psychiatrist Martin Dysart's treatment of Alan Strang, a teenager who has admitted to blinding six horses with a metal spike.[2] The therapy sessions reveal that the boy had transferred his mother's Christian teachings and other bits of his life into a secret worship of horses that is both spiritual and sexual. The doctor ultimately learns that Alan blinded his jealous gods because he dared to defile the sanctity of the stables by bringing a girl, Jill, there for what would have been his first encounter with the opposite human sex.[3] Unable to perform, he drives her away and then, feeling the wrath of his gods, blinds them to end their accusatory stares.

Equally as important as the "whydunit" is the effect Alan Strang has on Dysart, who becomes more and more unsettled as he treats Alan. The boy has in abundance what the doctor lacks: passion. Yes, the boy is ill and needs help, but the cure will kill the worship and the passion. In discussing his treatment options with a colleague, Dysart questions the goal of curing the boy and relieving his pain: "[T]hat boy has known a passion more ferocious than I have felt in any second of my life.... That's what his stare had been saying to me all this time. '*At least I galloped! When did you?*'"[4] If Dysart is successful in his patient's rehabilitation, Alan will trade in his horse for a mini-scooter, his doctor predicts, and go "puttering off into the Normal world where animals are treated *properly*: made extinct, or put into servitude, or tethered all their lives in dim light, just to feed it! I'll give him the good Normal world where we're tethered beside them — blinking our nights away in a nonstop drench of cathode-ray over our shriveling heads!.... With any luck his private parts will come to feel as plastic to him as the products of the factory to which he will almost certainly be sent.... Hopefully, he'll feel nothing at his fork but Approved Flesh. *I doubt, however, with much passion!*"[5] If Dysart is passionate about nothing else, he is passionate about having no passion — and about his envy of Alan. Saddled with his own "eternal timidity," Dysart yields to the harness of professional duty to which he is a lamenting slave.[6] As Ennis and Jack do in *Brokeback Mountain*, Dysart ultimately decides to carry out his prescribed duty in service to his society, thus favoring the rational and the normal over the instinctual and the passionate: Apollo tops Dionysus.[7]

Existential Perspectives

Playwright Shaffer acknowledges that uniformity of thought and behavior is something "they" (governments, churches, and allies) encourage because it makes the populace easier to control — many opiates for the masses. Shaffer reflects, "To me the greatest tragic factor in History is man's apparent need to mark the intensity of his reaction to life by joining a band. For a band, to give itself definition, must find a rival or an enemy."[8] From the perspective of the band — the herd —"you are either with us or against us." Sociologist Erving Goffman argues that this oppositional urge allows the self to emerge: "Without something to belong to, we have no stable self, and yet total commitment and attachment to any social unit implies a kind of selflessness. Our sense of being a person can come from being drawn into a wider social unit; our sense of selfhood can arise through the little ways in which we resist the pull. Out status is backed by the solid buildings of the world, while our sense of personal identity often resides in the cracks."[9]

Because these "bands," these "solid buildings," these herds write their own scripts, draw their own maps, and set their own cadences, they are unreceptive to too much creativity and deviation. While they offer security, they restrict freedom: the age-old tradeoff. Such concerns have been examined by existential philosophers of the twentieth century as they focus on the nature of being, the search for meaning, conformity, alienation, homelessness, and godlessness.

From an existential perspective, Sheldon Litt offers a succinct summary: "One can always choose, as many do, to be an 'outsider,' to go against the grain of social coercion. Indeed, this is the Kierkegaardian existential dilemma facing humanity ... the core conflict we all must face — and the root of existential angst. Whether to go along passively with society and 'do what everyone else expects' (Heidegger's Das Man, following the crowd) or to resist the others and risk suffering existential anxiety of uncertainty (and freedom)."[10] In *Equus* Shaffer has illustrated this existential dilemma in vivid theatrical terms, pitting socially responsible existence against passionately lived life, the acculturated self against the natural self (or the *authentic* self in existential terms). Famous for his declaration that existence precedes essence, Jean-Paul Sartre helped to define existentialism. Paul Livingston writes of Sartre's philosophy, "In the challenge to determine, and create, what we are, we can do so either authentically — with integrity and honesty — or inauthentically. We act inauthentically when we forget our own difficult freedom, and rest with pre-established patterns for life or pre-given answers to the questions of what we should be...."[11]

Much of the appeal of both *Equus* and *Brokeback Mountain* lies in their presentations of existential themes undeniably relevant to the twenty-first century. This focus also explains, in part, why Annie Proulx, Larry McMurtry, Diana Ossana, and Ang Lee's *Brokeback Mountain* appeals to such a wide range of audiences, for authenticity and freedom — and their appeal to our idealism and romanticism — resonate with more than the closeted and the out. Whereas Shaffer presents one character as the passionate primitive and his adversary as the responsible citizen, each of Proulx's characters finds these combating forces within himself. Jack reveals a greater willingness to buck the constraints of society, while Ennis sticks to the script of convention to avoid the label *queer*. In Ennis we see a man who as a child was shown what could happen to people who are different. Here is a man who gets engaged at age 19 because he is a male and lives in Wyoming in 1963. Here is a man who gets married because he is already engaged, even though he has found someone much more engaging. Their boss Joe Aguirre warns them when they are hired, "SLEEP WITH THE SHEEP, hundred percent, NO FIRE..."(SS 2; emphasis hers). But ignite, they do. In spite of that summer flame, Ennis's sense of conformity sends him back to his November bride, yet in his heart, as he walks away from Jack Twist, he "felt like someone was pulling his guts out hand over hand a yard at a time" (SS 9).

In the motel room after their passionate reunion sex, they talk about their last four years and about the future. No longer protected by the privacy of acres of mountain timberland, they hear the phone ringing off and on from the room next door (SS, 14–15) — the outside world trying to make a wake-up call to two naked men in bed together.[12] When Ennis admits to Jack that they should have never parted, Jack is eager for them to begin a new life together now. But Ennis stops him: "I doubt there's nothing now we can do.... What I'm sayin, Jack, I built a life up in them years. Love my little girls. Alma? It ain't her fault. You got your baby and wife, that place in Texas" (SS 13). When Jack persists, Ennis refuses again, explaining: "I'm stuck with what I got, caught in my own loop. Can't get out of it." In actuality, the loop is not his but society's, but stuck is stuck. Jack's "loop" may have tripped him up that summer on Brokeback, yet with wife and children, Ennis now defines himself as the breadwinner serving his family — the traditional nest-building narrative to which Jack succumbs as well. In Goffman's terms, Ennis allows his authentic personal identity — one directly connected to Jack — to form "in the cracks" rather than in "the solid buildings" of his world.

"Heidegger" would probably sound like a new line of farm equipment to Jack, but he innately senses that what Ennis and Alma have is not an authentic life — "You and Alma, that's a life?" (SP 52). One of the twentieth century's leading philosophers, Martin Heidegger, is well served by Ilan Gur-Ze'ev who explains the former's basic concepts: "To be authentic the human subject must overcome the governing world of facts, the realm of self-evident or 'proved' truths and resist the threats and temptations of security, pleasure, and success offered by the Other, by society."[13] Only then can a person overcome "the infinity of nothingness and of homelessness" as he finds a transcendent freedom, as well as an "unconcealment" — "dis-covery, un-covering, un-veiling"[14] — un-closeting? (It is interesting to note that Heidegger sees authentic Man as "the *shepherd* of Being" in a state of "ecstatic homelessness."[15]) In Heidegger's terms the normalized world where Jack, Ennis, and their families reside is the essence of "Das Man," the generalized public body of humankind, which is grounded in *concealment* of the true self. Das Man affords each person a place to hide from death, and there we spend our time in *Gerede* ("idle chatter") — the "groundless" public exchange of previously expressed ideas, fostering not genuine disclosure but a closing-off into an inauthentic exercise of generic language.[16]

Jack is willing to risk nonconformity although he has no mental blueprint for assuring their success at living together; his desire to be with Ennis is an emotional and visceral impulse not a rational one. Like Dysart's observation of himself in *Equus*, Jack and Ennis must deal with something they cannot even identify much less accept: "All reined up in old language and old assumptions, straining to jump clean-hoofed on to a whole new track of being I only suspect is there. I can't see it, because my educated, average head is being held at the wrong angle. I can't jump because the bit forbids it...."[17] Even the imagery is appropriate for Ennis and Jack: "All reined up in old language and old assumptions...." As Ennis observed in his visit to Jack's boyhood room when he looks out the window at a gravel road stretching south, "for his growing-up years that was the only road Jack knew" (SS 25). Ennis also knew how fatal a curve in the road can be; the only curve in 43 miles cost his parents their lives. Trying to walk his own narrow and straight path, Ennis is terrified of Jack's proposal.

Why is it so difficult for Ennis and Jack to break away, to step out of their respective closets, off their respective islands, out of the cracks, and to start a life together? Why is living one's freedom difficult? Because — from a romanticized perspective — it is flying blind, fueled by courage and piloted by instinct. Because the opiates are not there. Because — from a more realistic view — it lacks the props of social consensus and countless cloned allies. Because it may even lack the vocabulary or the labels necessary to negotiate in a free existence. "Gay" suited neither Ennis nor Jack. Since bisexuality was then unheard of, low-profile, or to many, oxymoronic, these two men perceive a society in which they have two choices: traditional heterosexuality or shameful homosexuality. In their minds, the latter entails stereotypical elements with which they would not be comfortable. Yet their heterosexuality, manifest in their successful breedings, does not encompass their sexual passion for one another: "the brilliant charge of their infrequent couplings" (SS 20). If they do name it, it becomes that; if they do not name it, it is what it does — or simply, it does.[18] So unidentified and unlabelled, they feel stranded, not at home with here or there — nowhere — the existential experience of homelessness.

Pattern Maintenance

From 1963 to 1982 when Jack died, he and Ennis had to alternately deny and face their nonconformity, even their isolation, without support except occasionally from each other — Ennis because he lacks the courage and the vision to do otherwise, Jack because he is waiting on Ennis. Such outsiders face a formidable challenge because the major institutions of our society work to promote the norm. Scholars in organizational communication use the label "pattern maintenance" to refer to schools, churches, and families, promoting "cultural and educational regularity and development within society."[19] These patterns are made by con/forming to the traditional narrative of employed consumers in procreative family units in an ongoing line of like descendancy. Other scholars have examined these same functions as "normalizing education," as Ilan Gur-Ze'ev does when he observes, "In the course of its production the 'I' is constituted as a focus of selfhood in a manner that ensures the identification of the subject with the present order of things, reinforces its justifications, and makes possible the invisibility of the violence which constructs and represents it as 'reality.'"[20] From a Heideggerian perspective, normalizing education "produces the subject as some-thing and prevents her from becoming some-one, the true [authentic] subject."[21] In Sartrian terms, this normalization involves inauthentically settling for "pre-established patterns" at the expense of a "difficult freedom." By extension, we can also consider employment as it relates to pattern maintenance. Businesses have a vested interest in the success of pattern maintenance because the norm generates stability and predictability as well as employees and customers. In *Brokeback Mountain* (as in *Equus*), we find characters at odds with pattern maintenance; their passions lead them off the path of conformity — with tragic results.

Limiting Education

Schools have immense power to shape youths into well patterned citizens. Gur Ze'ev observes that contemporary education is "part of this process of dismantling possibilities for self-constitution, of life as unconcealment [in Heidegger's terms]. Instead life becomes a concern and a response to the call of instrumental, calculated thinking and its fabrications."[22] Ennis del Mar and Jack Twist had enough pre-secondary education to assure that their lives remain concealed in social prescriptions. Ironically, they think that in their sexual friendship they are concealing what are actually their unconcealed selves. As high school dropouts, they were thrown into the lower end of social opportunity. After his parents were killed in a car accident, Ennis at age 14 took the initiative to get a hardship license which allowed him to drive the well used family truck to high school an hour away from home. When the transmission went out on the truck, the family could not afford to fix it so his schooling ended in the ninth grade. Explaining his disappointment, Proulx writes, "He wanted to be a sophomore, felt the word carried a kind of distinction, but the truck broke down short of it, pitching him directly into ranch work"—low pay, long hours (SS 2). A few more years of school might have brought him in contact with the word *condiments* as well as opening more significant opportunities. For Ennis and Jack, their lack of education certainly has a significant impact on who they are and how they spend their existence, narrowing their perspectives and limiting their options—keeping them far away from concepts such as alternative narratives.

Judgmental Religion

The family lives of Ennis and Jack are rooted in Christian fundamentalism which has also shaped the communities where they live and, fertile soil for Ennis's paranoia, where they could be judged. Ennis and Jack live in a time and place where the simple warning sign on an employment office trailer might claim religious space as well: "Trespassers will be shot ... Survivors shot again." On the mountain Jack shares with Ennis a song called "Water Walking Jesus," apparently one he heard his mother and others sing in the Pentecostal church of his youth. The son of Methodist parents, Ennis asks Jack what the Pentecost is. Jack does not know, but he guesses that "it's when the world ends and fellas like you and me march off to hell." Ennis corrects him, "You may be a sinner, but I ain't yet had the opportunity" (SP 17). He is only hours away from one such opportunity to sin—at least in the eyes of the majority of Americans in 1963 and perhaps even today.

In August after Jack's departure, when words failed them both, the camera leaves a grunting, anguishing Ennis on his knees and takes us to a small church where ironically the congregation, Ennis, and his bride are repeating in unison some of the most widely recited words in history, "The Lord's Prayer": "...and forgive us our trespasses as we forgive those who trespass against us. Lead us not into temptation but deliver us from evil." It is likely that Ennis at times views his passion for Jack as an evil from which he needs to be delivered; no wonder he has such shame. A joking preacher gives Ennis a sanctified reminder to marry and breed: "You may kiss the bride ... and if you don't, I will." The kiss seals their new marriage; so begins this new family's traditional narrative.

We know that in their earlier years the Del Mars maintain some sort of church-going life. In 1969 Alma Jr. reminds her father that the church picnic is next weekend so he should plan on being back from his fishing trip by then. As Ennis loses belief in religion, he loses one of the major social girders for easing the pain of existence — one opiate lost. By 1973, Ennis prefers to stay at home on the couch, drinking beer and watching the newer opiate, television, rather than to go to the church social as Alma suggests. He views them as "that fire-and-brimstone crowd" and knows how they regard homosexuality: "If a man also lie with mankind as he lieth with a woman, both of them have committed an abomination; they should surely be put to death" (Leviticus 20:13).

In the 1970s the majority of churches, even those not readily identified as fundamentalists, saw homosexuality as a sin; Bible literalists would say it is a sin punishable by death (a fate also prescribed for those who work on Sundays; Exodus 35:2). However, Proulx may be metaphorically providing an alternative perspective, one of universal embrace. After the hailstorm, Ennis and Jack ride to the herd only to find that the flock of some Chilean shepherds has gotten mixed in with the Aguirre herd. They spend five days separating the sheep from the sheep. The god of Brokeback Mountain is not a god of judgment like the one Jesus describes in the Bible: one who separates the sheep from the goats, welcoming the surprised sheep into heaven and sending the equally surprised goats to hell (Matthew 25:31–46). It's a parable the "fire-and-brimstone crowd" knows well in their them-against-us mentality.

Employment as Priority

While communication scholars view employment in terms of its "economic orientation," nonetheless all jobs serve pattern maintenance as well for without an income, taxes, and tithes, where would homes, schools, and churches be? Employment, housing, and money play a dominant role in the lives of the characters in *Brokeback Mountain.* "Makin a livin's about all I got time for now," Ennis informs Jack (SP 49). Such is the standard truth — often an empty one — of billions of our planet's "existers." Both Ennis and Jack have the same dream of becoming a cowboy; as Proulx observes, "Both wanted to be cowboys, be part of the Great Western Myth, but it didn't work out that way. Ennis never got to be more than a rough-cut ranch hand and Jack Twist chose rodeo as an expression of cowboy. Neither of them was ever a top hand, and they met herding sheep, animals most real cowboys despise."[23] Their summer job on Brokeback Mountain not only brings them together but also gives them unexpected opportunities to flirt with freedom and to challenge convention. While Jack complains of the boss, "Aguirre's got no right makin' us do somethin' against the rules" (SS 7), ironically he soon finds himself recommending that they break the rules: shooting a sheep for food, switching jobs (herder and camp tender), and indulging their sexual rebellion. When a spying Aguirre arrives with news about Jack's uncle, reminding him of his family obligations below, Jack, the displaced herder, stands his ground, "Ain't much I can do about it up here, I guess" (SP 22). When summer ends, down they go to the flatlands of convention.

Marrying Alma in November, Ennis begins his existence as a wage earner for his new family, one whose low-paying jobs initially keep them in small rural areas. His income is not sufficient to take care of his family in the way that Alma expects: she wants an apartment over the laundromat in town. Her job at the grocery store makes a move to town possible. Eventually her concerns over income join them in bed. Ennis moves to begin intercourse, still trying for that son he wants. Alma stops him: "As far behind as we are on the bills, it makes me nervous not to take no precautions." With his incentive removed, Ennis is bluntly honest: "If you don't want no more of my kids, I'll be happy to leave you alone." Alma chokes the words up from her gut: "I'd have 'em, if you'd support 'em" (SP 60–61). Three (sexless?) years later, Alma files for divorce from Ennis, and the judge orders him to pay $125 a month in support of each child, a responsibility he accepts.

Jack's early employment history is checkered: a couple of summers herding sheep on Brokeback Mountain, helping his dad at the family spread, and after moving to Texas, bullriding at rodeos, which one year earned him an income of $2,000 (or $3,000 in the movie). A dropped cowgirl hat and a first-place bull ride bring Jack the opportunity for a financially secure life. When Jack asks a bartender who that girl is, he identifies her as Lureen Newsome: "Her dad sells farm equipment. I mean big farm equipment. Hundred-thousand-dollar tractors, shit like that" (SP 40). Jack's main motivation for allowing Lureen to rope him is debatable. Does he fall in love with her? Does he need to test out his heterosexuality now that Ennis is nowhere to be found? Or coming off a year of making $2,000, does he like the idea of courting a rich girl? He is probably motivated to some extent by all three.

Two scenes that did not make the final cut of the film and one that did, underscore why he might want to try heterosexuality. We do see vividly Aguirre's contempt for Jack when he returns in the summer of 1964 to seek another summer on Brokeback. Viewers did not see what happened when he leaves the trailer: apparently filled in on what Aguirre had seen the previous summer, a couple of mechanics in the nearby garage stare accusingly at him. Nor did viewers see an even more menacing scene in the bar after the rodeo clown, disturbed by Jack's sexual vibes, walks off to the pool table to tell his buddies. The cut scene shows them on the parking lot confronting Jack as he heads for his truck, but then letting him pass, in derisive laughter.[24] That triple dose of ridicule and danger certainly had some motivational kick to it, and of course, not having to worrying about money would be a great thing too. Wedding bells.

The priority of employment leads to the final confrontation between Ennis and Jack. Saving the news to the very end of their trip, Ennis informs Jack that he won't be able to make the planned August trip, one that was to have been a long one, nine or ten days. Instead August will find Ennis running the baler. Shaken by the news, Jack complains, putting Ennis on the defensive: "You ever heard of child support? I been payin out years and got more to go. Let me tell you, I can't quit this one. And I can't get the time off. It was tough getting this time — some a them late heifers is still calvin. You don't leave then. You don't." (SS 20). For Ennis, the divorced husband and father, existence has become earning a paycheck by performing a series of events that relate to the life cycles and needs of cows and horses — washing horse blankets, feeding livestock, castrating calves, midwifing heifers. Jack cannot accept that priority: "Never enough time, never enough" (SP 81), nor can he bear the sad truth of their separate existences, too much of which is unshared. So again they part, deferring the dream of living together. Down the mountain again they go. Conformity wins again. Security is victorious. Chalk up another mark for predictability. The script prevails.

Cruelly Jack's final return to the real world will prove how vehemently some enforce the patterns of convention. If Ennis's suspicions are correct, Jack was beaten to death with a tire iron by men who hated "perverts." His nonconformity cost him his life.

Traditional Narratives of Family

The family is the key social pattern of our society; it supports and populates the churches, the schools, and wage-earning/wage-spending employment. While the American family nowadays may show greater diversity, in the 1960s and 1970s it still held on to many of its traditional beliefs in terms of roles, power, rights, needs, and limits. Proulx writes of the families in *Brokeback Mountain*, "I strove to give Jack and Ennis depth and complexity and to mirror real life by rasping that love against the societal norms that both men obeyed, both of them marrying and begetting children, both loving their children, and, in a way, their wives."[25] While their marriages begin routinely enough, the reunion of Ennis and Jack as witnessed by Alma has a devastating effect, but one she doesn't speak of for years. Their marriage is one in which Ennis rules the bed, turning Alma over for a position reminiscent of his couplings with Jack; one also wonders who prefers Alma's arm pits being unshaved (SS 9).[26] Jack's marriage, too, is one in decline from its inception as Lureen comes to spend more and more of her time at the adding machine and at the beauty parlor, painting herself as the portrait of a successful Texas businesswoman of the 1970s.

During the course of the story, we get glimpses of the parenting skills of both Jack and Ennis. Jack lets his son Bobby steer a tractor in the parking lot, following a typical father-on-son bonding pattern, although much later in the story Jack admits he never wanted to have any kids — not a normal wish in the eyes of a society of breeders. Ennis is generally presented in a favorable light as a parent. He seems willing to do his share of child-rearing duties in a house "full of the smell of old blood and milk and baby shit, and the sounds ... of squalling and sucking and Alma's sleepy groans, all reassuring of fecundity and life's continuance to one who worked with livestock"(SS 9) — the breeder's duty and his pride. He would be prouder if Alma were to give him a son, but he loves his girls, his "little darlins," and they love him. After his divorce from Alma, he takes seriously his obligations of child support and visitation weekends.

However, Ennis lives a constant lie with his wife and daughters. He never takes them on vacations as a family because all of his spare time blocks are reserved for "fishing trips" with Jack. Undeniably, Ennis has shortchanged them. In addition, he seems willing to accept the male chauvinism of his era, place, and ilk, as we see in the scene where the angry husband tells his wife, "No one's eatin' it unless you're servin' it, Alma" (SP 54) while she hurries off to pick up an extra shift at the grocery store where she works to supplement their income.

The screenplay clearly situates the Del Mar and the Twist families in Americana. Even in the opening scene outside Aguirre's trailer, Director Ang Lee subtly establishes the traditional American context as a steepled church rises in the background. Several years later the town's Fourth of July fireworks display offers Ennis the opportunity to flex his tough-guy muscles as he violently chases a pair of foul-mouthed outlaws away as fireworks erupt behind him. Thanksgiving, another all-American holiday, becomes a showcase for each family, allowing Jack to confront his father-in-law L.D. who considers himself the "stud duck" and therefore the man who does the carving of the Thanksgiving turkey. An argument over a football game on television gives L.D. a chance to reiterate the party line: "You want your son to grow up to be a man, don't you, daughter? Boys should watch football" (SP 66). Jack turns off the television and demands that L.D. sit down, leaving the rest of carving to the newly dominant male of the house.[27]

For Ennis, that same Thanksgiving begins quietly, as he has joined his daughters, his now ex-wife Alma, and her new husband Monroe around their table. Alma is pregnant with Monroe's child. The dinner conversation seems a bit uncomfortable and forced, but we do see how Alma Jr. and Jenny dote on their father. (It is interesting to note that Ennis, who has always wanted a son, makes one nominally by calling his first-born "Alma Junior.") As Monroe and the girls gather around the television set, Ennis carries in some dishes to the kitchen where Alma performs her wifely "duty" as dish washer. Any seasonal feelings of goodwill soon dissipate into threatened violence when she finally confronts her ex-husband about "Jack Nasty" and fishing trips where no one fished. The fact that she waits until now to reveal what she knows is a sign of how important it was to her to maintain the pattern of the family. For eight years, she kept silent about what she had seen outside their apartment because it was too far outside the normality she knew and wanted.

When we last see Ennis, he is paid a visit by Alma Jr., whom he now calls simply "Junior," still looking for that son. She tells her father of her upcoming marriage to a roughneck (like the husband of her aunt, Ennis's sister) and invites her dad to her June wedding at the Methodist Church where Jenny will sing and Monroe will cater, the elements of tradition already falling into place. His immediate response is that he is scheduled to be on a roundup in June. Stepping to his refrigerator, he only needs a couple of seconds to remind himself of his lesson on priority: "You know what? I reckon that they can find themselves another cowboy.... My little girl ... is getting' married" (SP 96). He then toasts, "To Alma and Kurt" and to one of life's most enduring patterns, marriage — and another familiar familial story will begin.

While Ennis and Jack try hard to be good fathers to their own children, we learn that their own fathers had made some costly mistakes in child rearing. When Ennis was nine years old, his dad took him and his older brother to view the corpse of Earl, the partner of Rich, both local jokes because in their living together the town assumed their homosexuality. Earl was beaten with a tire iron and dragged "around by his dick till it pulled off" (SS 14). One cannot overestimate the impact of that image on Ennis as he weighs his options with Jack. From a Freudian perspective, the normal boy feels threatened by his father, who he believes wants to castrate him.[28] Seeing a man with a bloody gaping hole where his penis used to be must have subconsciously magnified that fear for young Ennis. Freud points out that to diffuse the threat, the son imitates the father, his body language, his speech, his thoughts, and his prejudices, hoping to protect himself by being like his father. The blatant message to young Ennis is: Queers get killed; the subliminal message is: Castration can happen. The suggestion that his father may have done it himself shows that on some level Ennis viewed his father as a potential castrater. During their reunion in the motel room, Ennis has no doubt that if his father was still alive and walked in on them in bed together, he'd go get his tire iron (SS 15).

After two or three beers at the bar in Signal in 1963, Jack turns the conversation — an easy steer because the topic is always right there — to his father: "[B]eats workin' for my old man. Can't please my old man no way" (SP 5) In pursuit of becoming more like his father to win his favor, Jack has become a bull rider as his father was, but the son never had the successes that his father did. Jack's hurt is almost palpable when he tells Ennis that Mr. Twist did not even teach his son any of his tricks of bullriding nor did he ever come to see Jack ride. The word *twist* is a rodeo term for the strength of thighs and butt muscles required for a bull rider to lock onto the bull.[29] Jack's failed rodeo career regularly reinforces his father's message: not enough twist. Still Jack returns every summer to help his father on the old family ranch. The short story gives us another snapshot of John Twist's behavior, a disturbing one and fraught again with Freudian significance. At age three or four, Jack had trouble using the toilet, and he often urinated on the toilet seat or the bathroom floor. One day his father went into a rage when he discovered some poorly aimed sprinkles around the toilet. Jack recalls, "Christ, he licked the stuffin out a me, knocked me down on the bathroom floor, whipped me with his belt. I thought he was killin me. Then he says, 'You want a know what it's like with piss all over the place? I'll learn you,' and he pulls it out and let go all over me, soaked me..." (SS 25). In the process young Jack notices his father's foreskin which he viewed, in Proulx's words, as "an anatomical disconformity." Experiencing the Freudian threat of castration by his father, toddler Jack sees that part of his penis has been removed: "I see they'd cut me different like you'd crop a ear or scorch a brand. No way to get it right with him after that" (SS 25). His perception of deformity must certainly undermine his confidence. In addition, psychologists have long known the effect of the self-fulfilling prophecy: Tell a kid he can't do anything right, and that's usually what he'll do. Poor Jack. He sure knows how to make love to Ennis, but he usually fails at bullriding, shooting (he misses a coyote and an elk), harmonica playing, cooking, opening a can, and catching keys. "Nothin' never come to my hand the right way," he tells Ennis in their last trip together, after admitting that he never wanted any children (SS 20). Father Twist is always right there.

We actually get to see Jack's parents in their stark surroundings, a cold and lonely house, where Mrs. Twist has learned to endure her husband, of whose life she was never a part. Jack's mother tolerates her husband's rude behavior, his menacing expression, and his hard words: "[Jack] thought he was too goddamn special to be buried in the family plot" (SS 24). She invites Ennis to go upstairs to view Jack's boyhood bedroom which she has preserved as it was 20 years ago. Before Jack departs, Mr. Twist announces his final decision on Jack's ashes: they will not be scattered on the mountain but "buried in the family plot." In the contexts of *Brokeback Mountain* and pattern maintenance, the term "family plot" suggests a meaning other than a patch of land in a cemetery. We are either part of the family plot, or we are outsiders, nonconformists unwilling to become characters in the planet's most overused story line (or its most ingrained conspiracy)—and waiting for a steed to carry us into some new and unexplored narrative.[30]

For Ennis and Jack, whose love is labeled a "force of nature," their relationship began as shepherds on horseback, playing at cowboys, in the escape afforded by the high meadows of Brokeback Mountain where they felt themselves "suspended above ordinary affairs" (SS 7). The far-distant barking of ranch guard dogs was an easy-to-dismiss reminder of the world where patterns are rigorously maintained and deviations dangerous. Brokeback became a separate reality and their true home. Within the sphere of their togetherness on the mountain they found a strength, a beauty, and a freedom, not dependent on previous perceptions of others. There were language-free truths there to be discovered and relished, not predetermined and inflicted. As to a child, their world there was a new geography of exploration and sensation. Life was play. On Brokeback the sun was the only clock they needed, and time was boundless permission, as to a child.

One can imagine that Ennis and Jack, their love on-growing, could have found a way to bring the cinemascopic freedom of the mountain into a small, newly built cabin on a ranch outside Lightning Flat, a fit name for a good place to domesticate so rich a passion and keep it glowing. The power of the patterns ruled otherwise. The family plot ensnared them both and offered them a safe, easy, and popular alternative way to spend most of the days of their lives. That plot confined their transcendent love to a week or two each year in the hidden shadows of Brokeback Mountain (and its neighboring peaks). That plot cost Jack his life and Ennis the love of his life. When Jack's ashes were buried in a cemetery plot, the ultimate *concealment* was achieved, covered in dirt, never to be corporeal again. For Ennis, so accustomed to finding his sense of personal identity "in the cracks"—now on the back of a closet door—Jack's death might have finally given him an authenticity, one anchored in his inconsolable grief. Freedom is indeed difficult.

Notes

1. In *Equus* the horse is a figure of both worship and sexual abandon. While Alan Strang calls Equus his "Godslave" and enchains his horse with "chinkle-chankle" (bridle), it is really the boy who becomes slave to this god. The slave/master paradox takes on psychological as well

as religious implications when one considers Freud's comparison of the ego (also viewed as the Apollonian, Dysart) and the id (the Dionysian, Alan) to a rider and his horse. Freud writes, "The horse supplies the locomotive energy and the rider has the prerogative of determining the goal and of guiding the movements of his powerful mount towards it. But all too often in the relationship between the ego and the id we find a picture of the less ideal situation in which the rider is obliged to guide his horse in the direction in which it itself wants to go" (*New Introductory Lectures in Psycho-Analysis* , ed. and trans. James Strachey [New York: W.W. Norton, 1933/1965], 96).

With Ennis and Jack, too, we see Dionysian forces at odds with the Apollonian as these men alternately embrace their sexual passion for one another and their obligation to their families. Ennis turns to his experience as a horseman to characterize the rampaging passion that can overcome them: "No reins on this one"—a Dionysian force unleashed (SS 13). He rightfully fears the danger that their unsublimated instincts invite.

2. Peter Shaffer, *Equus* (London: Penguin, 1973), 2.35, 108. For a more complete analysis of these themes in *Equus* (also shared by another Shaffer play, *The Royal Hunt of the* Sun), see James R. Stacy, "The Sun and the Horse: Peter Shaffer's Search for Worship," *Educational Theatre Journal* 28, no. 3 (October 1976): 325–337.

3. In the original New York production of *Equus*, Jill was played by Roberta Maxwell, who thirty years later played Jack Twist's mother in *Brokeback Mountain*.

4. Shaffer, 2.25, 82.

5. Shaffer, 2.35,108.

6. Shaffer, 2.25, 82.

7. In *The Birth of Tragedy* (1872) Friedrich Nietzsche explores the interplay of the Dionysian and the Apollonian in ancient Greece, with Dionysus representing the ecstatic, passionate, spontaneous, and preverbal impulses in humankind and Apollo acting to counter the chaos with reason, form, and language. See *Nietzsche: The Birth of Tragedy and Other Writings*, ed. Raymond Geuss and Ronald Speirs (Cambridge: Cambridge University Press, 1999).

8. Shaffer, "'To See the Soul of Man...,'" *New York Times*, Oct. 24, 1965, sec. 2, p. 3.

9. Erving Goffman, *Asylums: Essays in the Social Situations of Mental Patients and Other Inmates* (Garden City, NY: Anchor Books/Doubleday, 1961), 320. While Goffman focuses on inmates, he specifically applies this observation to "free society" as well.

10. Sheldon Litt, "The Impact of Existential Philosophy on Modern Psychology," *Positive Health*, <http://www.positivehealth.com/permit/Articles/Regular/litt40.htm> (accessed Mar. 14, 2006).

11. Paul Livingston, "Martin Heidegger: 'The Letter on Humanism," *Homepage*, Mar. 2, 2005, <http://www07.homepage.villanova.edu/paul.livingston/martin_heidegger%20-%20letter%20on%20humanism.htm> (accessed April 10, 2006).

12. The outside world has a way of insisting itself into Ennis's insecure conscience whether it's a ringing phone, a white pickup truck slowly cruising by, or distant barking dogs (heard that first summer as they head for their first conversation over drinks at the bar and later in their tent on Brokeback). Ennis admits to Jack that sometimes he's so paranoid that he thinks everyone in town knows their secret (SP 71).

13. Ilan Gur-Ze'ev, "Martin Heidegger, Transcendence, and the Possibility of Counter-Education," in *Heidegger, Education, and Modernity*, ed. Michael A. Peters (Lanham, Md.: Rowman & Littlefield, 2002), 71.

14. Ibid., 70–71.

15. Heidegger, "Letter on Humanism," in *Basic Writings* (London: Routledge, 1996), 242.

16. Heidegger, *Being and Time*, trans. John Macquarrie and Edward Robinson (New York: Harper & Row, 1962), 213.

17. Shaffer, *Equus*, 1.1, 18.

18. For a more in-depth look at the power of naming, see "Love and Silence, Penguins and Possibility," beginning on p. 205 of this anthology.

19. Judy C. Pearson et al., *Human Communication*, 2nd ed. (New York: McGraw Hill, 2004), 245

20. Gur-Ze'ev, "Martin Heidegger," 65–66.

21. Ibid., 74.

22. Ibid., 66. By extension, one could propose that labeling also turns the "true subject" (the authentic self) into a something rather than a someone.

23. Annie Proulx, "Getting Movied," in *Brokeback Mountain: Story to Screenplay* (New York: Scribner, 2005), 130.

24. Brief identifications of these and other cut scenes (40 minutes worth) are listed at http://www.hometheaterforum.com/archive_forum/showthread.php?postid=2963204 (posted Mar. 10, 2006; accessed Sept. 23, 2006).

25. Proulx, "Getting Movied,"132.

26. Proulx's choice of the name *Alma* is an interesting one because while most Americans think of it as a female's name, it is also a male's name — most evident in this country in the Book of Mormon where Alma, which means "nurturer," is a leading prophet and Alma the Younger is his son.

27. Shrewd screenwriters, McMurtry and Ossana use the Thanksgiving scene to show Jack at his strongest in asserting his macho dominance — an immediate, audience-pleasing "rehabilitation" of Jack's image in the two preceding scenes: crying behind the wheel of his truck and picking up a male prostitute in Mexico.

28. Freud, *Introductory Lectures on Psycho-Analysis*, ed. and trans. James Strahey (New York: W. W. Norton, 1920/1966), 459–461.

29. Gyllenhaal, "WANTED (preferably alive): Gyllenhaal and Lee," interview by Camille Ricketts, Dec. 8, 2005, *Chicago Tribune*, <http://metromix.chicagotribune.com/news/Celebrity/mmx-0609050387dec05,1,57738477.story> (accessed Jan. 12, 2005).

30. Given the detachment of many gays and lesbians from the demands of procreation and child-rearing, alternate life narratives may be more readily available in today's society. See Judith Halberstam, *A Queer Time and Place: Transgender Bodies, Subcultural Lives* (New York: New York University Press, 2005).

4

Love and Death in an American Story: A "Vulgar" Reading of *Brokeback Mountain*

by John Kitterman

In 1960 Leslie Fiedler's controversial work on American fiction, *Love and Death in the American Novel*, offered a sweeping characterization of American literature as reflecting a specific theme: a fear of heterosexuality which drives men into the wilderness to escape domesticity and into the company of their "dusky" brothers, those who have been cheated out of their birthright by the genocide whites practiced on Native Americans and by their exploitation of Africans. Beginning with a 1948 *Partisan Review* essay on *Huckleberry Finn*, Fiedler suggested that Twain's narrative conceals in an adolescent adventure a recurring myth of America as a new Eden already fallen from innocence.[1] Continuing his thesis through the trilogy of *Love and Death in the American Novel* (1960), *Waiting for the End* (1964), and *The Return of the Vanishing American* (1968), Fiedler traced the trajectory of what he saw as a failure of American writers to deal with heterosexual love, substituting instead a romanticized homosexual encounter in the wilderness between the white man and the red or the black.[2] For anyone familiar with Fiedler's work, the themes and symbolism of Annie Proulx's short story "Brokeback Mountain" or the film based on it cannot come as a surprise. In some ways we could say that the story is a culmination of Fiedler's thesis in which the "innocent" male sexuality implicit in the myth comes out of the closet and declares that this is, indeed, as so many of its critics would wish not to call it, a "gay cowboy" film. By examining the details of Fiedler's American myth and applying them to the story and film versions, and by updating Fiedler's Freudian model to include its Lacanian interpretation, we can see that the power of Proulx's narrative

45

LIVERPOOL JOHN MOORES UNIVERSITY
LEARNING SERVICES

ıg Lee's film lies not just in the language and imagery of the writer's
⁀rector's art, but also in the representation of an enduring myth always
held in unconscious abeyance in the American psyche.

Fiedler's Interpretation of Classic American Novels

If we look first at the American myth Fiedler describes, we can then turn
to the way the "Brokeback Mountain" narrative contains and offers a culmination of key elements in his theory. In the preface to the 1966 Second Edition of *Love and Death in the American Novel*, Fiedler remarks that he hopes
new readers will find his book "still as lively, and in the best sense of the word,
as vulgar as ever."[3] His use of the word "vulgar" alludes both to his unconventional argument about sexuality in classic American literature and to the assault
he withstood for creating a new kind of criticism, very different, as he puts it,
from the "genteel tradition, with its emphasis on textual analysis, its contempt
for general ideas, and its fear of popular culture," meanings of the word kept
alive in this essay. Since the 1960's, of course, under the influence of postmodernism, literary analysis has undergone a sea change from the New Criticism
of John Crowe Ransom and Robert Penn Warren. Today we are not surprised
by an interdisciplinary approach to interpreting texts, literary or cinematic,
one which is grounded in the social and cultural context of the times.

However, coming as it did at the end of the Eisenhower era, Fiedler's
thesis was roundly attacked and often dismissed by those on the right as reductive and unproven. After the initial scandalized reactions to Fielder's argument that *Huckleberry Finn*, *Moby Dick*, and *The Last of the Mohicans* were
founded on a repressed homosexual desire, the main argument against Fiedler
eventually came from the left. It centered on his use of a now compromised
Freudian tenet, the orthodox assumption that there is a so-called "normal"
developmental sequence for males which involves leaving behind adolescent
fantasies of freedom from responsibility and of homosexual desires so that men
can engage in adult, committed, heterosexual relationships. Fielder was a
product of his time and could not completely avoid the repressive tendencies
of 1950s Freudianism toward sexual conformity, a neo-Victorian psychoanalysis which French theorists like Lacan worked over in the 1960s. Fiedler astutely
pointed out the latent homosexual themes in the great tradition of American
literature, but he shied away from endorsing overt homosexuality as a viable
component of the American identity. By recounting the virtues of the frontier encounter between the European American and the "primitive" man of
color while avoiding the sexual implication that American homosexuality
might be normal behavior, he seemed to want to have his cake and eat it too,
and contemporary critics have taken him to task for his ambivalence.[4]

Fiedler believed there was something in the early American character that turned writers away from the ideals of the European sentimental love tradition with its emphasis on heterosexual marriage and domestic life and toward youthful adventure, a case of arrested development in the collective psyche of these new people. He writes:

> In this sense, our novels seem not primitive, perhaps but innocent, unfallen in a disturbing way, almost juvenile. The great works of American fiction are notoriously at home in the children's section of the library, their level of sentimentality precisely that of a pre-adolescent.... Our great novelists, though experts on indignity and assault, on loneliness and terror, tend to avoid treating the passionate encounter of a man and woman, which we expect at the center of a novel. Indeed, they rather shy away from permitting in their fictions the presence of any full-fledged, mature women, giving us instead monsters of virtue or bitchery, symbols of the rejection or fear of sexuality.[5]

The reason for this avoidance of heterosexual themes, he suggests, lies in the American unconscious, where an unresolvable conflict gets repressed, the conflict between America as natural paradise and America as howling wilderness. North America was a kind of Garden of Eden, a prelapsarian world filled with primitive people, but the westering Europeans also needed to subdue the wilderness and formulated an ideology of superiority that allowed them to exploit Indians and Africans. Inheriting a sense of doom from the Calvinistic Puritans, early Americans were at the same time obsessed with sin in the untainted woods: "The American writer inhabits a country at once the dream of Europe and a fact of history; he lies on the last horizon of an endlessly retreating vision of innocence — on the 'frontier,' which is to say, the margin where the theory of original goodness and the fact of original sin come face to face."[6] Finally, because of these conflicts American fiction tends to be symbolic rather than realistic like its European counterpart, finding in allegory a way of both repressing and representing the unconscious, the truth that dare not be told: "That tradition [of symbolism] was born of the profound contradictions of our national life and sustained by the inheritance from Puritanism of a 'typical' (even allegorical) way of regarding the sensible world — not as an ultimate reality but as a system of signs to be deciphered."[7] In the case of *Huckleberry Finn*, for example, the fact that a black man fleeing from a tyrannical system of enslavement loves a white boy escaping the restrictions of "petticoat government" necessitates a new kind of relationship on the margins of American society, in a still-pristine river landscape. It is a relationship which runs counter to the civilizing effects of society, and for Fiedler it is an immature one: "So buried at a level of acceptance which does not touch reason, so desperately repressed from overt recognition, so contrary to what is usually thought of as our ultimate level of taboo — the sense of that love can survive only in the obliquity of a symbol, persistent, archetypical, in short, as a myth: the boy's homoerotic crush, the love of the black fused into a single thing."[8]

"Brokeback Mountain" and the film that followed it in many ways culminate these themes, resonating with the American public precisely because they expose these contradictions in American culture inherent from the very beginning, indeed, even before the discovery of America in the imagination of the European as an unfallen paradise to the west where those rejected from conventional society might find the freedom to live a new life. There are several important areas where Fiedler's groundbreaking work can be usefully connected to the story and film: the nature of the Western as genre, the idea of wilderness and how a mythical nature forms a fitting background for expressions of homosexuality and the avoidance of the female, and the way a Freudian interpretation might be opened up through a Lacanian paradigm. Finally, Fiedler's thesis is useful in exploring the controversy as to whether or not this is a "gay cowboy" film.

Fiedler's Thesis and the Brokeback *Narrative as Western*

Contending that American writers have tended to describe themselves topographically by the points of the compass, Fiedler defines a Western as:

> a fiction dealing with the confrontation in the wilderness of a transplanted WASP and a radically alien other, an Indian — leading either to a metamorphosis of the WASP into something neither White nor Red (sometimes by adoption, sometimes by sheer emulation, but *never* by actual miscegenation), or else to the annihilation of the Indian (sometimes by castration-conversion or penning off into a ghetto, sometimes by sheer murder). In either case, the tensions of the encounter are resolved by eliminating one of the mythological partners — by ritual or symbolic means in the first instance, by physical force in the second [emphasis Fiedler's].[9]

According to Fiedler, the metamorphosis of the white man through his encounter with the native produces "at last the cowboy — or maybe next-to-last, for after him comes the beatnik, the hippie, one more wild man seeking the last West of Haight-Ashbury in high-heeled boots and blue jeans."[10] Because Proulx's short story begins in 1963, just before this transformation of white man into native becomes commodified by the counterculture into pseudo-Indian, cowboys in "Brokeback Mountain" are still cowboys, or rather they are the last cowboys. With the disappearance of the Indian from the American consciousness, the cowboy represents the last of the dying red blood of the new continent, and with really nowhere else to go except into a pseudo-native, hippie subculture, the cowboy or Western novel becomes what it has always threatened, according to Fiedler's thesis, to become — a story of overt homosexual love.[11] The gay cowboy represents, in effect, the return of the repressed: what American fiction was always hinting at but dared not reveal. The "vanishing American" Indian, as Fiedler calls him, or we could even say the "dusky other" of whatever non-white color, reappears in "Brokeback Mountain" as the two gay men finding each other through a blood brotherhood in one of the few remaining unspoiled landscapes in the country. The movie version goes further than the story in suggesting the symbolism of white and dark: Heath Ledger as Ennis is blonde and wears a white hat, while Jake Gyllenhaal as Jack is dark featured and wears black. Jack too is associated, it might be argued, with an ethically dark "other," the Mexican male prostitute whose company he seeks as a substitute for Ennis.

If we follow this thread of reasoning, Fiedler's speculations become even more relevant, for he observes that in the traditional Western it is *never* through intercourse that the "natural" man and the WASP establish a bond, and that if the white man is not changed by the red man then the Indian must be eliminated, perhaps as a kind of sacrifice to propitiate the threat of miscegenation. Here we begin to see how Proulx's Western culminates the genre by overturning it: the taboo against interracial mixing, heterosexual or homosexual, that Fiedler points out, is still in place in 1963 when the narrative begins, but it can be broken in the changed climate of the late 90s when the story was written, and in 2005 the public is even ready for a movie version. This particular plot was the last canyon the Western could ride off into, and finding itself against a stone wall, it could turn to face its enemy, the bourgeois status quo, and say, in effect, all right, you have been asking for this for four centuries, now you can see what this bond of love actually means in sexual terms.

But of course, there is a price: the price that still has to be paid because America may be tolerant enough to allow the film to be made, but not enough to believe what it says. Jack Twist must die, and he must die a horribly violent death, perhaps by "castration-conversion" as Ennis imagines it, based on his memory of the body of the gay cowboy his father showed him as a warning, "drug ... around by his dick until it pulled off" (SS 14). It seemed a reasonable fear that their homosexual encounter on Brokeback Mountain would lead to death; this is an American story, after all, set in the West. From the moment of their first intercourse, the possibility of sudden violence and death hangs over the story like cigarette smoke, so that even this most open-range, hard-bitten story has the feel of the Gothic about it, a genre, as Fiedler points out, that lends itself well to the American preoccupation with love and death. The argument is that homoerotic love in classic American fiction always exists in the shadow of death, because it primarily concerns a love between men who cannot articulate their feelings in a society indoctrinated in what the feminist poet Adrienne Rich calls "compulsory heterosexuality."[12] The transition in the film from the tent of Ennis and Jack's lovemaking to the scene of the slaughtered sheep provides the symbolism to confirm the feeling that nothing good can come of their love. The film seems, in effect, to be saying, yes, they were supposed to be watching the sheep, and like a couple of immature adolescents they weren't, but they too are sheep in American society, and who is watching them? Only Joe Aguirre with his spy glasses, a kind of snake in the garden.

The Wyoming landscape of course becomes another major character in the story and the film. Annie Proulx's writing and Ang Lee's cinematography are simultaneously so lyrical and so unsentimental that they go a long way toward restoring an American wilderness that signifies both an original innocence and a fallen reality. Consider the effect of this passage from the story right after the two have announced to each other that they are "not no queer[s]": "There were only the two of them on the mountain flying in the euphoric, bitter air, looking down on the hawk's back and the crawling lights of vehicles on the plain below, suspended above ordinary affairs and distant from tame ranch dogs barking in the dark hours. They believed themselves invisible, not knowing Joe Aguirre had watched them through his 10x42 binoculars for ten minutes one day..." (SS 7). Clearly this is an Edenic dream that is being laid before us, a dream of godlike beings living freely high above the plain where ordinary mortals crawl about like tame dogs. It echoes the passage from the first page when Ennis in his trailer remembers "that old, cold time on the mountain when they owned the world and nothing seemed wrong" (SS 1). Then he hears the wind hit the trailer "like a load of dirt coming off a dump truck," and he is buried under his memories which become the twenty-year narrative of their love. The imagery and language evoke a dream world, an optimistic world befitting two nineteen-year-old lonely young men who find themselves surrounded by a natural environment that encourages and sustains their sexual openness, but at the same time the dream is already a nightmare, nature is tainted by surveillance, the cold air is both "euphoric" and "bitter" in the same breath.

In this way the short story and the movie retell the mythic account of the conquest of America, the story of Adam before Eve. It is almost as if, set against the backdrop of Brokeback Mountain, homosexual love becomes naturalized, acceptable. That is the underlying message, but it is both hopeful and doomed. After all, it is on the frontier that the imagined encounter between the white European American and the darker "other" takes place, in the space between what is primitive taboo and what is conventional practice. Even Brokeback Mountain itself takes on a mythological, imaginary quality, as if it were not a real place. It is not a real mountain in Wyoming, as Proulx has admitted, and to some not even a real place in the history of the story, as Lureen suggests when she tells Ennis after Jack's death, that "knowing Jack, it might be some pretend place where the bluebirds sing and there's a whiskey spring," alluding to the folksong "Big Rock Candy Mountain," which describes a fantasy place where libidinal desires can run rampant (SS 23). The Wyoming mountains, in the movie especially, symbolize an eternally unfallen space, a Zarathustran abode where time stands still. The story and the movie represent homosexual love as a part of nature, just as the mountains and the rivers are part of the character of this continent. It makes sense that gay love is natural in a natural environment, and the message that there is some natural, biological origin to such love is hopeful, but at the same time how much natural environment in America is left and accessible?

The story conveys this message of doom as well: Because the reader or the viewer realizes that Brokeback Mountain is in some sense a fictional and idealized place, he can see homosexual love too as impossible. Then the dream of this wild, idyllic place slides back into the unconscious like the "panel" of his dream about Brokeback that Ennis recalls upon awakening at the beginning of the short story. Like the adolescents Fiedler recounts in his books — the Tom Sawyers and Huck Finns, the young Natty Bumppo and Ishmael, even the married Rip Van Winkle — Ennis and Jack represent a longing in American identity that must be denied, that is doomed to tragedy if it is not denied. But because it is a tragedy originating on the "last horizon" and played out in the natural world, the scenery of Brokeback Mountain lends it a grandeur and majesty that few domestic tales can rival. Because of this ambiguity between the real and imagined qualities of a homosexual love, the film is not likely to change many people's minds about how they view same-sex relationships, but it is likely to affect them on an unconscious level in ways which they will not be aware of and which may produce unpredictable results.

One such unconscious effect is an understanding of the relationship between women and men who discover that they are gay. In Fiedler's thesis male erotic bonding is usually combined in American mythic literature with a stereotyping of women into "monsters of virtue or bitchery."[13] It is true that the women in the story and the film do not come off as sympathetically as the men, perhaps because they are not as well developed, but the important question to ask is this: Do Ennis and Jack flee from Alma and Lureen, from their brand of "petticoat government," into each other's arms, or do the women get the short end of the stick, as it were, because the cowboys are already gay? One commentator has gone so far as to say that without the encounter on Brokeback Mountain, these two young men may have never realized they were gay,[14] a claim which, while quite possibly valid, still misses the point that the tragedy occurs because they are gay. Another, Stephen Hunter of the *Washington Post*, takes a moralistic stance and criticizes Ennis and Jack for their failure as fathers: "Generally, the movie is cruel to family. It seems to think family is a bourgeois delusion," implying perhaps that Ennis and Jack had better buckle down and sublimate their homosexuality or else their children will suffer, like Alma Jr. who "ends up in a gaudy Trans Am owned by her fiancé, a harbinger of roughneck disaster to come."[15]

In contrast to the implications of these critics, it can be argued that Jack is not escaping from domesticity or family responsibility into the wilderness — he does not even meet Lureen until after the first encounter with Ennis — while Ennis and Alma, although engaged when he meets Jack, apparently have not lived together and certainly have no kids yet. The imagery of stifling domesticity, particularly in Ennis and Alma's home, and the cool lack of intimacy in Jack and Lureen's are at least partly the long-term result of the way homoerotic love is viewed in American society. These men hide their sexuality and are forced to lead double lives, compromising their marriages. If they do not conform to society's expectations of cowboys, they might possibly die. As Ennis states, "We do that in the wrong place we'll be dead" (SS 13). In other words, in this culmination of Fiedler's American myth of frontier homoeroticism, the men no longer have to flee the "sivilizin'" effects of women because the homosexual element once hidden in the background has now come front and center. There has been a kind of reversal in consciousness, so that men who are attracted to other men no longer have to use women as an excuse to leave home. But they and their families still are made to suffer because America is not yet ready for this "myth" to come true.

So is this then a "gay cowboy" story? To listen to the filmmakers and most of the critics, it is not. The DVD extras include repeated commentaries from the writers, actors, and director about how it is "so much more than a gay cowboy movie." Daniel Mendelsohn, writing in the *New York Review of Books*, quotes Ang Lee as saying, "This is a universal story. I just wanted to make a love story."[16] The campaign to present *Brokeback Mountain* to the public tried hard to cover up the gay elements, but this repression, of course, is part of the psychological process of making people more aware of what is there by virtue of its denial, as Fiedler himself accomplished when he strictly ruled out "miscegenation" as a way for the white and dark to bond in his typology of the myth. Despite his protestation that homosexuality is only a stage in psychosexual development, Fiedler's account may be seen as nothing less than this: The Western, the most explicit of the Indian — white encounters in the American narrative, has always been a gay story waiting to happen. *Brokeback Mountain* is not a "gay cowboy" film in any conventional sense; it is not a Village People parody of cowboys much less a pornographic depiction of rough trade. It is not even a story about cowboys who happen to be gay.[17] Rather, it is an end stage in the working out of a national myth in which cowboys, as the literary offspring of the WASP and the Indian, make manifest what has been, until 1997 when Proulx wrote her story, only latent in the unconscious of the American psyche — a current of same-sex love befitting a land of promise with its democratic ideals and uncivilized landscape.[18]

A Lacanian View of the Brokeback Narrative

One of the problems with Fiedler's thesis, as mentioned earlier, is that he relies on an orthodox Freudian notion of sexuality, in which the fulfillment of sexual development consists of subsuming the demands of the id, the "natural" man, under the control of the ego or superego, the "civilized" man, so that man's sexual nature serves the societal status quo. (That is why anal intercourse cannot be acceptable except as an aberration and why the Indian must die if no satisfactory metamorphosis with the white man takes place.) Lacan replaced Freud's tripartite id/ego/superego divisions of human subjectivity with a different model, one which took into account the primary role of language in the formation of the subject: the terms he used are the Real, the Symbolic, and the Imaginary orders.[19] Instead of the Freudian nineteenth-century, mechanistic model in which the superego tries to keep a lid on the boiling cauldron of the id, Lacan adopted some of the language theory developed in the twentieth century to show how human beings use words to deal with a loss. Lacanian psychoanalysis defines human desire as a lack instead of a libidinal force, a lack brought on by what Lacan playfully called the "castration" or separation of the infant from the only world he has known — the mother, or (m)other, an "other" with whom he has been fused as an infant — when he begins to use language as a child. Language, that is to say, is what separates the child from the mother. The early, infantile, pre-symbolic state of identification with parts of the mother — her voice, her gaze — that precedes the use of language makes up the Imaginary, while the categorizing effects of language itself, passed on within the network of one's society, constitute the Symbolic. In effect, human beings stitch up the "wound" they have experienced of being "castrated" into separate subjectivities by fantasizing imaginary unifications with the world outside themselves, at the same time using words to explain and cover up the lack that is at the core of their identity, the lack of the (m)other, the missing oneness. The Imaginary and the Symbolic work together, in other words, to avoid the Real: all that is non-human, the state of nature or being that precedes the entrance into both the Imaginary and the Symbolic human world. The Real is impossible to describe in words or to imagine and therefore too terrifying to be confronted. For

Lacan, the Real is not at all the same as "reality." Instead, "reality" is the human world the Imaginary and the Symbolic construct, and as such, can of course be described and imagined. However, the Real does leave a residue or remainder of itself, a slight connection to human reality, as we shall see later when we examine the symbolism of the shirts.

Using this newer psychoanalytic formulation, we can perhaps obtain a clearer view of the dynamics of the mythopoeic elements in the film narrative than we could using Fiedler's Freudian model. The idyll in the mountains, for example, especially the originating experience on Brokeback Mountain but including too the subsequent "fishing" trips Ennis and Jack take together, represents the Imaginary order at work: they are trying to circumvent in their fantasy life society's injunction against homosexual love, the Symbolic function. The Symbolic function, in a predominantly patriarchal society like the American one, largely falls to fathers, and in this respect the case of Ennis and Jack is painfully instructive. Both young men grew up with fathers who not only problematized their duty in distributing society's codes about how to be a man, as if somehow they already knew their sons were gay, and cast them into the Imaginary where they had to find their own way (a process Lacan calls foreclosure), but they also went out of their way to symbolically "castrate" their sons through non-language threats. For Ennis it was the spectacle of the castrated gay cowboy that his father made him witness, while for Jack in Proulx's story it was the moment his father pissed on him and he saw that his father had not been circumcised while Jack was "cut." After that kind of intimidation, the fact that Jack's father's denied him any of his knowledge about rodeoing seems fairly tame: "Jack said his father had been a pretty well known bullrider years back but kept his secrets to himself, never gave Jack a word of advice, never came once to see Jack ride, though he had put him on the woolies when he was a little kid" (SS 6). The effect of the primordial castration anxiety on Ennis is his inarticulateness, which accounts, much more convincingly, for his strained relationship with his children than any shirking of his fatherly role: the movie makes clear that he loves them; he just cannot put his feelings into words. The effect of the foreclosure on Jack is his insistence to become what his father has denied him — a rodeo regular, part of the Western myth that he feels he must measure up to in order to be a man.

Departing from Fiedler's Freudian model, the Lacanian model of psychoanalytic interpretation avoids privileging of heterosexual love as the normalizing behavior for civilized human beings. Seeing homosexuality as a case of arrested development, as Freud and Fiedler do, turns gays into irresponsible children at best, perhaps an appropriate image for a story about an Edenic new land, but not for the narratives of a first-world nation. However, examining how Symbolic codes categorizing gay people are formed, passed along in society from father to son, and proliferated puts the burden on society to rethink the codes. Ironically perhaps, restructuring the Symbolic order, which includes the behavioral and physical sciences, allows the possibility of seeing homosexuality as a natural, not cultural, product as it becomes part of the status quo. That restructuring also takes the classic American narrative we have been discussing out of the realm of myth, out of the Imaginary where we left it on Brokeback Mountain, and puts it squarely back into the social order.

The Real, which has been excluded for the most part in the story and film, makes its appearance in the imagery of the embracing shirts (the shirts from their Brokeback summer, Jack's and Ennis's, the one Jack cherishes so much that he steals and puts on a hanger in his closet under his own.) The shirt scene at the end of the movie is one more piece of evidence that the story, while painstakingly realistic, is also highly symbolic, even allegorical, like so much of classic American fiction. The conventional symbolism of the shirts is tragic enough: Ennis now holds Jack in his arms as he did in the flashback scene on Brokeback Mountain, "when Ennis had come up behind him and pulled him close, the silent embrace satisfying some shared and sexless hunger.... Later that dozy embrace solidified in his memory as the single moment of artless, charmed happiness in their separate and difficult lives" (SS 22). The notion of "sexless hunger" seems to suggest that this is, indeed, a universal love story, until we remember that the two young men have been having sex all over the mountain for days. But the pathos is clear enough, and the realization that time has stopped but will start again as soon as they descend to the plains, is a truly tragic view. It is mostly tragic because they have no future; their love lives in the Lacanian Imaginary, like Brokeback Mountain itself.

On the other hand, it is not completely part of the Imaginary order; it might be more accurate to say that it partakes of both the Imaginary and the Real. It is in the Imaginary because they are living in a dream world above the clouds where society cannot see them until Joe Aguirre arrives with his binoculars. They have few words to describe what grips them; it is mainly in their innocent dream that such a love can exist. However, it is part of the Lacanian Real because this process of hiding the fatal nature of their impossible love in the ideal world of Brokeback Mountain leaves what might be called a scar, a remnant of its existence. Freud called this piece of the Real *das Ding* (the thing) and Lacan termed it *objet a*, the object which takes the place of the missing other left behind after the fall into individual subjectivity. It is what temporarily fills the lack in the self. Ennis and Jack's homoerotic love produces, as it were, the little piece of the Real which their imaginary identifications and their language cannot suture, a tangible reminder around which Ennis's world will revolve now that Jack is dead. Lacan argued that there is always a remnant of the Real which cannot be covered over by the Imaginary and Symbolic orders, and this remnant is the two intertwined shirts, more than just a symbol of their homosexual love and their idyll in the mountains. The shirts, in other words, are the material remainder of what happened in one singular point in time on the mountain. Ennis has a hard time putting their homosexual passion into language, as if he recognizes on some level that it is terrifyingly real in a way which language cannot describe: In the short story he alludes to it as "what happened back there" (SS 13), while in the film he actually uses Freud's words when he says, "*This thing* grabs hold of us at the wrong place, wrong time, and we're dead" (SP 52; emphasis added). The short story opens in Ennis's trailer where the shirts, hanging on a nail, "shudder slightly in the draft," as if they are ghosts stirred up by the wind which "rocks" the trailer. In fact, they are ghosts; they mark the return of the repressed, the piece of the real thing which sets the whole plot in motion, like an unburied body in a Greek tragedy. Their status as the Lacanian *objet a* is what gives them such incredible power to affect us emotionally. The shirts also outline the space of the empty subject, which in this case is the gay subject, in his traditional identity as an excluded other, a powerless sub-citizen in American society. In this story there cannot be one gay subject; there must be two, stained with the blood of their violent encounter on the frontier, their blood brotherhood in the American mythos, as Fiedler first pointed out.

The short story opens in Ennis' trailer, when he wakes after dreaming of Jack, and the rest of the narrative is a memory which fills out the "temporary silence" left when the wind stops blowing, ending where it began with the dream again. The movement of time in the story is thus circular. The movie, however, begins with the first meeting of the two ranch hands, and ends in the trailer with the framing of the two totemic objects — the shirts and the postcard of Brokeback Mountain — and the view out the window. The temporal flow is linear, with a future implied by the new relationship Ennis has with his daughter, his willingness to quit a job to attend her wedding. The film seems more hopeful than the story; it offers both the past and the future, and the future is there for Ennis to choose: his gesture to his daughter suggests that he has turned a corner, that possibly he will live for the future seen through the window. The story is much more relentlessly tragic — there is no escaping the cycle of dream, only stoicism in the face of an eternal recurrence, a kind of Nietzschean acceptance that dovetails with the Zarathustran majesty of the Brokeback idyll. Ang Lee provides a kind of Hollywood way out — a magnificently framed shot, nonetheless — but Proulx offers only more struggle for Ennis: "There was some open space between what he knew and what he tried to believe, but nothing could be done about it, and if you can't fix it you've got to stand it" (SS 28). Open space, perhaps, is at the heart of American mythmaking, and characters like Ennis and Jack personify the tragedy that befalls people when society does not give them the same freedom that the land does.

Notes

1. Leslie Fiedler, "Come Back to the Raft Ag'in, Huck Honey!," in Adventures of Huckleberry Finn: *A Case Study in Critical Controversy*, 2nd ed., ed. Gerald Graff and James Phelan (Boston: Bedford/St. Martin's, 2004), 519–525.

2. Fiedler's trilogy consists of *Love and Death in the American Novel*, rev. ed. (New York: Stein and Day, 1975), *The Return of the Vanishing American* (New York: Stein and Day, 1969), and *Waiting for the End* (New York: Stein and Day, 1964).

3. Fiedler, *Love and Death*, 8.

4. See Christopher Looby, "'Innocent Homosexuality': The Fiedler Thesis in Retrospect," in Adventures of Huckleberry Finn: *A Case Study in Critical Controversy*, 526–541. Contemporary scholarship has pointed out that Freud himself was quite liberal in his own assessment of homosexuality. As Henry Abelove notes in his essay "Freud, Male Homosexuality, and the Americans," the founder of psychoanalysis believed homosexuality was not a disease, did not need treatment, and should not be illegal. He did, however, tend to view homosexuality as "a variation of the sexual function produced by a certain arrest of sexual development" (Abelove, in *Lesbian and Gay Studies Reader*, ed. Henry Abelove, Michele Aina Barale, and David Halperin [New York: Routledge, 1993], 381). Although Freud (and Fiedler) believed that gay people perhaps were not fully developed sexually, he remained throughout his life at odds with American psychoanalysts who were decidedly more conservative in viewing homosexuality as a medical problem; the American Psychiatric Association did not remove it from its list of illnesses until 1973.

5. Fiedler, *Love and Death*, 24.

6. Ibid., 27.

7. Ibid., 29.

8. Fiedler, "Come Back to the Raft," 522.

9. Fiedler, *The Return*, 24.

10. Ibid., 25.

11. See also what Native American writer Sherman Alexie has done to the Western, redefining it from the natives' point of view, particularly in a story like "The Toughest Indian in the World" in the collection of the same name in which the male Indian protagonist has a homosexual one night stand with an Indian boxer.

12. Adrienne Rich, "Compulsory Heterosexuality and Lesbian Existence," *Signs: Journal of Women in Culture and Society* 5, no. 4 (1980): 631–660.

13. Fiedler, *Love and Death*, 24.

14. Mick LaSalle, quoted in Daniel Mendelsohn, "An Affair to Remember," review of *Brokeback Mountain*, New York Review of Books 53.3 (2006), 13.

15. Stephen Hunter, "A Picture of Two Americas in 'Brokeback Mountain,'" Rev. of *Brokeback Mountain*, Washington Post, Feb. 2, 2006, C1.

16. Quoted in Mendelsohn, 13.

17. As for the "cowboy" part of this categorization, notwithstanding Annie Proulx's insistence that Ennis and Jack are merely "ranch hands," they are, at least for the general public anyway, cowboys, or at any rate they represent cowboys in this contemporary Western (see Matthew Testa, Interview, *Salt Lake City Weekly*, Dec. 29, 2005, <http://www.slweekly.com/article.cfm/closerange.html> [accessed June 30, 2006], 2).

18. For more on homosexuality among Native Americans, see some suggestions in Looby's essay, "'Innocent Homosexuality': The Fiedler Thesis in Retrospect."

19. Mindful of being trapped in the Symbolic order, Lacan made his lectures notoriously hard to understand. However, in Book I of *The Seminar of Jacques Lacan*, "Freud's Papers on Technique, 1953–1954" in chapter VII, "The Topic of the Imaginary," he discusses the three orders (Lacan, *Seminar*, ed. Jacques-Alain Miller, trans. John Forrester [New York: W.W. Norton, 1991]). For a clearer presentation, see Ellie Ragland-Sullivan, *Jacques Lacan and the Philosophy of Psychoanalysis* (Urbana: University of Illinois Press, 1987), in chapter 3, "A Lacanian Theory of Cognition."

5

The "Gay Film" That Wasn't: The Heterosexual Supplement in *Brokeback Mountain*

by Lisa Arellano

The movie *Brokeback Mountain*, of course, is based on Annie Proulx's short story of the same title. A close reading of Proulx's short story in conjunction with the screenplay reveals that the spare original text was expanded through the addition of multiple narrative elements whereby both Ennis and Jack are made intelligible through their reintegration into a heterosexual economy. In the story both characters are marked by their failed fatherhood, respectively evidenced by Jack's impotence as a father and Ennis's abandonment of all but the barest expressions of obligation. In the screenplay, Jack and Ennis are carefully redrawn as competent and caring father-figures, reassuring audiences of their "all but normal" masculinity and their "but for an aberration" sexual normalcy. This difference is apparent as the film reaches its penultimate resolution when Ennis "understands" the importance of attending his daughter's wedding, thus marking his simultaneous incorporation within, and capitulation to, a heteronormative world. The screenplay's 69 additional pages are comprised of precisely these kinds of heteronormative re-framings of the characters, resulting in a film that is centrally about heterosexuality and committedly resistant to the characters' sexual "misconduct." As a result, *Brokeback Mountain* constructs gay characters as powerless and tragic victims of forces beyond their control; simultaneously, the film preserves heterosexual privilege by obscuring the ways that heteronormativity produces an abjected other through social erasure and exclusion.

Larry McMurtry and Diana Ossana adapted Annie Proulx's "Brokeback Mountain" for the screen, drawing the spare 28-page original story into a 97-

page screenplay.[1] In an account of their first discussion about the project, Ossana recalls asking McMurtry if he had concerns that *Lonesome Dove* fans might revile this newer, potentially controversial material.[2] But to Ossana's delight, McMurtry expressed no such concern; Ossana cheerfully concludes it "was the only time we ever spoke about any political implications to making a film of 'Brokeback Mountain.'"[3] Relying on a close reading of the original short story and the screenplay, this essay seeks to do precisely the opposite — in effect, to examine at length the "political implications" of creating the "Brokeback Mountain" screenplay. For it is arguably the case, whether Ossana and McMurtry discussed the political implications of this adaptation either extensively or at all, that the stakes of the project are unusually high. This film — in all of its seeming promise of gay representation — comes at an historical moment when issues of sexual difference, normative relationships, and kinship are crucial within the political movements of sexual minorities as well as for normalizing legal and political institutions.[4] Within this highly charged context of debates concerning values, rights and recognition, "political implications" might be quite different for sexual minorities and heterosexual viewers (let alone for individuals within either of these groups). While Ossana's recounting is intended, arguably, as representative of McMurtry's (and her own) good intentions in pursuing this project, the lack of extended (or any) consideration of this political historical context produces a film that lays claim to gay representation when the movie is in fact saturated with heteronormative ideology and images.

Ossana's recollection may be little more than a casual claim to liberal intention, but her assertion also reveals the two central mechanisms whereby *Brokeback Mountain* does its normativizing work. First, the casual pass over political implications is grounded by a naïve belief that representations of sexual difference are somehow interchangeable — that the film would "be gay" in the same way that Proulx's short story is. On the contrary, while both versions of Brokeback Mountain "represent gayness," Proulx's short story is manifestly queer while Ossana and McMurtry's screenplay is patently heteronormative. Ossana's second and related assumption is that all such "gay" representations are, de facto, off-putting to certain kinds of viewers. These viewers, represented by Ossana as fans of *Lonesome Dove*, stand in for an unspecified heterosexual collectivity potentially unable or unwilling to digest or comprehend sexual difference. If the first obfuscation demonstrates the ways in which sexual diversity is monolithically compressed into an undifferentiated category of sexual deviance, this second obfuscation demonstrates the simultaneous process whereby heteronormativity acts as the unmarked category against which deviance is defined, and through which deviance is punished. It is both too simple and potentially dangerous to suggest that *Brokeback Mountain* is merely a consequence of this structure of normalcy and deviance; in fact, the adaptation and screenplay reveal the process through which the polarities of normative and deviant are produced.

"Straightening" the Story

The most crucial issues concerning the adaptation take place in the ways that McMurtry and Ossana expanded the short original text in order to create a feature-length film — in what McMurtry calls the "augmenting and amplifying" and what Ossana more explicitly names as "creating new scenes [and] fleshing out existing ones."[5] To make the point most simply, the "augmenting, amplifying, creating and fleshing out" involved interjecting innumerable heteronormative conventions and norms into a text that had originally focused entirely on one man's complicated struggle with his desires for another man. It is worth noting how this happened — for it is in the "straightening" of this narrative that the film's overall ideology is radically transformed into a context for the erasure of queer agency and subjectivity. The film's nominal claim for gay self-recognition is not only foreclosed, but replaced by a demand that queer viewers accept *Brokeback's* heteronormative world wherein queer desire is invisible, impossible, and deadly.

While the majority of the story's expansion takes place in the center of the film, it is worthwhile to begin with the film's opening scenes. For here the groundwork is laid for the film's thoroughgoing commitment to the representation of heteronormative kinship. After meeting Aguirre and procuring summer employment, Ennis and Jack speak to one another for the first time. The passage in the short story is characteristically brief:

> They found a bar and drank beer through the afternoon, Jack telling Ennis about a lightning storm on the mountain the year before that killed forty-two sheep, the peculiar stink of them and the way they bloated, the need for plenty of whiskey up there. He had shot an eagle, he said, turned his head to show the tail feather in his hatband [SS 3].

The screenplay, on the other hand, finds Jack and Ennis exiting Aguirre's trailer and engaging in the following exchange:

JACK: Jack Twist
ENNIS (shakes hands): Ennis
[a beat]
JACK: Your folks just stop at Ennis?
ENNIS (after a moment): Del Mar [SP 4].

This initial iteration of identification through normative kinship — here marked through Ennis's surname — is reiterated as Jack tells Ennis that working for Aguirre "beats working for [his] old man," and as he asks Ennis, "You from ranch people?" Ennis's response, wherein he narrates his own parents' deaths and discloses that he has been raised by his brother and sister, completes this inaugural framing of Jack and Ennis as normatively contextualized sons and siblings 5–6). The addition of these exchanges immediately suggests an interpretative framework for viewers as both characters are made recognizable through recourse to familial relationships; in effect, they are introduced to the viewer as "normal."

The difference between the two texts here is actually quite significant. At a comparable narrative moment in the short story, some of this information has been provided for the reader (the death of Ennis's parents, his engagement to Alma, both men's plans to earn and save money), *but this heteronormative orientation has not passed between the two characters.* In the film, Ennis and Jack's engagement with one another is rerouted through familial details that locate them within a world where their desire will be marked, from its inception, as impossible. While neither character discloses a joyful family past, the men's narratives are easily legible as, respectively, an orphan story and a conventional tale of the tensions between father and son. At the same time, the possibility that these men might have something to say to each other outside of the routine disclosure of familial details disappears. In the short story's inaugural dialogue, Jack boasts about his manliness (legitimately interpretable as sexual prowess) through a story of the feather in his hat, his knowledge about the mountain, and (in a section following the one cited above) the fact that he was "infatuated with the rodeo life" and successful enough that he "fastened his belt with a minor bull-riding medal" (SS 3). The idea that these two men can be made comprehensible through their birth families is quite distinct from the idea that they are posturing and preening for each other; the first notion makes recourse to the universality of relationships defined by heteronormative kin structures — the second acknowledges the existence of desires and relationships outside of, and defiant of, these norms. This pattern of erasing the queerness of the men's relationship and replacing it with legibly heterosexualized representations continues throughout the film. In fact, the overwhelming majority of additional pages in the screenplay derive from a series of scenes in the middle of the film that find the characters relocated within their respective heterosexual contexts.

Heteronormativity and the Closet

In Proulx's telling, Ennis's marriage and early life with Alma requires only one paragraph:

In December Ennis married Alma Beers and had her pregnant by mid-January. He picked up a few short-lived ranch jobs, then settled in as a wrangler on the old Elwood Hi-Top place north of Lost Cabin in Washakie County. He was still working there in September when Alma Jr., as he called his daughter, was born and their bedroom was full of the smell of old blood and milk and baby shit, and the sounds were of squalling and sucking and Alma's sleepy groans, all reassuring of fecundity and life's continuance to one who worked with livestock [SS 9].

The passage suggests that it might be heterosexual marriage that is marked by discordance or unfulfilled expectation — the marital bedroom smells of blood, sour milk, and shit. The passage also makes explicit recourse to the queer denigration of heterosexuals as "breeders" as Ennis is reassured by the seeming similarity between his marriage and the ranches where he works. This noticeably grim characterization is replaced in the screenplay by a series of scenes that portray an infinitely more pleasing picture of heterosexual couplehood. We see, for example, Ennis and Alma's wedding ceremony which concludes with a trite rendition of the post-ceremony kiss. Following the minister's particularly corny version of the prompt, "'...you may kiss the bride (wink, smile) and if you don't, I will...'," the direction makes it clear that *this* version of sexual relating is universal: "Everyone titters. Ennis and Alma, both nervous and shy, smile, kiss one another" (SP 29). "Everyone" titters, of course, because "everyone" here is presumptively heterosexual. The presumed familiarity and humor of the joke, wherein one man ribs another by violating his sexual claim to a woman, is a particularly good example of how heteronormativity works to constrain deviant sexual subjectivities. It is impossible, within this heterosexual world, *not* to laugh — which means, of course, that it is impossible to imagine Ennis's desire for Jack, or the literally shitty conditions in Ennis and Alma's bedroom.

The cheerful re-visioning of Ennis and Alma's life is amplified by the following scenes, marked in the screenplay as occurring sometime the following year. Here, we find Ennis and Alma playing in a toboggan. As they start down the hill, the direction tells us, "Alma squeals in delight; Ennis whoops it up." The scene concludes when they overturn at the bottom of the hill and "Very young, they laugh, throw snow on each other" (SP 29).[6] Some time later the same year, we find Ennis and Alma at a drive-in movie: "Alma has her head on Ennis's shoulder. Ennis has his arm around her. She cuddles in closer. She's pregnant, just showing. Feels the baby move. Takes his hand. Places it on her tummy" (SP 30). The visual cues are overwhelming at this point in the film — this couple is young and in love.[7] While these events occur after Ennis and Jack's summer on the mountain, Ennis's prior sexual deviance seems not only forgotten here, but forgettable. While it would be possible to read the wedding scene as implicitly self-critical (i.e., to imagine that we are being shown that Ennis is experiencing a profound alienation from the principal public rite of heterosexual normalcy), it is far more difficult to bring this reading to bear on the young couple's antics in the snow or their tender caresses at the drive-in. These scenes include no witness by the church, State, or community — Ennis's seeming heterosexuality has been created by Ossana and McMurtry exclusively for the viewer's benefit. All of which raises the question: What might these benefits be?

These benefits can be partially understood through Michael Warner's assertions about "the closet": "Common mythology understands the closet as an individual's lie about him- or her-self. Yet queers understand, at some level, that the closet was built around them, willy-nilly, by dominant assumptions about what goes without saying, what can be said without a breach of decorum, who shares the onus of disclosure, and who will bear the consequences of speech and silence...."[8] Indeed, what we see in the screenplay throughout these scenes is the building of a closet, i.e., the introduction of normative and thus *normativizing* representations. But it is important to note that the closet is not only being built around Ennis — for nominally, the film is concerned with depicting the ways that Ennis is hogtied by a culture of masculinity and heterosexuality — it is also being built around non-normative viewers. The scenes depicting Ennis's life with Alma — even those representing the challenges of their working class rural existence — offer a series of conventional and familiar tableaus. This is precisely what makes the heterosexual supplement in the screenplay dangerous. As Warner suggests, it is heteronormativity that "goes without saying." The possibility that these scenes were added to Proulx's project without *extensive* reflection about the political implications for queer viewers exemplifies Warner's assertion that it is the queer subject who inevitably bears the responsibility for negotiating the rules of silence and disclosure.[9] Moreover, these normative and normativizing scenes produce two potential effects for heterosexual viewers. First, these viewers are invited to recognize and identify with Ennis and Alma; they are, in effect, encouraged to understand Ennis as familiar. This invitation produces a second, corollary effect — a necessary aversion to Ennis's persistent desire for Jack. For the film, having engaged in its own form of seduction is poised to enact a reversal on the viewer wherein this familiar on-screen world will be undone by Jack's return. Proulx's masterful and minimal paragraph about Ennis and Alma produces nearly the opposite effect — a proportional distribution of the story's text in which Ennis's life with Alma is a painful and discordant distraction from the time he spends with Jack.

In Proulx's "Brokeback Mountain," Jack never appears outside of his encounters with Ennis and the details of his life in Texas appear only as they are reported to Ennis during their periodic reunions. In this sense, the screenwriters' addition of scenes depicting Jack's life with Lureen is even more conspicuous, as this rewriting changes not only the proportional significance of the men's relationships but the extent to which the original story was about Ennis del Mar rather than about Ennis and Jack. Arguably, in dissipating the narrative between two parallel characters, the impact of Ennis's struggle with his desires is lost and the story becomes more generically about (as the popular phrase suggests) "gay cowboys." But it is certainly the case that the scenes involving Jack's life in Texas make him, like Ennis, recognizably and reassuringly heterosexual.

Ideal Masculinity and Fatherhood

In addition to being redrawn as fully functioning heterosexuals, the film re-imagines both characters as committed and competent fathers. Early in the film, Ennis is seen "cradling" and "rocking" his daughter Jenny, "patting" and "soothing" Alma Jr., and suggesting to Alma that he take the girls to town to "get 'em an ice cream" (SP 33). Later in both versions of the story, Ennis joins Alma and her new husband for Thanksgiving dinner and we are told that Ennis does his best not "to be a sad daddy" (SS 16).[10] The screenplay supplements this awkward familial encounter with a reassuring note of direction, "His girls love him, their faces [are] rapt when their daddy speaks" (SP 67). The film's characterization of Ennis is markedly different from the one in the story wherein we find Ennis saying, "I used to want a boy for a kid ... but just got little girls" and, by way of explaining to Jack why he can't get away, "You forget how it is being broke all the time.... You ever hear of child support? I been payin' out for years and got more to go" (SS 20). In fact, Proulx's Ennis is an awkward and cynical father, more bound by the legal mandates of divorce proceedings than any genuine commitment to, or affection for, his daughters.[11]

Similarly, Jack's secondhand stories about his mostly failed attempts at fatherhood are replaced in the film with iconographic representations of father and son. In a scene now infamously depicted on one of the movie's promotional posters we see Jack "breathlessly" entering the room following the birth of his son. In response to an unwelcome intrusion from Lureen's parents, the direction tells us that she "gives Jack a what-can-we-do expression." Making recourse to yet another inevitable convention of heterosexual kinship, we are shown the young couple colluding against the pesky in-laws. Later, we are taken to the family ranch and shown Jack and his son driving a tractor, the child positioned in his father's lap.[12] As the inevitable conclusion to this predictable father/son tableau, Jack removes his hands from the wheel and encourages his son, "Whoa, son, there you go. No hands! It's all yours, Bobby. It's all yours" (SP 59). The film's Jack is a devoted and playful father, not merely conventional but ideal in his care for his young son.

While the short story suggests that Ennis fails at fatherhood as a result of disinterest, Jack is characterized by a genuine but thwarted commitment to his son. Proulx's Jack tells Ennis that he is "worried about his boy who was, no doubt about it, dyslexic or something, couldn't get anything right, fifteen years old and couldn't hardly read, *he* could see it though goddamn Lureen wouldn't admit to it and pretended the kid was o.k., refused to get any bitchin kind a help about it. He didn't know what the fuck the answer was. Lureen had the money and called the shots" (SS 19). Ossana and McMurtry's Jack has an entirely different relationship to his son's condition which we are shown during one of the additional scenes between him and Lureen:

> JACK: Speaking of Bobby, did you call the school back yet about getting him a tutor?
> LUREEN: I thought you were gonna call.
> JACK : I've complained too much, his teacher don't like me. Now it's your turn [SP 57].

The revised Jack is both interested and active in parenting his son — if anything, the screenplay tells us, a little *over* interested. Jack's impotence as a father is again reversed in the film when he is shown manfully challenging his father-in-law over the Thanksgiving table. After Jack orders his son away from the television and back to the table against his father-in-law's wishes, he explicitly claims his patriarchal territory: "This is my house! This is my child! And you're my guest! So sit the hell down, or I'll knock your ignorant ass into next week..." (SP 66). The direction notes that Lureen "is secretly pleased" (visually represented as another conspiratorial expression — this time a smile) and undoubtedly the audience is pleased as well. For this Jack is not only an interested father but a manly one. While the gendered dynamics in the scene veer towards chillingly patriarchal (Jack's marked use of "my" and Lureen's pleasure over his chest-thumping), the scene clearly suggests that whatever Jack's deviant desires may mean, they do not compromise his ability to engage in normative kinship.

The Impossibility of Queer Love

There are further examples of the ways that Ossana and McMurtry created a "heterosexual supplement" to the short story, but the most striking distinction between Proulx's understanding of Ennis and Jack's relationship and the screenwriters' misunderstanding actually involves a seemingly miniscule, but symbolically enormous, deletion. When Jack initially arrives to see Ennis after the men have been apart for four years, the film shows Ennis, "bounding down the stairs two at a time to Jack. "[The men] [s]eize each other by the shoulders, hug mightily, squeezing the breath out of each other, saying sonofabitch, sonofabitch…. Then, as easily as the right key turns the lock tumblers, their mouths come together" (SP 46). The direction here replicates Proulx's text exactly except for the fact that Ossana and McMurtry decided to eliminate Proulx's most significant detail. In Proulx's version, the men strain towards, and against, each other in a fierce embrace (legitimately depicted visually in the film) "until they pulled apart to breathe and Ennis, not big on endearments, said what he said to his horses and daughters, little darlin" (SS 10). This endearment, uttered by the notoriously unspeaking and emotionally silent Ennis, is a testament of his *love* for Jack. That the men might sexually desire one another — that they might grope each other, wrestle with each other, and fuck each other — is ultimately insignificant in comparison to this momentary but life-altering declaration. It is both banal and extremely necessary to observe that *this* constitutes what is un-representable about Ennis and Jack on film. *Brokeback Mountain* is credited with bringing male-male sexual desire to the big screen for mainstream viewers. This attribution of representational achievement is based on the fact that viewers are privy to, in particular, a scene wherein Ennis anally penetrates Jack and a scene where the two men kiss. But again, the film attempts a normative recontextualization on this point by also including a number of crucial scenes in which Jack and Ennis approach each other through masculine aggression and violence (most conspicuously during their final afternoon on Brokeback). Having reassured us that these men are fully capable of normal fatherhood, the film also reassures us that Ennis and Jack are normatively gendered; colloquially speaking, they are "manly men." Proulx complicates this overwrought rendition of gender normativity and masculine desire with the addition of Ennis's uncharacteristic endearment. As a result, the Ennis in the short story is a genuinely vexing but profoundly real character, simultaneously hyper-masculinized and subject to emotional vulnerability. Without this crucial detail, Ennis is reduced to being a gender archetype. Moreover, in removing this moment from the film, Ossana and McMurtry capitulated to and perpetuated a world wherein it is impossible to represent queer *love*.

Arguably, this erasure of queer love finds its parallel in the film's most conspicuously heteronormativizing moment — the penultimate scene between Ennis and Alma Jr. In a rare visit to her father's trailer, Alma Jr. tells Ennis she is getting married and thus inaugurates the film's decisive ideological statement. Ennis initially declines his daughter's invitation to the wedding, letting her know he has planned to attend a roundup. Noting his daughter's disappointment, Ennis then quickly revises his plans. This scene — invented by Ossana and McMurtry for the screenplay — contains a particularly resounding account of Ennis's capitulation to heteronormativity. The final lines of direction and dialog are telling:

> (He stands. Goes to the fridge, opens it. Takes out a half-empty bottle of cheap wine, a legacy of Cassie.)
> ENNIS: (smiles at his daughter) You know what? I reckon they can find themselves another cowboy. [...] My little girl ... is gettin' married. [...]
> ENNIS: (raising his glass) To Alma and Kurt.
> (ALMA JR. smiles, and clinks her glass with her daddy's.)
> (ENNIS smiles back at his luminous daughter. But his smile can't hide his regret and longing, for the one thing that he can't have. That he will never have.)
> [SP 95–96].

It is no coincidence that Ennis toasts his daughter with the vestigial wine from his failed courtship with the local bar waitress Cassie. This metonymic substitution resounds as the relic of Ennis's failed heterosexuality is taken back up as the symbol of his capitulation to his inevitable obligations as a father and as the abject other of the heteronormative structures of love. Of course Alma Jr. is luminous because her subjectivity is both produced and amplified by her impending status as a bride. And of course Ennis is consumed with his own regret and longing, because — and this is the point that *Brokeback Mountain* makes repeatedly as a film — queer desire and queer subjectivity precipitate tragedy. Given Alma's pending nuptials, it is possible to understand that the "thing that Ennis can't have" is a socially sanctioned and secure partnership with Jack. But the description of Alma as luminous also suggests that what Ennis regrets here is his exclusion from love and desire. Social norms notwithstanding, it is worth noting that Jack himself believed that he and Ennis might inhabit their desire and love for one another, despite social constraints. But Ennis is precluded from either one or both of these options by virtue of the determinative logic of heteronormativity that governs the world of the film. This scene's homage to queer tragedy is visually repeated as the film closes with the image of Ennis fondling snap shirts in his sparsely furnished trailer.

In the short story, on the other hand, Ennis's queer subjectivity is not foreclosed. In Proulx's version, the narrative moves from Ennis's visit to Jack's parents, to his purchase of the postcard of Brokeback Mountain, to a closing sketch of Ennis's dreamlife. From these dreams, he:

> ... would wake sometimes in grief, sometimes with the odd sense of joy and release; the pillow sometimes wet, sometimes the sheets.
>   There was some open space between what he knew and what he tried to believe, but nothing could be done about it, and if you can't fix it you've got to stand it [SS 28].

Neither romantically banal nor unrelentingly tragic, Proulx's conclusion captures the ambivalent future of the queer subject through an exquisitely drawn contradiction. While Proulx's Ennis elects to "stand" rather than "fix" his location within the normative conventions that mute his desire, he is cognizant of the open space between his constrained existence and the possibility of pleasure and queer fulfillment. Notably, Proulx begins and ends "Brokeback Mountain" by locating Ennis in the liminal space between sleep and consciousness. In the first paragraph of the story, we are told that regardless of the grim conditions into which he awakes, Ennis is "suffused with a sense of pleasure because Jack Twist was in his dream" (SS 1). Proulx's Ennis, even at the chronological conclusions of the events in the story, retains the capacity for desire and pleasure.

This open space can also be understood as the space of queer subjectivity itself—characterized, as are Ennis's somnolent reflections, by an amalgamation of fear and desire. Here Ennis's tragedy is simultaneously social and personal; the foreclosure of his subjectivity is defined by the intersection of the social conditions that produce a very real threat of violence, *and his own failure to act within the open space that he knows to exist.* This is precisely the nature of the queer subject's position in this historical moment—a socially constrained location for agency. The possibilities for Ennis, and for queer subjects (and viewers) more generally, range from extrasocial sexual fulfillment (symbolized by Ennis and Jack's time on Brokeback Mountain) to gay revisionings of heteronormative relationships (symbolized by Jack's proposition that he and Ennis start a ranch on their own). In the film, Ennis is *forbidden* from exploring either of these options or anything in between. In the short story, Ennis *chooses* to give into his fears fully knowing that his tragedy, while social, is also of his own making. With Proulx's complex rendering of queer subjectivity, queer readers are not only invited to identify with Ennis's predicament, they are challenged: if we as queer subjects are to choose freely among these options, it is our obligation to fix, rather than stand, the social conditions that constrain us.

Notes

1. Insofar as the original short story was also contained in the collection *Close Range: Wyoming Stories* (New York: Scribner, 1999), the screen adaptation simultaneously compresses Proulx's work—a re-sizing that is equally problematic. In this instance, Proulx's self-professed "geographic determin[ism]" is rendered anemic, as the remainder of the collection disappears from view, leaving only a fragment too easily recognizable within conventional narrative genres ("the Western," "a love story"). *Close Range*, to borrow Proulx's assessment, "is ostensibly concerned with Wyoming landscape and making a living in hard, isolated livestock-raising communities dominated by white masculine values, but also holding subliminal fantasies" ("Getting Movied," in *Brokeback Mountain: Story to Screenplay* [New York: Scribner, 2005], 129.) The remainder of the stories in the *Close Range* collection are about economy, gender, and fantasy in numerous and complicated ways—the attempted metonymic transition fails in the adaptation insofar as the part really does not stand in for the whole.

2. Ossana, "Climbing Brokeback Mountain," in *Brokeback Mountain: Story to Screenplay*, 143–145.

3. Ibid., 145.

4. This stance might be regarded generally as a "sex panic" or more precisely as a "marriage panic"—a social and political moment characterized by a heightened if not obsessive scrutiny of the relationship between sexual practices and the controlling mechanisms of the State.

5. McMurtry, "Adapting Brokeback Mountain," in *Brokeback Mountain: Story to Screenplay*, 140; Ossana, "Climbing Brokeback Mountain," 146.

6. Arguably, Ennis's gentleness with Alma during these scenes offers audiences a legible equation of heterosexual coupling and love, and thus an explicit counterpoint to the aggression Ennis exhibits in his encounters with Jack.

7. The language in the screenplay's direction is also striking: The use of "cuddles" and "tummy," as opposed to the less conspicuously precious "moves" and "stomach," seems almost like an expression of Ossana and McMurtry's fondness for this imaginary couple.

8. Warner, *The Trouble with Normal: Sex, Politics, and the Ethics of Queer Life* (Cambridge: Harvard University Press, 1999), 180.

9. One of the possible consequences of deviant speech is, inevitably, being unheard. Perhaps this explains Ossana's assertion, in the *Village Voice*, that *Brokeback Mountain* "is a story that was waiting to be told and no one had ever told it, as if it were understood but never spoken" (Jessica Winter, "The Scripting News," *Village Voice*, Nov. 29, 2005.) There is nothing about *Brokeback Mountain's* story of heteronormative exclusion — including its rural setting — that is "new" for queer subjects. It would seem, then, that queer narrations of this exclusion have remained inconsequential and that this story is only audible now as it is spoken by normative voices and/or for a heterosexual audience.

10. In the short story, even Ennis's assertions of fatherly pride are awkward. When Jack arrives, the men disclose the details of their family lives to each other. In response to Jack's "You got a kid?" Ennis responds "Two little girls ... Love them to pieces" at which point, Proulx tells us, "Alma's mouth twitched." Proulx's artful insertion of the spare but discomfiting detail of Alma's mouth alerts her readers to the fact that the familial relationships here are far from ideal.

11. In "Getting Movied," Proulx expresses a specific commitment to depicting Ennis and Jack's commitment to fatherhood as a point of regional — i.e. "rural" — authenticity (132). Nonetheless, the two men in the short story are marked by both implicit and explicit parental failures.

12. The language in the direction here is, like that used earlier in the screenplay to describe Ennis and Alma, conspicuously precious, noting that "little Bobby" is "on his daddy's lap."

6

Gay Cowboys Close to Home: Ennis Del Mar on the Q.T.

by Hiram Perez

> Obviously not all gay, lesbian, and transgender people live their lives in radically different ways from their heterosexual counterparts, but part of what has made queerness compelling as a form of self-description in the past decade or so has to do with the way it has the potential to open up new life narratives and alternative relations to time and space.
> — Judith Halberstam, *In a Queer Time and Place: Transgender Bodies, Subcultural Lives*

> You boys found a way to make the time pass up there, didn't you.
> — Joe Aguirre to Jack Twist, "Brokeback Mountain"

Their first summer together on Brokeback Mountain, Ennis del Mar and Jack Twist famously proclaim that they are not queer. Ang Lee's film powerfully adapts this anxious exchange between the two protagonists of Annie Proulx's short story: "Ennis said, 'I'm not queer,' and Jack jumped in with 'Me neither. A one-shot thing. Nobody's business but ours'" (SS 7). Gay pundits too numerous to count and several major newspapers "jumped in" as well, eager to corroborate the nervous denunciations uttered by these two teenage protagonists. Representing an ideologically wide spectrum, writers weighed in on why Ennis and Jack — and the film itself — are not gay, much less queer. A headline from the gay and lesbian website *Advocate.com* decreed, "Not a gay movie."[1] Sometimes citing the movie's transcendence of identity categories, other times impugning the political viability of identity categories altogether, critics across the country and internationally echoed the *Advocate*'s headline.[2] It is remarkable that such overwhelming consensus about the meaning of gay and queer identities should greet the anxious repudiations of

71

characters Proulx herself describes as, "...inarticulate, confused Wyoming ranch kids ... [who] find themselves in a personal sexual situation they did not expect, understand, nor can manage."[3]

Questions about its political disposition (queer or mainstream) and the proper identity categories for its characters (straight, gay, or otherwise) loomed larger in the film's critical reception than its powerful affect, which for many viewers persists well beyond the devastating conclusion. (That affect in fact became grounds for dismissing the film as melodrama or "chick flick.") This essay offers a queer reading of *Brokeback Mountain*, focusing on the character Ennis del Mar, so often (mis)read as repressed homosexual. Arguably, the "not a gay movie" response to *Brokeback Mountain* is symptomatic of unimaginative turns in gay and queer politics. Rather than opening new possibilities for identity, "not a gay movie" rules out any engagement with the inherent contradictions of identity, in effect foreclosing the alternative life narratives toward which *Brokeback Mountain* gestures.

The "not a gay movie" reading inadvertently naturalizes heterosexuality as well as quashing differences — contradictions even — that may inhabit "gay" or "queer." Furthermore, it risks making the violence in the film unnamable. The dispute over the film's queer identities calls for the revitalization of what Judith Halberstam finds most compelling about queerness, "the way it has the potential to open up new life narratives and alternative relations to time and space."[4] In that spirit, this essay contests the prevailing reading of Ennis del Mar as repressed homosexual, instead inviting his difference to help open both "gay" and "queer" to new narratives. Ennis's queerness is concentrated unexpectedly in the cowboy ethic that guides his life; because nationally that ethic is memorialized as heroically and uniquely masculine, its queerness has dissipated from legend. This essay restores the queer in cowboy, insisting that we situate Ennis close to home (Wyoming, ranch labor, rural) in order to fully appreciate his difference. Proulx offers that Jack and Ennis are "beguiled by the cowboy myth"[5]; this essay proposes that queerness is a quietly beguiling aspect of the myth.

Don't Fence Me In ... or Out

In addition to critiques that either impugn or claim to transcend identity, yet another argument appeals to a gay authenticity presumably violated by *Brokeback Mountain*. Novelist Adam Mars-Jones, writing for the British paper, *The Observer*, lambastes the film for its lack of a gay consciousness and complains that the project foregoes an authenticity he deems realizable only through the "actual testimony" of gay men.[6] Curiously, despite the nature of his protest, Mars-Jones himself overlooks "actual testimony." Such disregard is typical of the entire body of "not a gay movie" criticism. Poised as self-appointed arbiters of what is gay or queer, these critics uniformly fail to consult potential archives for testimony from men similarly situated to the characters in the short story and film. Apparently it is not necessary to leave New York or San Francisco or London to write about Wyoming's "ranch-country" queer populations. Such testimonials, gathered by only a handful of reporters, disturb the identity fence-posts staked by either gay liberalism or postmodernist queer theories. Much of the interpretation of Ennis's identity reads his silence as a relic of a bygone era when gay men were less likely to publicize their sexuality. This criticism ignores the significance of contemporary identifications with Ennis del Mar. Are the identifications articulated by Wyoming ranchers then also relics or might they document instead counternarratives of gay identity? Where else might the trajectories of these identifications lead us?

Guy Trebay's *New York Times* report from Lusk, Wyoming, is one of the few newspaper or magazine accounts of reception to the film that bothers to seek the response of a gay rural audience. After a special screening in Jackson, Wyoming, Trebay quotes a thirty-three year old rancher, Derrick Glover, who proclaims, "That could have been my life." Glover's roots in Wyoming are deep, his family having "worked the land around Lusk for generations."[7] His identifications complicate how we assess the choices Ennis makes. While critics repeatedly cite Ennis's repression, even judging him a "coward,"[8] Glover's testimony suggests alternative narratives. Defying the dominant narrative of queer desire to migrate from rural to urban, Glover explains, "I never had any intention of leaving the cowboy lifestyle.... Ranching is who I am." Criticism of the film, even when proclaiming the protagonists "not gay," privileges a narrowly defined terrain of sexuality as the primary locus of identity for queer subjects. For example, the nature of Ennis's relationships with Jack and Alma as well as his one pronouncement against queer identification function to disqualify him from the classifications "gay" and "queer," but the criteria for sanctioning what counts as evidence needs to be reevaluated. Our frame of reference for making determinations about sexual identity is too narrowly focused. Both humanist and posthumanist interrogations of sexuality may inadvertently collude with the hegemonic specification of individuals, as described by Foucault, through the truth of sex.[9] How are boundaries naturalized for the delimited field of activities, desires, and identifications that constitute sexuality? Might the narratives of *Brokeback Mountain*, including the testimonies it generates, broaden our frame of reference for determining sexual identities?

Glover's testimony defies categorization under the binary "in/out":

"They always define it as coming out of the closet, but I don't consider myself to be out of the closet," Mr. Glover explained. There is a reason for that, he said. "Where I live, you can't really go out and be yourself. You couldn't go out together, two guys, as a couple and ever be accepted. It wasn't accepted in the past, it's still not, and I don't think it ever will be." That he and some of the others interviewed for this article were willing to be named and photographed was not without social and physical risk.[10]

Glover's experience resists the language of the closet. He distances himself from the dominant narrative for modern gay and lesbian identities, noting the canonization of the closet but attributing it to a hegemonic authority: "*They* always define *it*" [emphasis added]. Glover presents a conundrum to the totalizing logic of the closet. He doesn't consider himself "out," yet, as Trebay points out, he remains "willing to be named and photographed" for a *New York Times* article on gay cowboys and the impact of *Brokeback Mountain*. The characterizations of Ennis in both the short story and film present comparable difficulties. Dominant narratives of gay identity fail to accommodate either Glover's testimony or Ennis del Mar's fiction.

Ben Clark, a "fourth-generation rancher from Jackson," also identifying with the film's protagonists, testifies to the lack of an identity on which to model his own: "I grew up with the same kind of fear and conflict.... Growing up, I never even dreamed that a real cowboy would be gay."[11] As a part of his interview with Clark, Trebay shares a joke he's learned from his local sources: "There's a joke out here about how one goes about finding a gay man on the frontier. The punch line is deadpan: Look for the wife and kids." The joke suggests the frequency of the circumstance; the gay man is commonplace on the frontier. But furthermore, it asks that we reconsider a place for queer life vis-à-vis heterosexuality. The coming out narrative fences in Ennis del Mar and fences him out as well. It canonizes the closet for queer life and imposes the binary "in/out" on Ennis del Mar regardless of whether or not that narrative construct translates meaningfully within the parameters of the story. A disputed interpretation of fiction is not all that is in question here. How we decide to read the fiction on this point may also impact how we greet sexual outsiders.

As Trebay's interviews reveal, the reactions to *Brokeback Mountain* unearth a potential archive. One part of that archive is comprised of the voices of Wyoming men testifying to their identifications with the film; another part is the cultural politics that the film ignites. But an archive only submits knowledge of other lives when it brings us into crisis, when we too arrive at a new understanding of ourselves and our desires. Halberstam's work on Brandon Teena, in which she shifts focus from the production of biography to an analysis of the stories told about him — what she designates as the "Brandon

Archive"— offers a creative critical approach to the archive. The stories that *Brokeback Mountain* stirs to the surface, like the Brandon archive, reveal "how little we actually know about the forms taken by queer life outside of metropolitan areas."[12] Halberstam proposes that "Brandon's story, while cleaving to its own specificity, needs to remain an open narrative."[13] The remainder of the essay reopens the narrative(s) in question through a series of provocations that nonetheless cleave to the specificities of the texts at hand.

Rather than acknowledge its content as potentially representative of a gay experience, the prevailing attitude seems to dictate that it is more radical to deny *Brokeback Mountain* status as a gay film because of its protagonists' resistance to naming themselves "gay" or "queer." John Wirt's review for *The Advocate* is typical in ascribing repression as the singular motivation for Ennis's choices within the narrative. According to Wirt, "the repressed Ennis is the one who argues that a life together is impossible, that he and Jack must continue their traditional family-man existences in the conventional world, no matter how grim."[14] Wirt ignores the fact that Ennis, unlike Jack, has already abandoned a "family-man" existence. Is it possible that the unhappiness of his marriage makes him averse to pursuing a relationship similarly modeled, whether that be a heterosexual or same-sex union? Might Ennis's refusal of a lifestyle modeled on the conventional heterosexual relationship in fact mark his queerness?

When a remarried and pregnant Alma tells Ennis that he should marry again, he responds sarcastically, "Once burned" (SS 16). Perhaps even more telling, standing in the kitchen helping Alma with the dishes after a family reunion over Thanksgiving dinner, Ennis "feel[s] too big for the room" (SS 16). He is not looking to settle down, committed instead to a cowboy's transience, making his home in a trailer out of economic necessity but also because of lifestyle. Only Jack directly expresses dissatisfaction with the course of their relationship. Ennis communicates his longing for an absent Jack and a desire to prolong their encounters, but, in the short story at least, he never expresses dissatisfaction with the nature of the relationship. Like the fourth-generation rancher from Jackson, Ben Clark, interviewed by Trebay, Ennis finds himself at a loss, searching for some model that will help him to comprehend his situation: "Shit. I been lookin at people on the street. This happen a other people? What the hell do they do?" (SS 15). Ennis then, hardly in denial or repressed, actively reflects on his difference and seeks (albeit unsuccessfully) an alternative expression of his identity.

In opposition to Jack's desire for domesticity modeled on marriage, Ennis's commitment in the relationship suggests an alternative (or queer) temporality. After all, the urgency and intensity of their desire is dictated by the fleetingness of their encounters. Readings of the film as a defense of gay marriage abound, yet there is no indication in either short story or film that Jack's and Ennis's passion can weather domestication. Ennis cherishes the ephemeral, a quintessentially queer measure of time and space. As if to confirm that he is as serious about his model for the relationship as Jack is about domesticity, he cites the magnitude of his sacrifices, reminding Jack that "[t]hem earlier days I used a quit the jobs" (SS 20). The idyllic space and time of Brokeback Mountain, enshrined in memory and rekindled during passionate but fleeting encounters, sustains Ennis. The pain and frustration of repeated departure perhaps enflames Ennis's pleasure, while Jack's pain remains unambivalent. Jack confronts Ennis on this point: "Tell you what, we could a had a good life together, a fuckin real good life. You wouldn't do it, Ennis, so what we got now is Brokeback Mountain. Everthing built on that.... You got no fuckin idea how bad it gets. I'm not you. I can't make it on a couple a high-altitude fucks once or twice a year" (SS 21). The prevailing reading of Ennis's resistance to Jack's proposition, perhaps due to the political imperatives of the current gay liberalism, interprets his refusal of the "good life together" to repression and self-loathing. Jack's accusations suggest an alternative reading. For Ennis, loss is tinged with pleasure. The transitory nature of the relationship is a comfort as well as burden.

The postcard memorializes precisely the transient nature of the relationship between the two men, one negotiated over long distances not by phone but by postcards used to arrange the dates and locations of their rare meetings. Again, this testifies to how Ennis is gratified by ephemera. Jack's absence provides a source of both pain and pleasure for Ennis; his attitude to their separation suggests more ambivalence than critics have allowed. It is essential also to recall, before assessing Ennis's position on his physical separation from Jack, how the experience on Brokeback Mountain idealized by both characters — but, as Jack charges, more so by Ennis — is one of desire repeatedly frustrated by distance, repeatedly rewarded with love. They never remain in camp together for longer than a night, as one must travel back and forth several hours a day to tend the sheep. If Ennis seeks to regain the fulfillment he experienced on Brokeback, it makes sense that he would pursue a script that calls for prolonged absences punctuated with abbreviated but intense reunions in favor of a script that realizes a more regularly dependable (i.e. domesticated) presence of the loved object. It is clear in both the short story and film that only Jack insists on permanence.

Gay Cowboys in Close Range

In an interview for a Wyoming newspaper, Proulx objects to the categorization of the film as a "gay cowboy" movie. "Excuse me ... but it is not a story about 'two cowboys.'"[15] Despite Proulx's objection, there is an argument to be made for considering Ennis a modern-day cowboy. If he's not yet a cowboy on Brokeback Mountain (where he works as a shepherd), he certainly becomes one in the remainder of the story. Jack, too, before settling into his bourgeois existence with Lureen, makes a living as a rodeo cowboy. In fact, Ennis's derision of the rodeo cowboy — more pronounced in the film — raises its own questions of authentic masculinity within both texts. If Ennis is the authentic cowboy, then we cannot expect him to settle down. Domesticity is anathema to a cowboy lifestyle, traditionally understood.

The invention of barbed wire, privatization of land, and modernization eventually restrict the original cowboy's habitat to Wild West shows. He disappears together with the open range; whether or not Jack and Ennis are cowboys is then also a matter of symbolism. The cowboy roams the popular imagination, well past his life driving cattle over large expanses of Texas and the American West. Apart from the specific historical register, the title of "cowboy" also marks a lifestyle, characteristically rugged and independent. Ennis's hard, itinerant work life arguably makes him a modern-day cowboy. "Itinerant" is used specifically to characterize the instability of his career, while geographically he remains stationed in Wyoming, his lack of mobility a matter both of choice and economics. Ennis tolerates the erratic lifestyle of ranch work in order to preserve his independence. As Proulx describes, "Ennis went back to ranch work, hired on here and there, not getting much ahead but glad enough to be around stock again, free to drop things, quit if he had to, and go into the mountains at short notice" (SS 16). Ironically, the itinerancy of ranch work allows Ennis his independence but ultimately also severely limits his mobility. He is subject not only to the possibility of ranch foreclosure or sale but also to the fluxes of seasonal work (the amount of work available to Ennis, for example, depends at times on whether or not cows are calving and how many). These conditions apply when we first meet him in the film (Aguirre hires Jack and Ennis as seasonal laborers), and they are true in the short story when Proulx introduces the reader to Ennis as he prepares once more to relocate and find new work. In McMurtry's and Ossana's screenplay, Alma proposes that Ennis apply for work at a power plant, a job with long-term security and benefits. Ennis balks at the idea. Likewise, in the short story, Alma resents "his failure to look for a decent permanent job with the county or the power company" (SS 16).

Proulx in fact describes Ennis's inclination toward ranch work as a "yearning" (SS 16). He is like the rancher Derrick Glover who affirms his devotion to the "cowboy lifestyle," insisting that *New York Times* readers regard his identity on terms he sets: "Ranching is who I am." His use of the word "lifestyle" resonates in this context due to its familiar usage in designating modern homosexuality, the "gay lifestyle." Might not all cowboys be just a little gay? In her more expansive understanding of queerness, Halberstam includes "people who live without financial safety nets, without homes, without steady jobs, outside the organizations of time and space that have been established for the purposes of protecting the rich few from everyone else" among those people who "could productively be called 'queer subjects'."[16] If we enlarge the word "queer" in the way that Halberstam suggests, the "cowboy lifestyle" indeed appears fundamentally queer. Readings that deny Ennis his queerness err by not accounting for his cowboy ethic. His values as a cowboy may prove elemental to his particular expression of queerness. Regarding the cowboy and his social status, historian Richard W. Slatta explains, "Cowboys held distinctive cultural values. These values and their way of life set them apart from others in society. In some cases, they occupied a unique legal status — that of rural outlaws or vagrants. By definition, they never owned land, exercised political power, or held high social position."[17] The designation "outlaw" need not imply criminality; the cowboy ethic of "use rights" suggests a radically different relationship to land, resources, and community in contrast to privatization. This ethic, however, clearly situates the cowboy outside the law. This same ethic is intrinsic to Ennis's queerness.

A historical examination of his career invites further queering. The American "cowboy" finds his forebear in the Spanish *vaquero*, or "cowman."[18] The translation from "man" to "boy" situates the cowboy out of proper reproductive time. He represents a kind of instability, marked certainly by the constant movement of his calling. The exclusively male world of the cowboy lifestyle also removes him from reproductive time. As a pejorative, "boy" also marks class and race differences. The *vaquero* originates in Mexico, a mestizo figure employed by white creoles; his U.S. successor, the cowboy, was often black. These class and race differences are sexualized and arguably also queer the body of the cowboy. It is striking really that "gay cowboy" should pose such a conceptual difficulty, at least for U.S. audiences.

While there is plenty to qualify the cowboy as a queer subject, he is also an iconic point of reference for American identity. Masculine, heroic, independent. A tension arises between the cowboy's historical queerness and his role as national symbol. His queer reputation is a secret entrusted to the national imaginary. Chris Packard argues persuasively for the cowboy's forgotten queer life in his study, *Queer Cowboys: And Other Erotic Male Friendships in Nineteenth Century American Literature* (2005):

> Particularly in Westerns produced before 1900, references to lusty passions
> appear regularly, when the cowboy is on the trail with his partners, if one knows
> how to look for them. In fact, in the often all-male world of the literary West,
> homoerotic affection holds a favored position. A cowboy's partner, after all, is his

one emotional attachment, aside from his horse, and he will die to preserve that attachment. Affection for women destroys cowboy *comunitas* and produces children, and both are unwanted hindrances to those who wish to ride the range freely.[19]

Queer passions, as Packard points out, are not necessarily self-evident. They become apparent *if* "one knows how to look for them." And if an entire era of renegade queerness can disappear from the sanctioned memory of the nation, is it so unusual really that the queerness of a single, fictional cowboy should evaporate with so little critical pressure? Knowing how to look requires also knowing where to look, and neither the dominant culture nor the larger body of queer scholarship are attuned to the potential queerness of spaces outside the metropole and temporalities not measured by "coming out." The terrain of what constitutes sexuality also needs to be destabilized if we are to pursue satisfactorily the question of what identities Ennis represents.

We need to reckon, for instance, with Ennis's "yearning for low-paid, long-houred ranch work" (SS 16). Some yearning clearly is satisfied by his ranch work, and some part of that satisfaction is sensual. The short story suggests a sensual gratification in the smells and sounds of ranch work, oddly, in its description of the conjugal bedroom after the birth of Alma Jr.: "...their bedroom was full of the smell of old blood and milk and baby shit, and the sounds were of squalling and sucking and Alma's sleepy groans, all reassuring of fecundity and life's continuance to one who worked with livestock" (SS 9). The passage both suggests Ennis's heterosexuality (he is comforted by his inclusion in that fecundity) and simultaneously undercuts any such reading, comparing the sounds and smells of his bedroom to that of livestock. But what should be emphasized here is his sensual pleasure, which need not be classified within the binary heterosexual/homosexual. Might not the sensuality of his work complicate how we assess Ennis's sexuality? How is his sexuality potentially channeled through his work as a wrangler and ranch hand? Why assume that his yearning for a cowboy lifestyle is not continuate with sexual desire? Jack hypothesizes an association between wrangling and sex when after intercourse he observes, "Christ, it got a be all that time a yours ahorseback makes it so goddamn good" (SS 12). Is it impossible that Ennis's labor on the ranch provides sensual — even sexual — gratification? Does the Proulx text suggest we include Ennis's cowboy lifestyle within his narrative sexuality? How does this square with the text's so-called "gay bona fides"?[20] If we allow for the sensuality of Ennis's work, we also need to consider the context of masculine camaraderie in which it transpires and the correlation then of sensual pleasure with male companionship.

Ennis's "cowboy lifestyle" in this modern context — which incorporates but cannot be reduced to queer sexuality — is arguably the greater threat to heteronormativity and the American way of life: migrant, exclusively homosocial, communal, anti-industrial. As documented in Proulx's collection, *Close Range: Wyoming Stories* (which includes "Brokeback Mountain"), the days of a Western frontier are long gone.[21] The cowboys disappear together with the open ranges (leaving us Proulx's "Close Range"). However, what remains unequivocally, if now anxiously, is the cowboy as style. That style is less certain of its masculinity after *Brokeback Mountain*, a consolation for those of us weary of hearing the words "gay cowboy" serve as their own punchline. Both film and short story rupture the iconic masculinity of the cowboy and thus destabilize what is perhaps the emblematic masculinity of American individualism and courage. Where have all the cowboys gone, indeed. They've gone fishing.

As the title *Close Range* provocatively implies, all of the stories are about place, violence, and intimacy. The violence usually is consummated; the intimacy remains frustrated. The title evokes both home on the range and the sight on a shotgun. As indicated, all the stories are set in Wyoming. In this sense, Ennis is of Wyoming, and the scope of Proulx's work will not release him from that place. Throughout Proulx's work, place figures prominently in the lives of her characters. She asserts in an interview, "Everything that happens to characters comes welling out of the place. Even their definition of themselves...."[22] The film too, with its languorous treatment of the mountainous landscape, performs a seduction, aligning the spectator's identifications with Ennis's and Jack's sensual — ultimately erotic — attachments to place. Ennis is indeed stuck in Wyoming, since mobility is not feasible, but is it not possible as well that other ties bind him to this place, ties that an urban queer bias especially may eclipse? Rather than merely stuck, he is perhaps rooted in the Wyoming landscape, its life and communities. The urban bias typical of gay and lesbian dominant cultures precludes recognition of the complex of identifications that may root someone like Ennis del Mar to a small town or rural setting. Recall Derrick Glover's testimony: "I never had any intention of leaving the cowboy lifestyle.... *Ranching is who I am*" [emphasis added]. As Halberstam observes, "Some queers need to leave home in order to become queer, and others need to stay close to home in order to preserve their difference."[23]

Comparisons of Ennis and Jack often ignore their differing socioeconomic statuses. Ennis is quick to point out these differences when Jack insists on meeting more regularly. Critics point to Ennis's resistance to relocate with Jack as evidence of his repressed identity, but they ignore that Ennis must forego meeting Jack, constrained by his economic circumstances. Repression does not explain Ennis's refusal to meet more regularly with Jack; the story indicates his desire to do so. The evidence in the story more strongly supports economic hardship and ties to place (including his relationship to his daughters) as Ennis's rationale for resisting Jack's demands for more than "a couple of high-altitude fucks once or twice a year." Ennis protests Jack's insensitivity to his economic situation: "Jack, I got a work. Them earlier days I used a quit the jobs. You got a wife with money, a good job. You forget how it is bein broke all the time" (SS 20). Economics and place also circumscribe what identities are available to each character, a condition also ignored by the film's critics. Jack's rise in social class through his marriage to Lureen enables his greater mobility. That mobility makes it possible for Jack to adopt an identity closer to what contemporary spectators, especially urban gay men, recognize as modern and gay.

The metanarrative for that modern gay identity is largely founded on migration — to metropolitan locales, such as New York and San Francisco — and on a certain gay cosmopolitanism. Jack's sex tourism in Mexico is inferred in the short story and literalized in the film. Following a frustrated attempt to join Ennis after learning of his divorce, we follow Jack to Mexico where he cruises for sex. His greater mobility, especially his ability to travel outside the boundaries of the nation, contributes to an articulation of sexuality that many viewers more readily label as "gay" in comparison to the narrative they confront in Ennis. That story complicates the metanarrative for modern gay identity by insisting on an unfamiliar context. The experience of a poor, white, rural ranch hand, settled far from any metropolis, disrupts the usual narrative. Jack's trip to Mexico similarly defamiliarizes the cowboy, in this case by reintroducing him to queer origins. Although much criticism is devoted to the authenticity of the movie and its characters (i.e. are they gay? are they really cowboys? what is masculinity?), there is no commentary on the story's own play on authenticity. Jack, a belt-buckle cowboy of sorts, finds his rodeo-ing disparaged as inauthentic by Ennis, who claims "the kind of riding that interested him lasted longer than eight seconds and had some point to it" (SS 6). In his travels, Jack retraces the migration of the original cowboys, the vaqueros, from American west to Mexico. If such migration was crucial to the identity of the cowboy, it proves equally crucial to a modern gay sensibility, as the conflicting characterizations of Jack and Ennis establish. Jack proposes to Ennis: "We ought a go south. We ought a go to Mexico one day" (SS 20). He disregards the economic restrictions on Ennis's mobility; as Ennis explains, "Mexico? Jack, you know me. All the travelin I ever done is goin around the coffeepot lookin for the handle" (SS 20). Jack's migrations — his class mobility, his actual mobility, his cosmopolitanism in the form of sex tourism in Mexico — constitute the modern gay identity, or a nascent form of it, that so many critics appreciate in him. He even identifies the classic gay migration, from rural or small town to urban, when — responding to Ennis's question about whether their situation is a common one — he proposes, "It don't happen in Wyomin and if it does I don't know what they do, maybe go to Denver" (SS 15). Demonstrating exactly the bias that renders Jack gay and/or brave and Ennis cowardly, repressed and/or "not gay," David Leavitt, in his article "Is *Brokeback Mountain* a gay film?" cites this passage to establish Jack's gay sensibility, claiming Denver as "possible urban refuge."[24] He does not ask whether the urban can ever really provide someone like Ennis refuge. Might Ennis be that kind of queer that needs "to stay close to home in order to preserve [his] difference?" Or does such yearning render him inauthentic?

What we discover in fact — further complicating the question of Jack's authenticity — is that the cowboy is predecessor to the gay cosmopolitan. The travels of both cowboy and cosmopolitan serve colonial interests in expansion and Westernization. The nation tolerates the cowboy's queerness in the nineteenth century as part of an unspoken compact. As Packard explains, "The cowboy is queer because audiences want him to be queer. America's official emblem of masculinity is not one who settles down after he conquests ... he moves on, perpetually conquering, and repeatedly affirming his ties to the wilderness and his male partner."[25] The Anglo cowboy's homosexuality is critical to Westward expansion. His sexuality is quietly sanctioned by the nation as is the racial violence he executes against American Indians, as well as Mexican ranchers who remained in Texas, and even Basque sheepherders. That violence will not be delayed by the demands of family life, and the cowboy fulfills his role in the colonization of the American West.

If the cowboy is recuperated as hero after his demise due to land privatization, it is perhaps due to a need to recast his role (and consequently that of the nation) in the violent settlement of the American West. The wildness of the Wild West was characterized by the absence of U.S. legal jurisdiction. The Anglo cowboy's theft of Mexican cattle satisfied U.S. colonial interests. His outlaw behavior, in terms both of his theft and his queer sexuality, proved fortuitous for U.S. imperialism. However, it would need to be recast after the formal annexation of the West in order to preserve the nation's heroic fictions. "Cow-Boy," according to James Wagner, was originally applied to cattle thieves as early as the Revolutionary War, when it also functioned as a derogatory name for British Loyalists or traitors.[26] This more ambiguous legend of cowboy as traitor, foreigner, thief, and homosexual is nonetheless memorialized in the persistence of the word "cowboy," for despite its etymology, it survives with greater currency than less historically conflicted titles, such as "stockman," "cowhand," or "cowpuncher." His turbulent career, including those queer days on the open prairie, becomes a national secret, encapsulated in the preservation of the "boy" in his title. Perhaps "gay cowboy" suggests a redundancy rather than a punch line.

Ennis and Jack on the Q. T.

It is precisely Ennis's refusal to accommodate Jack's demands for domesticity that may disturb some gay assimilationists. In this time of gay and lesbian assimilation, such a rejection is read as reactionary when it might also be read as queer. The story's Brokeback Mountain is all about queer time and space. It is the site where two "high school dropout country boys with no prospects" (SS 1–2) etch out a time "when they owned the world and nothing seemed wrong" (SS 1). Ultimately, Jack Twist embraces a bourgeois lifestyle (this is especially true in the film's expanded vision of Jack's life in Childress). His plans for Ennis and himself, for example, remain contingent on patriarchal logic in the form of the anticipated inheritance of property from his father and the potential payoff from Lureen's father, disdainful of his daughter's interclass marriage. Hence, the future he imagines with Ennis does not so much reflect the subversion of traditional constructions of space and time that characterized the season on Brokeback Mountain. Jack aspires rather to a more conventional temporality premised on the inheritance of his father's ranch and his assumption of domesticity together with Ennis instead of Lureen. Ennis, on the other hand, organizes time against the demands of normative temporality — he ultimately succumbs to those demands but stakes his oppositionality nonetheless, acquiescing for example to Jack's demands that he take additional days off work and extend his leaves from Alma and family duty. That oppositionality is also staked by his "cowboy lifestyle," refusing for example the power plant job.

It's possible that the domesticity that Jack projects as the appropriate shared desire might also represent in the story the end of Ennis's relationship to Jack as he knows and cherishes it. Ennis's time with Jack is time stolen from the demands of family and labor. Jack's time with Ennis is a lien on future time premised on a more conventional way of being. On Brokeback Mountain, Ennis and Jack share the same conception of time; they resist the demands of capital accumulation, defying Joe Aguirre's instructions to maintain separate camps in order to secure the highest return on his flock. Aguirre's only interest is in preserving a privately owned flock of sheep on public land. Unknown to Ennis and Jack, Aguirre spies on them with binoculars. Having purchased their labor, in Aguirre's eyes, the two have foregone any privacy; their labor and hence their bodies become leased property. When Jack returns the following year once again seeking seasonal labor on Brokeback Mountain, and clearly hopeful to reunite with Ennis, he is confronted by a contemptuous Aguirre. Jack's inquiry for work is met with the foreman's sarcasm: "You boys found a way to make the time pass up there, didn't you" (SS 13). It is not a question. Aguirre's retort is meant as an accusation. Although Jack does not report the remainder of the encounter to Ennis, the foreman made it clear that he understood fully how "the boys" passed their time: "Twist, you guys wasn't getting paid to leave the dogs baby-sit the sheep while you stemmed the rose" (SS 14).

The prevailing gay liberal reading of the story eulogizes the relationship as the unrealized marriage between Ennis and Jack. But Ennis does not lose Jack to societal prohibitions against gay marriage; he loses Jack to a gay bashing, a fact which makes the "not a gay movie" reading somewhat baffling. In the short story, Ennis's memories of the relationship are not morbid, and there is no indication of regret. There are alternative ways to recall the relationship, alternative narratives that also recast the story's significance to cultural politics. Aguirre's condemnation serves to remind us that Jack and Ennis are also two queers cruising each other in a public park. As such, they subvert state and dominant culture prohibitions against not only same-sex desire but also public sex. "They never talked about sex, let it happen, at first only in the tent at night, then in the full daylight with the hot sun striking down, and at evening in the fire glow, quick, rough, laughing and snorting, no lack of noises...."(SS 7) These boys can hardly represent the decent, upstanding citizens of gay assimilationism.

Aguirre's classification of Ennis and Jack as "boys" places them outside of reproductive time (raising the specter of that queer cowboy). The foreman's accusation about how they "pass the time" impugns Ennis and Jack for mingling work time with private time (they are just passing time, as opposed to working) and for their proscribed homosexual activity, conducted during working hours and on a public campsite. Ennis and Jack subvert the logic of time and space formally allocated for either private labor or public recreation. It is the queer time and space of Brokeback Mountain, repeatedly invoked, that lends its name both to Proulx's and Lee's texts. If we focus on the time and space of the mountain and the value subsequently attributed to it throughout the story, the case for queer readings of both texts hardly seems controversial. In order to dispute *Brokeback Mountain*'s status as gay or queer, critics focus instead on an unrealized (and definitively more conventional) future projected onto the story. The queer time and space of Brokeback Mountain subverts the respectable gay morality of contemporary assimilationist politics. We should not be surprised then that the film's queer content has been suppressed by a gay liberalism so intensely devoted to establishing gay and lesbian respectability to the exclusion of any other queer articulations of experience and identity. When first assigning his workers their charge, Aguirre explains that one of them will have to sleep with the sheep. One of the men will have to camp illegally, outside of the Forest Service designated campsite. Pointing to Jack, Aguirre instructs, "pitch a pup tent on the q.t." (SS 2). What their foreman does not anticipate is that the "boys" will translate "q.t." as queer time. Aguirre requires that Jack and Ennis violate Forest Service regulations on the quiet. Sanctioning this one transgression of the state regulation of public lands, Aguirre inadvertently sets in motion subsequent transgressions. Brokeback Mountain represents a rupture of the normative strictures of masculinity, labor, and publicity. What emerges on the horizon of that rupture is a queer time and space.

It must be noted that the relationship on Brokeback Mountain duplicates the gendered roles of traditionally conceived marriage, the husband performing the labor outside the home/camp, while the wife cooks, tends home/camp, and faithfully awaits his return. Jack at one point arrives at an empty campsite (no dinner, no wife), and when Ennis — delayed by his encounter with a bear — returns, Jack stereotypically explodes. Clearly, Jack and Ennis disagree over their futures, but perhaps also their recollections of Brokeback Mountain are not as harmonious as may superficially appear. The tension in the story may be defined in the following way: Jack Twist commemorates Brokeback Mountain as a rehearsal for marriage; Ennis del Mar commemorates Brokeback Mountain as a queer time and space, an evasion and deferral of the law in classic cowboy style. Jack privileges the permanence rehearsed on the mountain, Ennis its transcendent moments.

However, Jack's own reverie, following his emotional confrontation with Ennis during their last meeting, both fuels and defies his fetish for permanence. "What Jack remembered and craved in a way he could neither help nor understand was the time that distant summer on Brokeback when Ennis had come up behind him and pulled him close, the silent embrace satisfying some shared and sexless hunger" (SS 22). In the film, the reverie takes the form of a flashback abruptly following the confrontation. The flashback disorients the viewer, incongruous both with the volatility of the previous scene and with the nature of Jack's demands. It is a moment marked by its singularity: "that dozy embrace solidified in his memory as the single moment of artless, charmed happiness in their separate and difficult lives" (SS 22). However much he craves it, the moment cannot be reiterated:

> They had stood that way for a long time in front of the fire, its burning tossing ruddy chunks of light, the shadow of their bodies a single column against the rock. The minutes ticked by from the round watch in Ennis's pocket, from the sticks in the fire settling into coals. Stars bit through the wavy heat layers above the fire. Ennis's breath came slow and quiet, he hummed, rocked a little in the sparklight and Jack leaned against the steady heartbeat, the vibrations of the humming like faint electricity and, standing, he fell into sleep that was not sleep but something else drowsy and tranced ... [SS 22].

The watch is Aguirre's, given to Ennis to ensure he promptly meet the supply truck Fridays at noon. A marker of normative time, it is absorbed into the transcendence of the moment, reclaimed by the queer temporality of the embrace, measured in burning sticks, heartbeats, humming, gentle rocking and slow breaths. Jack and Ennis's q.t. engulfs the normative function of the watch. The interruption of the action with this flashback produces a momentary incoherence in the film. Jack's most profound longing refuses to cohere with the normative temporality for which he pines.

In this sense, Ennis seems to intuit something about his desire that Jack cannot. Ennis longs not only for Jack's companionship but for the conditions of Brokeback Mountain. Their encounters, eventually to Jack's protest, replicate those conditions. Ennis wants to remain outside — in every way. His particular attachment to Brokeback Mountain represents a way of life (consistent with a cowboy ethic) occluded in the prevailing readings of the film by the preeminence of another lifestyle narrative, the gay lifestyle as it is being narrowly defined by a dominant gay and lesbian constituency. If we regard Ennis as gay, then we also reopen the narrative for what "gay lifestyle" and "gay" can mean. Classifying Ennis as gay does not necessarily mean uncritically imposing on him an identity metanarrative; it can also constitute an invitation for men like Ennis to expand our understandings of "gay" and "queer" identities. Certainly, if we are not attentive to the constitutive power of identity politics, we risk the foreclosure of alterity, but "not gay" forecloses without the engagement that makes new, alternative narratives for identity intelligible. Ennis's difference remains "close to home" and far from the dominant narrative for gay identity. Movements that bear the names "gay" or "queer" are obligated to represent outsider sexualities; they should in fact welcome the contradictions an Ennis del Mar introduces to the under-interrogated truth of sex. The representations in *Brokeback Mountain* prevail on that "truth" to remain productively incomplete; they urge us to approach identity politics not with hostility but imagination. Ennis, "too big for the room," ruptures the claustrophobic strictures of the "not a gay movie" debate. As gay cowboy he reopens a range for identity long-rived by the barbed wire and property claims of closed narratives for sexual intelligibility.

Notes

1. Ryan James Kim, "Not a Gay Movie," in *Advocate.com* (Dec. 9, 2005), <http://www.advocate.com/exclusive_detail_ektid23265.asp> (accessed Sept. 10, 2006).

2. See for example, Manohla Dargis, "Masculinity and Its Discontents In Marlboro Country," *New York Times,* Dec. 18, 2005, 13; Neva Chonin, "Midnight Cowboys," *San Francisco Chronicle,* Dec.18, 2005, 14; Meghan Daum, "A Breakthrough Called *Brokeback,*" *Los Angeles Times,* Jan. 7, 2006, B17; Paul Gessel, "*Brokeback Mountain* Is 'Just Another Chick Flick,'" *Ottawa Citizen,* Dec. 19, 2005, D3; Caryn James, "The Winner Is Only Acting Gay," *New York Times,* Nov. 20, 2005, sec.2:1; David Leavitt, "Men in Love: Is *Brokeback Mountain* a Gay Film?" in *Slate* (Dec. 8, 2005), <http://www.slate.com/id/2131865/> (accessed Sept. 10, 2006); Adam

Mars-Jones, "Out Takes," in *The Observer*, Dec. 18, 2005, 1; Joanna Weiss, "Considering the Source: *Brokeback Mountain* Turns a Short Story Into a Hollywood First," *Boston Globe*, Dec. 11, 2005, N13; John Wirt, "*Brokeback Mountain* Tells an Unconventional Love Story," *The Advocate*, Jan. 13, 2006, 17.

3. Quoted in Dargis.

4. Judith Halberstam, *In a Queer Time and Place: Transgender Bodies, Subcultural Lives* (New York: New York University Press, 2005), 1.

5. Quoted in Dargis.

6. Mars-Jones.

7. Guy Trebay, "Cowboys, Just Like in the Movies," *New York Times*, Dec.18, 2005, sec. 9:1.

8. Ryan James Kim, for example, pronounces Ennis's cowardice: "By the end of the film it's the expressive Jack we consider brave and the silent Ennis we find cowardly." Such criticism ignores more complicated queer identifications with Ennis, including class-based identifications.

9. According to Foucault, "the notion of 'sex' made it possible to group together, in an artificial unity, anatomical elements, biological functions, conducts, sensations, and pleasures, and it enabled one to make use of this fictitious unity as a causal principle, an omnipresent meaning..." (Michel Foucault, *The History of Sexuality, Volume I: An Introduction* [New York: Vintage Books, 1978, 1990], 154).

10. Trebay, 1.

11. Ibid.

12. Halberstam, 35.

13. Ibid., 25–26.

14. Wirt.

15. Quoted in Dargis.

16. Halberstam, 10.

17. Richard W. Slatta, *Cowboys of the Americas* (New Haven: Yale University Press, 1990).

18. In English, "cowman" is in fact reserved for the landowning rancher, in contrast to the unpropertied "cowboy." James Wagner, "Cowboy — Origin and Early Use of the Term," *West Texas Historical Association Yearbook* 63 (1987): 91-100.

19. Chris Packard, *Queer Cowboys: And Other Erotic Male Friendships in Nineteenth Century American Literature* (New York: Palgrave/Macmillan, 2005), 3.

20. Manohla Dargis comments on the controversy over the film's authenticity: "A lightning rod for attention even before it opened, the film has earned plaudits from critics' groups along with predictable sneers, and provoked argument over its gay bona fides."

21. Annie Proulx, *Close Range: Wyoming Stories* (New York: Scribner, 1999).

22. Steinberg, "E. Annie Proulx: An American Odyssey," *Publishers Weekly* 3 (June 1996): 58.

23. Halberstam, 27.

24. David Leavitt, "Men in Love: Is *Brokeback Mountain* a Gay Film?" in *Slate* (Dec. 8, 2005) <http://www.slate.com/id/2131865/>.

25. Packard, 13.

26. Wagner, 91–92.

ACKNOWLEDGMENTS: *I am grateful to Sarita See for providing invaluable feedback through several versions of this essay. Janet Cutler and Elaine Roth each read early drafts and I heeded their insightful suggestions. Special thanks to Jim Stacy for his careful editing and generous intellect.—* Hiram Perez

7

"When This Thing Grabs Hold of Us...": Spatial Myth, Rhetoric, and Conceptual Blending in *Brokeback Mountain*

by Jen E. Boyle

In a highly moving moment in *Brokeback Mountain,* Ennis del Mar explains to Jack Twist that any open commitment to the sexual love the two men share is impossible: "When this thing grabs hold of us, at the wrong place, the wrong time, and we're dead" (SP 52). The "thing" here, of course, is a placeholder for the emotional, sexual, and psychical bond between the two men, an attempt at verbally encapsulating all the socially illicit elements of their relationship that put them at danger in a homophobic environment. Yet "this" also carries with it one of the central problems of the film itself. What are the verbal and visual descriptors that can adequately signify what the film is about? What is the "this" that forms the aesthetic and social message of *Brokeback Mountain,* and to what extent is the film made legible to both a marginalized and a mainstream audience?

Critics and audiences alike have struggled, on the one hand, to define *Brokeback Mountain* as a progressive film that challenges conventional biases and assumptions about homosexuality, and on the other, to claim it as a "universal" space, a story that transcends the bounds of any particularized sexual or social identity. The vigorous debate that has ensued over what rhetorical spaces to attribute to the film is as interesting and layered as the film's narrative elements. This essay, then, offers a reading of the film's cognitive and rhetorical structures, which refer to the film's expressive and persuasive forms rather than its more immediately recognizable representational or thematic content. The focus is on how forms — genre, spatial metaphors, and rhetorical and conceptual framing — inform the film's power as a cultural event. These are forms that produce meaning that supplement the narrative elements of the story. In the case of *Brokeback Mountain*, for example, the Western genre evokes a relationship to space and nature that has the power to transform the emotional identifications made with the characters and storyline. To this end, the work of two theorists who take up the issue of how social power and aesthetic power emerge within cognitive and rhetorical locations is of importance here. Both Bryan Reynolds, cultural and performance theorist, and Mark Turner, cognitive linguist, provide bases for thinking about cultural change in terms of cognitive and rhetorical spaces — spaces that augment the more legible and transparent elements of representation and audience identification (character, action, and authorship). Turner's thoughts on "conceptual blending" in storytelling will help to illuminate how *Brokeback Mountain* functions as an experiment with cognitive and rhetorical structures and how this experiment plays out as a transformative filmic and social experience. This essay concludes with a consideration of whether these rhetorical and structural aspects of *Brokeback Mountain* reinforce more familiar ideological perspectives — perspectives that reinforce subjective categories of meaning through identifications with individual character, identity, and emotion — or challenge the viewer to inhabit a space of "transversality," an active performative space that plays off the intersection of text, culture, and identity to produce "fluid and discursive phenomena." Transversal events allow for movement beyond one's "subjective territory," a "conceptual and emotional spatial range from which a given subject perceives and experiences the world."[1]

The debates surrounding the film's meaning give us some insight into how a critical approach grounded in cognitive and rhetorical space differs from, say, a discussion of the film's representations of identity in terms of character or social context. In April 2006, the *New York Review of Books* (*NYRB*) published a lengthy exchange between Daniel Mendelsohn, author and reviewer of the film for the *NYRB*, and James Schamus, one of the producers of *Brokeback Mountain*. In the editorial exchange, Schamus takes issue with Mendelsohn's criticisms of the film's marketing campaign, a program of advertising that Mendelsohn claims rhetorically frames the film as a "universal love story," in effect minimizing any appeal to the film's gay themes and content. Schamus counters with his own charge of "rhetorical shortcuts" being taken by Mendelsohn, pointing out what Schamus characterizes as a far more complicated layering of "universal appeal" and the "gay story" at the center of the film's narrative structure. Where Mendelsohn observes equivocation around gay issues on the part of the film's producers, Schamus insists that the "universal" space and the space of "gay identities" are not registers — "sites," as he phrases it — that can be maintained as easy oppositions once there is an attempt to bring gay knowledge out of the closet. Two quotes from the exchange, one from Mendelsohn and one from Schamus, offer clear examples of the rhetorical locations that each takes up in criticizing and defending the film. James Schamus writes:

> One thing this means is that we solicit every audience member's *identification with* the film's central gay characters; the film succeeds if it, albeit initially within the realm of the aesthetic, *queers* its audience ... as a profound and emotionally expansive experience, understandable by all. The power of a cultural moment such as that signaled by the reception of *Brokeback* is that in shattering the "epistemology of the closet" we run the risk of destroying the nonuniversal, specifically gay knowledge previously hidden inside it. Think of it this way: if the phrase "You wouldn't understand — it's a gay thing" is now met with the retort "But I think I *do* understand!" what, we need to ask, becomes of "the gay thing" itself? ... [I]n the process of removing gayness from the closet and "mainstreaming" it ... *Brokeback* appears in the midst of new, and confusing, displacements of the sites of gay and, more broadly, GLBT identities — in the vast and disorienting space between the closet and the wedding altar.

And Daniel Mendelsohn replies:

> Simply because a narrative has universal appeal, however, doesn't mean that the story it tells is universal.... To say the story of *Brokeback Mountain* is universal because in some general way it concerns "love" is to say nothing at all; it's like saying that *Schindler's List* is a universal love story because we all know what it's like to lose a family member. (And imagine the response if critics were to claim that the Holocaust were incidental to that movie, or slavery to *Beloved*).[2]

The exchange between Schamus and Mendelsohn is instructive. In particular, because it mirrors in form many of the difficulties in locating meaning within the film itself. The rhetoric that figures most prominently in their exchange is structured around the "sites" of the "universal" "love" story and "the gay thing." Interestingly, the seemingly most elusive aspects of the film for a mainstream audience — its gay content and representation of gay experience — find expression in both the film and the *NYRB* exchange as a "thing." It is unclear, however, whether the thing in question here is an act (sexual or otherwise), an identity, a social event, or a broader abstraction.

The rhetorical phrase set in opposition to the "gay thing" is a bit less vague, yet no more transparent in detail: the "universal love story." The two contested sites here are framed as generic rhetorical and cognitive structures. The "universal love story," while lacking any specificity as to what actions and characters inhabit such a story, still appeals to a fairly ubiquitous pathos of human emotional and sexual success, an imaginative space where one finds their soul mate within the vastness of the universe. The "gay thing," though it lacks the immediately recognizable pathos of the universal love story, also serves as a spatial and rhetorical construct for the social identifiers of gayness within non-gay mainstream culture. Neither Schamus nor Mendelsohn seems particularly interested in exploring in any depth what the gay "thing" and "universal love" might actually look like, and indeed how they may constitute and reinforce one another. Instead, these shorthand phrases are invoked as placeholders for what both clearly find to be more substantive components of their argument; namely, in what way and to what extent can the gay thing and universal love be *represented* together. The unrepresentable space between their arguments is ultimately that "disorienting space between the closet and the wedding altar," as Schamus terms it. This unrepresentable space is between two conceptual paradigms that do not directly speak to or for one another. What sort of "thing" is this, then?

Spatial Rhetoric and Conceptual Blending

What emerges within this debate between film producer and film critic is an example of the difficulties that ensue when two rhetorical sites intersect yet do not quite overlap in a way that would allow a separate conceptual site or identification to emerge. This point requires an introduction to the recent work of Mark Turner and Gilles Fauconnier on "conceptual blending."[3] Conceptual blending is the process by which two very distinct conceptual sites are blended together to take on an entirely different form. According to cognitive theorists like Turner and George Lakoff (with whom Turner has collaborated over the years), metaphor serves as an example of how conceptual blending takes shape in the formation of new knowledge.[4] A summary example provided by Joseph Grady, Todd Oakley, and Seana Coulson is the following:

The Committee has kept me in the *dark* about this matter.[5]

This statement seems unremarkable at one level since it is so familiar as a colloquial analogy or metaphor for being isolated from information in a given social context. Yet, according to Lakoff and Turner, it is precisely the familiarity of this analogical device that exemplifies the power of conceptual blending for innovations in thinking. While the statement itself is a familiar colloquialism, the conceptual operations implied in being able to make sense of such an analogy are really quite formidable. In this instance, there is a "source" domain and a "target" domain that are blended to alter knowledge. The source, the experiential immediacy of the visual domain, is here mapped onto a source domain; in this case, information in a given social context. A compelling transformation occurs, according to conceptual blending, when something as abstract as being kept in ignorance in the context of a committee meeting is integrated with the very visceral experience of standing in the dark, cutoff from a visual interplay with one's environment. As Grady et al. describe the process, "[T]he relevant conceptual metaphor [is] a 'mapping'— presumably stored as a knowledge structure in long-term memory — which tells us how elements in the two domains line up with each other. In this metaphor, knowledge structures that concern seeing have been put into correspondence with structures concerning knowledge and awareness.... In fact, thanks to the general mapping between visual perception and intellectual activity, nearly any concept related to the experience of vision is likely to have a clear counterpart in the realm of knowledge and ideas."[6] The most relevant aspects of this cognitive phenomenon can be summarized as follows. First, dramatic shifts in the deep structures of knowledge are made possible through this mapping. While the example above employs a fairly general metaphoric construct, as Fauconnier, Lakoff, and Turner have discussed elsewhere, this kind of conceptual integration informs many different kinds of aesthetic, rhetorical, and social reformations in accessible knowledge.[7] Second, while the operations involved appear rather simplistic with respect to their familiarity as rhetorical devices, they imply a fairly complex array of operations at a cognitive level between linguistic and conceptual orders of meaning. This last point should be stressed, as the theory of conceptual blending asserts that the mapping of two domains typically involves a spatial or experiential pattern in relation to a more abstract set of concepts. In the example above, for instance, a mental "space" that imagines standing in the dark serves as a surrogate for the visual experience of darkness. This last point opens up a space for us to think differently about the function of rhetoric in these examples.

Conceptual blending is a means for understanding what is at work in the example of the rhetorical exchange between Schamus and Mendelsohn. As Schamus indicates, the real "thing" in thinking about the film's social location is not the oppositional registers of the "gay thing" and "universal love," but that "disorientating space" in between them. Yet, according to conceptual blending, it may be that the cognitive and rhetorical spaces of the "gay thing" and "universal love" form the outline of a third conceptual space that manages to blend and integrate the experiences surrounding both. We can proceed, then, to consider how such rhetorical effects provide another way of thinking about the representational efficacy of the film (character, plot, and action, for example). Thus, rhetorical space becomes a means for investigating both the film's communal persuasiveness and the film's potential impact on cognitive associations of myth, rhetoric, and space.

As Gilberto Perez has argued, the power of rhetoric in filmic experience is often overlooked in favor of more directed instances of individual identification.[8] Perez asks us to think beyond a model of identification in film-going experience which emphasizes an individualized experience that is informed by identifying *with* a given character in a given set of circumstances. Building off of Kenneth Burke's *Rhetoric of Motives*, Perez takes up the issue of how films function rhetorically, and, in particular, the way in which films and their persuasive constructs imply a more varied and nuanced engagement with identification.[9] Moving away from personal identification, Perez draws on the cognitive theory of Murray Smith to explore how the persuasiveness of character and context in films is about both "alignment" and "allegiance." Alignment refers to a spectator's experience of the actions and feelings of a given character and context, without necessarily feeling a strict allegiance to a character. Allegiance is a feeling *with* experience that "pertains to the moral and ideological evaluation of characters by the spectator."[10] The approach to rhetoric as a communal phenomenon is helpful in that it allows some interpretive room that takes us beyond thinking of the social power of texts (visual and verbal) in terms of character identification amid conventional (or counter-conventional) moral or ethical evaluations. By expanding this a bit further, we can look specifically at how the communal, very public rhetorical effects of a film like *Brokeback Mountain* are further mapped onto various cognitive sites. Focusing on rhetorical space and conceptual blending in *Brokeback Mountain* takes us between communal space and cognitive space, in such a way to steer clear of questions of individualized identity. This makes the "gay thing" and "universal love" at once ideological, rhetorical, and identity spaces, and sites perpetually in process of re-constituting and instituting the origins and meanings of the "gay thing" in relation to ideological, rhetorical, and biographical spaces.

To really get a sense of how relevant this process is for the film as a cultural event, we need to look more closely at the movement between experiential spaces in *Brokeback Mountain* and the rhetorical operations within the film. As Perez has noted, the rhetorical persuasiveness of a film is bound up in a combination of verbal and visual spaces and gestures — natural environments, camera angles, speechmaking, implied myths, and iconic scenes, sounds, and objects — that combine to inform a film's persuasive affect. Perez offers the example of two young lovers in a meadow as a demonstration of how this works. A young couple seen walking in a meadow are at once a romantic cliché and an embodiment of a rhetoric that asks the viewer to see the couple as part of nature, and thus their heterosexual love becomes aligned with the beauty and simplicity of nature. The two dominant rhetorical structures in *Brokeback Mountain* are the Western/Frontier genre, with its attendant myths, scripts, and spaces, and, to a lesser extent, the romanticization of nature.

Romanticizing Nature

Looking first at the romanticization of nature as rhetorical structure, we can identify a pretty clear message about the natural environment in *Brokeback Mountain*, one aligned neatly with the general myths and ideological stirrings of a romantic view of nature. Jack and Ennis discover an almost Edenic pastoralism in the natural environment of the mountains of Wyoming. We have the one scene right before the two initiate their sexual connection, where the camera lingers on a full moon nightscape that serves as a kind of foreboding of darkness and danger, but even in this instance, the scene is ambiguous as to whether we are to align ourselves with the nightscape as a sign of bad omens or as a symbol of the inexorable changeability of both social and natural order. Aside from this moment, where attention is directed to the rhetoric of nature in relationship to a key moment in the narrative, Jack and Ennis, along with the audience, are treated to a visual feast reminiscent of every aspect of pastoral simplicity: caring and productive labor amid the unfettered landscape; the discovery and re-creation of social, natural, and domestic order; and the promise of plenty inherent in the depictions of vast, unclaimed natural expanses.

At one level, this myth of natural simplicity is not as naïve as it might seem — indeed, the filmmakers seem perfectly aware of our potential responses to the rhetoric of a romanticized nature. While we are being swept up in the mythos and spatial rhetoric of the natural expanse, we are also being asked to follow the social and domestic evolution of Jack and Ennis's relationship. To this end, the Edenic myth is pushed into terrain it is not conventionally asked to inhabit, queer partnering and domesticity. The rhetorical mapping of domesticity onto the natural landscape is fairly forceful. From the earliest shots of Jack and Ennis heading up the into the mountains with their herd of sheep, we see an aspect of this pastoral labor that is not typically emphasized in Western fiction: the nurturing and caring that accompanies the tough, virile activities of cowboying. Indeed, much of what we see of both amid the iconic portrayals of pastoral herding is Jack and Ennis carrying smaller and less able-bodied sheep in their arms or over their saddles, and even the mending and caring of wounds and injuries.

We are from the outset being persuaded to connect the natural pastoralism of the film with the underlying domestic and caring labor of both Jack and Ennis. This association is pushed further with the negotiations that occur between Jack and Ennis over "home" labor — cooking, cleaning, and mending — and the "public" labor of caring for the herd. The genre of pastoral is in itself a potentially ironic set of constructs, to the extent that pastoral draws attention to nature not as a romantic backdrop to the emotional life of fictional characters, but as a means for critically investigating how nature is deployed in constructions of idealized emotional and physical space.[11] Indeed, some of the more interesting historical and contemporary work with the genre uses the conventions of "pastoral" and "urban" space to draw attention to how these categories are both fictionalized and redeployed to critique social hierarchies. Such appropriations of the pastoral employ the conventions of this mode to raise questions about our cultural assumptions about nature and the origins of human social organization. Along these lines, there is a rich tradition, from Virgil's *Eclogues* to John Milton's *Lycidas*, of using the pastoral to explore homoerotic desire and its communion with the instituting of "civilized" forces that "naturalize" heteronormative sexuality.[12] And while *Brokeback Mountain* does present a subtle exploration of the dialectic between "home" and "public" labor via its use of pastoralism, there is still a predominantly romantic connection established between the pastoral life and a simpler, less complicated "original" mode of existence.

At one level, we could say that the rhetoric of landscape and domesticity function as an implied critique of the ideology surrounding the naturalization of gendered social and sexual relationships. That is, the relatively socially neutral and natural setting for the initiation of their relationship serves as a kind of blank canvas for painting the division of labor as a function of practical, context-driven choices rather than essentialist traits linked to one's gender or sexuality. Yet, at the same time, the appropriation of the more subtle and experiential rhetoric of the natural landscape carries with it some fairly fraught mythical terrain — mythical constructs that are bound to the most prominent rhetorical construct in *Brokeback Mountain*, the Western/Frontier genre.

Spatial Myth and the Western/Frontier Genre

As Richard Slotkin has illuminated, the Western landscape is one of the most powerful American mythic spaces. Slotkin, in his exhaustive study of the complicity between Frontier and Western myths and the colonial imperialism of American culture, traces the significance of spatial setting and genre to a comprehensive visual rhetoric that becomes a surrogate for a complex intersection of national, personal, and historical myths:

> When fully developed, the mythic space of a genre invests even the sketchiest characterization or setting with resonance, as if it were part of a larger culture, with its own spatial architecture, manners, folkways, and politics.... Genre space is also mythic space: a pseudo-historical (or pseudo-real) setting that is powerfully associated with stories and concerns rooted in the culture's myth/ideological tradition. It is also a setting in which the concrete work of contemporary myth-making is done. This is particularly true of the Western, whose roots go deeper into the American cultural past than those of any other movie genre.[13]

The rhetorical flexibility of the Western genre as both a personal experience and as a space that is transformed into a hybrid of myth and history is central to its power as a cultural experience. That is, the Western is a communal experience in American culture, a recognizable frame for masculine, self-sufficient world making, which also serves as rhetorical shorthand for an imagined history of the progress of American culture. The progressive myths that emerge within the Western assimilate social, economic, and racial conflicts and re-frame them as problems to be resolved within the Western formula. The effects of building upon a collective rhetoric of personal value, mythology, and history made possible by a genre space like the Western allow for "a complex system of historical associations by a single image or phrase."[14] "Pearl Harbor," "The Frontier" (we can now add "9/11" to this list) permit a complicated and divergent set of emotional, political, historical, and cognitive sites to become compressed into a single rhetorical, mythical entity: "myth expresses ideology in a narrative, rather than discursive or argumentative structure.... The movement of a mythic narrative, like that of any story, implies a theory of cause-and-effect and therefore a theory of history (or even of cosmology)."[15]

On a rhetorical level, Turner would refer to this phenomenon as "cognitive compression."[16] In other words, the historical and mythical elements of the Western become conceptually blended with an experiential and cognitive immersion in the "openness" and "freedom" of the unfettered, natural landscape, and further, those visual signifiers for progressive freedom then become affixed to the biographical details of the cowboy as a form of authentic American consciousness. This form of conceptual blending, which is heavily dependent on the rhetorical structure of a genre, points to a different form of character identification. Here, the issue is not a projection of personal judgments or morals in order to identify *with* a character, but a more subtle systemic alignment of personal consciousness, historical and political ideology, and, moreover, a blending of historical and mythic narratives with "biographical performance."[17] Biographical performance in this context draws attention to "identity" as a function of conceptual and linguistic blending weaved into the fabric of historical and cultural myth.

This form of blending may seem auspicious in the case of *Brokeback Mountain*, where queer love and sexuality are mapped onto idealized pastoral and Western rhetorical settings. Yet, these multi-layered associations, while pointing to a subtle re-ordering of the terms of audience identification, can carry with them the accumulated mythic spaces of the genre. It is certainly the case, as Slotkin has described it, that "as stories accumulate and are mnemonically linked to a particular visual setting, the imaginative possibilities of the generic terrain are both expanded and mapped for future reference."[18] It is equally the case, however, that reliance on the rhetoric of genre "invokes a set of fundamental assumptions and expectations about the kinds of events that can occur in the setting, the kinds of motives that will operate, the sort of outcome one can predict."[19] It is these less transparent alliances that should draw our attention along with the potential for *Brokeback Mountain* to re-institute a connection between American myth and biographical perform-ance.

Brokeback Mountain's force, then, is derived less from its promotion of individual identification with a viewer than it is a communal form of persua-sion that draws on queer biography mapped onto the Western genre and the rhetoric of the romanticization of nature. Yet, there is a rhetoric of individ-ual "authenticity" that is evoked in the film. The success of taking something as conventionally scripted as the Western genre and fusing it with queer space is contingent upon the film's convincing depiction of the authenticity of the genre. In order to be persuasive, the film must be viewed without too much irony. To achieve as much, Jack and Ennis must register as authentic embod-iments of the most persuasive elements of the genre. And here again, we are asked to immerse ourselves in some powerfully persuasive aspects of the West-ern/Frontier myth. Throughout the film, Jack is linked with the desires of the rodeo cowboy. Specifically, Jack's struggles to embody the masculinity associated with the cowboy become projected onto his performances *as* a cow-boy on the rodeo circuit. Jack's persona increasingly becomes tied to both the authentic measures of the cowboy (roping and riding) and the performances necessary to maintain the illusion of Western, masculine ideals. Ennis, on the other hand, is more closely aligned with mastery over the techne of guns and vehicles. Our very first introduction to both characters, and indeed the open-ing frames for the movie, bring us from a wide-angle shot of mountainous landscape — pierced by the lights from a truck moving slowly over the land-scape — to our first look at Ennis. We see Ennis making his way from the truck that has brought him to Signal for work, and then propped against a trailer, his body occluded in montage by a passing train. When Jack arrives on the scene, he stumbles from his truck, offering a swift kick to the tires of a vehicle whose clutch has obviously given him grief. This imbrication of rural landscape and the technologies of mobility and transportation returns throughout the film as a kind of sub-narrative. Indeed, the truck(s) becomes a kind of scenic backdrop throughout the film, overshadowed only by the landscape of the mountain and the claustrophobia of domestic spaces.

Jack has pursued the life of rodeo cowboy. Ennis can shoot an elk and fix a truck. Both registers of authenticity, modes of being that connect with the autobiographical myths of the authentic Western cowboy as self-sufficient and ruggedly individualistic (not to mention masculine) create an opening

LIVERPOOL JOHN MOORES UNIVERSITY
Aldham Robarts L.R.C.
TEL. 0151 231 3701/3634

for the audience to develop an allegiance with Jack and Ennis as iconic representations of the Western mythos. But it is also through the play with technology, mobility and transportation, and rural self-sufficiency that another set of autobiographical and historical myths are aligned within the film. Both Jack and Ennis are caught within a kind of dialectic of rural, pastoral simplicity and the advent of mid-twentieth-century American values. These are not just the emergent American values associated with the nuclear family and compulsory heterosexuality. Throughout the film we catch glimpses of the progressive machinery of American life (literally and metaphorically) amid the cultural transition from the 50s into the early 60s, and alongside a very understated back-story on the Vietnam War. Jack even makes reference at one point to the Army getting hold of him. Exposed to the pressures of being caught between American "progress" and pastoral simplicity, both characters evolve into virtual embodiments of Teddy Roosevelt's rough-riding ethos of "regeneration through regression."[20]

Regeneration through regression refers to a political and historical ideology based in the desire to return to the plebian roots of American democracy to recapture the simplicity of the "democratic life of the cowboy."[21] As Slotkin demonstrates, cowboyism represents the entitlement of a "successor class" in American consciousness, a place where competitive, imperialist motives of Frontiersman can be rescripted as the "stages of civilization," drawn down to an autobiographical experience. In this sense, we can re-conceive Jack's and Ennis's development in the film as characters who have discovered a map of an earlier stage of history, an earlier phase of civilized life where they are free to create a world of their own. But we cannot lose sight of the fact that this "contract," if you will — the promise contained in the rhetoric of the Western/Frontier mythos — is inseparable from its history as a genre that justifies and rationalizes the ascendancy of white, American men taking control of savage terrain for their own economic and social advancement. Entitlement becomes the subtext for Jack and Ennis' freedom in the landscape of Brokeback Mountain, a directed line of metaphoric and real descent that implies that men who can aspire to the authenticity of the Western are entitled to their place as members of the successor class — the "gay thing" aside. The merging of spatial and experiential immediacy of the Western landscape with these historical and class accumulations allows for Jack and Ennis to emerge as powerful icons of American imaginative space.

The mythos of the "democratic life of the cowboy" is a framework as linked to the complicated history of American colonialism and manifest destiny as it is to any reification of self-sufficiency, individualism, and democratic values. In a fascinating redirection of the pastoral simplicity of Ennis and Jack's earlier moments on Brokeback Mountain, their return to "modern" social life becomes a rhetorical scene of frustrated love and obstructed progress toward the full realization of the myth of Western progressivism. The association of the images of the Western landscape and all its attendant mythologies of social, historical, and individual progress have prepared us for a connection with Jack and Ennis as representatives of Western, progressive ideals. The nostalgic rhetoric of such ideals sets forth the expectation that Jack and Ennis, as representatives of the "authentic" Western hero, will be allowed to realize the simplicity and progressive energy of their earlier pastoral existence as a way of life, as a new form of social order. The further play off of mobility and Western landscape, juxtaposed with the suffocating and static energy of modern social life, instill in us a sense that what Jack and Ennis are being asked to sacrifice is not "universal love" so much as the interrupted progress of the Frontier myth.

Remaining mindful of the fraught ideological underpinnings to the Western/Frontier mythos, we are confronted with the possibility that apart from projecting the simplicity and democracy of Western individualism onto two queer characters (that is, the familiarity and purity of the Western ethos cast onto the private, individual pathos of two men in love), we are asked to re-imagine the sexual and emotional bond of these two men as embodiments, indeed avatars, of American social and economic progress as distilled through the lens of the Western genre. Jack and Ennis's obstructed love story is rhetorically fused with our own collective history with Western progressivism (race wars on the Frontier and failed wars, Vietnam in particular). We are being nudged toward the cognitive and rhetorical compression of our own nostalgia for and frustration over the fulfillment of Western progressivism vis-à-vis the impeded love of Jack and Ennis.

This alignment between historical and social ideology and homosexual love is reinforced in even more direct ways within the representational economy of the film itself. The most prominent example is Ennis's connection with the artifact of the horse. Amid the pastoral simplicity of the two men's slowly evolving love, Ennis clutches and whittles away at a small woodcarving of a horse. The object is a kind of fetish that mediates the psychical and emotional complexity of Ennis's growing desire for Jack, but is also an icon of the horseman and cowboy in the larger cultural sense. We know as well that the figure of the horse represents Jack's struggles with his authenticity as a cowboy; a point made salient by his settling for the life of the bull-riding, rodeo cowboy. Ennis's love for Jack is imperceptibly mapped with one of the most powerful signifiers of Western authenticity. Jack and Ennis's failed love becomes our loss as well. A further implication of this rhetoric is that permitting the narrative of their love to advance unimpeded might re-generate those lost idealizations of Frontier consciousness, that it just might put the West right with itself again.

LIVERPOOL JOHN MOORES UNIVERSITY
LEARNING SERVICES

Ang Lee's extensive use of Fordesque sky panoramas raises the question of the extent to which *Brokeback Mountain* is attempting a more reflexive, critical appropriation of aspects of the Western genre. John Ford's *Stagecoach* (1939) is well known for its very self-aware engagement with the Western as a genre and its concern with democratic ideology and social progressivism. *Stagecoach* employed the vast skyscapes of Monument Valley as a way of drawing attention to the emblematic power of open landscape in reinforcing the stereotypes and myths of the Western. As Slotkin argues, Ford employs the vastness of the open sky and terrain of Monument Valley to invent such landscape "as a cinematic (and American) icon."[22] The power of authenticity that prevails in Ford's film is generated out of the landscape's familiarity as a space representative of "the West," but also from its very strangeness and alien form. Ford combines these elements into a film experience that simultaneously generates the myths of the Western and critiques them, drawing attention to the mobility and openness of the stagecoach journeys as a way of inducing reflection on the "civilized," democratic spaces of the town and way station scenes in between. The "narrative of the journey"—a progression through "stages" and stations — across the open Western landscape serves as an "archetypal, ... allegorical movement" that becomes a "tool [for] ... exploring and questioning the fundamental assumptions about American communities that underlie self-congratulatory formulas of the epic Western and the history textbook."[23]

Enough similarity with Ford's stylized techniques is seen in the use of sky panoramas in *Brokeback Mountain* to suggest that the film is rhetorically aligning itself with Ford's critical engagement with the Western genre. Yet, the open-sky landscape scenes in *Brokeback Mountain* are frequently used as transition shots that rapidly move the viewer into close-up and framing angles indoors within domestic space. Domestic space in *Brokeback Mountain* is representative of limiting, claustrophobic environments where characters are trapped and constrained. Where Ford uses the way stations along the stagecoach journey as microcosms that parallel the emblematic and ideological spaces associated with the open landscape scenes, Ang Lee uses the skyscapes in *Brokeback Mountain* as a space that resists or contrasts with the closeness and even stifling atmosphere of domestic space. In this case, we are not asked to think critically about the iconic, emblematic function of open Frontier vistas and how they reinforce or challenge our assumptions about social communities, but to embrace these vistas experientially as spaces that give both viewer and characters relief from the oppressiveness of domestic heteronormativity. As *Brokeback Mountain* progresses, open landscapes are increasingly used as still shots set in stark contrast with the confinement of domesticity. This is an appropriation of Ford-like big-sky vistas that further idealizes the notion that the Western genre offers a form of escape from the restrictive conventional expectations of normalized American social communities. The rhetoric of "openness" that serves as a metaphor for an idealized American way of life is re-formed as a space of confinement. In this context, the physically "open" spaces of the big-sky panorama promise relief from such confinement.

Interestingly, the way in which space prevails as a metaphoric encapsulation of the closet in *Brokeback Mountain* actually further reinforces Western individualism in fraught terms as well. Ennis in particular is a character who comes to embody the epistemology of the closet, and this embodiment is further caught up with Western individual authenticity. Ennis' individualism is made nearly impossible by the social scripts he is worked into upon his return from Brokeback Mountain, and throughout the remainder of the film we see the oppression of indoor, domestic spaces begin to materialize as an internal psychology. The cloying effect of domestic space is absorbed by Ennis to the point where the claustrophobia of the physical spaces becomes a troubling feature of Ennis' character. Behind such compression, the self-sufficient cowboy is literally transformed before us into a caricature of the trapped gunfighter of earlier "B" Westerns. The trapped gunfighter is a figure whose personal struggles are always tied up with history. The gunfighter is a character whose drive to embody the Frontier myth has put him at odds with his own comfort and progress. "Despite his discipline and skill," the trapped gunfighter is "vulnerable" and "trapped by his history and his identity."[24] This character type enters the narrative of the Frontier as "limitless in its possibilities for social and personal perfection," and comes to the realization that it is a "mirage."[25] Yet, in the case of Ennis, this inner pathology and suffering is romanticized as a kind of ethos of self-repression that betrays moral steadiness.

Western Myth "In" and "Out" of the Closet

We can have little doubt, however, that there is an active appropriation of the visual rhetoric of expansiveness juxtaposed with the oppressiveness of domestic space in *Brokeback Mountain* and that much of this is meant to invoke a visceral experience of "the closet." The concept of the closet conventionally refers to the state of being either "out" with one's minority sexual practice or identity, or "in the closet" and thus hiding one's sexual identity. Eve Kosofsky Sedgwick's foundational queer theory text, "Epistemology of the Closet," expanded the discussion of the closet to include a more encompassing exploration of the categories of knowledge versus ignorance within Western epistemology. That is, Sedgwick focuses on how the rhetorical interplay between knowledge and ignorance informs Western knowledge production in a much broader context. The closet is certainly about the explicit and implicit signifiers of homosexuality and heterosexuality, but it is also about the productive confusion that emanates from within the dialectic of two oppositional categories of meaning. Homosexuality and heterosexuality are not clear markers or limits on experience or identity, much in the same way that the "universal love story" and the "gay thing" lack delineation and relief. Yet, as Sedgwick points out, it is the play between seemingly fixed, transparent categories of meaning that informs our sense of the very possibility of making meaning in the world. For example, gay versus straight and black versus white, masquerade as knowable entities even though they are nebulous, contingent, and fluid rhetorical constructs. The binaries that inform how we come to knowledge are conceptually incoherent, then, but yet give the appearance of a kind of progress inherent to coming out of ignorance and into knowledge.[26]

The difficulty, of course, in bringing the closet forward as an experiential and visual rhetoric in *Brokeback Mountain* is that the spatial immediacy of being "in" the closeted spaces of heteronormative domesticity and "out" in the expansive Western landscape is infused with the ideologies of the Frontier. Ang Lee's framing of this dialectic aligns the Frontier-scape with the promise of being "out," of being brought from ignorance into knowledge, in Sedgwick's terms. Thus, being part of the progressive mythos of the Frontier offers an escape from the limiting spaces of modern domesticity and heteronormativity. A further problem here lies in restraining meaning within *Brokeback Mountain* to the very epistemology of the closet that Sedgwick identifies. That is, beyond the rhetorical and mythical accumulations attendant upon the Frontier and Western myths, there is rhetorical affirmation of the closet itself as a conceptual structure leading to personal liberation. This space offers the promise of release from closeted homosexuality, which is then translated into the liberating idealizations of a pastoral and re-purified American normativity. Indeed, the film ends with Ennis standing before the closet in his trailer, adjusting the buttons on Jack's shirt, caught up in bitter nostalgia and pain over the constraints on his emotional life, of being trapped in the closet for so many years. The final shot takes us away from the closet and back outside to bask in the spatial rhetoric of big sky and mountainous landscape. The conceptual blending at work here creates nostalgia in us for the possibility that Jack could have been allowed to "come out," allowed to map his identity onto the promise of the unclaimed Western expanse. The danger implicit in this formulation is the further reinforcement of a collective belief in the possibility of a liberating transparency that follows "coming out." As Sedgwick has described this phenomenon, "the image of coming out regularly interfaces the image of the closet, and its seemingly unambivalent public siting

can be counterposed as a salvational epistemologic certainty against the equivocal privacy afforded by the closet."[27] Salvation in these terms results in an
untenable paradox: on the one hand, the reaffirmation of "knowing" as a
function of moving from secrecy into the supposedly clear, transparent space
of the "gay thing"; and on the other hand, assimilation into the communal
rhetoric of Western, American Progressivism. Not only is "identity" in *Brokeback Mountain* hinged to the closet door, it makes the possible siting of the
"gay thing" an experiential and mythical space located between an over-
idealized romance with Edenic origins, authentic individualism, and Frontier consciousness.

In many senses, the rhetoric of the film is quite effective in moving mainstream audiences into a communal space that is framed as a complex layering of historical, cultural, and biographical registers. Moreover, the films's
social and historical associations are merged with both the immediacy of the
spatial rhetoric of the natural Frontier and the very visceral experience of the
closet. *Brokeback Mountain* is an example of how fluid conceptual blending
is in restructuring the relationship between biographical narratives or performances and larger historical and mythical ideologies. The film is successful as
well, one could argue, in shifting audience allegiance around issues of morality and character in the conventional sense of those terms into more generic
alignments of biographical performance, history, and myth.

Bryan Reynold's concepts of "subjunctive space" and "transversal performance" create another set of questions about *Brokeback Mountain*'s capacity to challenge some of the ideologies it regenerates. Subjunctive space is a
performative and discursive space that allows for a form of "hypothetical ...
empathy" where "as if" and "what if" become sites for considering experience beyond one's cultural or personal comfort zone. Subjunctive space can
emerge in response to a traumatic or moving experience through "emotional,
conceptual, and bodily performances" that follow from historical, cultural,
or aesthetic events.[28] We can hear in Reynolds' descriptions of the subjunctive categories of "what if" and "as if" echoes of the categories of "allegiance"
and "alignment" in thinking about audience identification. The power of
Reynolds' formulations along these lines is in their embrace of cultural change
in terms of performances that operate simultaneously at the level of cognition and communal experience. Rather than envisioning *Brokeback Mountain*
as an experiment with identity and the individual viewer, we can broaden
our understanding of the film's import as an event capable of re-constituting
the "gay thing" as part of a much broader collocation of historical, mythical,
and biographical performance.

Yet, transversal performances, while capable of re-forming individual
and collective knowledge and experience, must give way to "self-activating"

movements that "work to stabilize, empower, or disempower the subject."[29] Certainly, on the one hand, the film evokes the spatial myths of the Western/Frontier genre for its persuasive power and conceptually blends these myths with the rhetorical spaces of the "gay thing" and "universal love." Moreover, experientially, it activates a visceral experience with these rhetorical spaces that becomes linked to the epistemology of the closet. On the other hand, the performative and rhetorical "text" of the film leaves space for the possibility for differing and more interesting *alignments* of autobiography, myth, and experiential space to emerge. Indeed, the very "transversal" act of bringing queer desire into contact with more conventional genres and spaces creates an unstable cultural site where these rhetorics may be read differently, may be "activated" along more critical and expansive lines. Perhaps the "thing" that best describes *Brokeback Mountain*, then, is a performance in progress between text, rhetoric, and American myth.

Notes

1. Bryan Reynolds, *Performing Transversally: Reimagining Shakespeare and the Critical Future* (New York: Palgrave Macmillan, 2003), 3.
2. James Schamus, Daniel Mendelsohn, "'Brokeback Mountain': An Exchange," *New York Review of Books* 53, no. 6 (Apr. 6, 2006), <http://www.nybooks.com/articles/18846> (accessed Aug. 18, 2006). Schamus wrote in response to Daniel Mendelsohn's review of *Brokeback Mountain*, "An Affair to Remember," in *NYRB* (Feb. 23, 2006).
3. Mark Turner and Gilles Fauconnier, *The Way We Think: Conceptual Blending and the Mind's Hidden Complexities* (New York: Basic Books, 2002); Mark Turner, "Compression and Representation," *Language and Literature* 15.1 (2006), 17-27.
4. George Lakoff and Mark Johnson, *Metaphors We Live By* (Chicago: University of Chicago Press, 1980).
5. Joseph E. Grady, Todd Oakley, and Seana Coulson, "Blending and Metaphor," on Mark Turner, 2006, <http://markturner.org/blendaphor.html> (accessed on May 15, 2006).
6. Ibid.
7. See Lakoff and Johnson; Turner, "Compression and Representation"; Turner and Fauconnier; Gilles Fauconnier, *Mappings in Thought and Language* (Cambridge: Cambridge University Press, 1997).
8. Gilberto Perez, "Toward a Rhetoric of Film," *Sense of Cinema* 5 (April 2000), <http://www.sensesofcinema.com/contents/00/5/> (accessed Apr. 3, 2006).
9. Gilberto Perez. "Saying 'Ain't' and Playing 'Dixie': Rhetoric and Comedy in *Judge Priest*," *Raritan* 23, no. 4 (2004): 34-54.
10. Perez, "Toward a Rhetoric."
11. Both Paul Alpers and, more recently, Thomas Hubbard offer extensive treatments of how the pastoral is a mode (or theme) used as a means not only of idealizing nature, but of drawing attention to how the pastoral serves as an ironic set of conventions to critique the concepts of origin (including authorship) and the instituting of "civilized" settings against "natural" environments. See Alpers, *What Is Pastoral?* (Chicago: University of Chicago Press, 1996), and Hubbard, *The Pipes of Pan: Intertextuality and Literary Filiation from Theocritus to Milton* (Ann Arbor: University of Michigan Press, 1998).
12. See Stephen Guy-Bray, *Homoerotic Space: The Poetics of Loss in Renaissance Literature* (Toronto: University of Toronto Press, 2002); Paul Hammond, *Figuring Sex Between Men from Shakespeare to Rochester* (Oxford: Oxford University Press, 2002); Valerie Traub, *The Renais-*

sance of Lesbianism in Renaissance England (Cambridge: Cambridge University Press, 2002); Rictor Norton, "The Homosexual Pastoral Tradition," *Rick Norton Homepage,* 1974/1997, <http://www.infopt.demon.co.uk/pastor01.htm> (accessed, July 1, 2006).

13. Richard Slotkin, *Gunfighter Nation: The Myth of the Frontier in Twentieth-Century America* (New York: HarperCollins, 1992), 233–234.

14. Ibid., 286.

15. Ibid., 6.

16. Ibid.

17. Turner, "Compression and Representation."

18. Slotkin, 233.

19. Ibid.

20. Ibid.

21. Ibid.

22. Ibid., 305.

23. Ibid., 309.

24. Ibid., 390.

25. Ibid.

26. Eve Kosofsky Sedgwick, "Epistemology of the Closet," in *The Lesbian and Gay Studies Reader,* ed. Henry Abelove, Michele Aina Barale, and David Halperin (New York: Routledge, 1993).

27. Ibid., 48.

28. Reynolds, 5.

29. Ibid.

8

From "Nature's Love" to Natural Love: *Brokeback Mountain,* Universal Identification, and Gay Politics

by Xinghua Li

Declaring the loss of a "center that holds," postmodernism has set free a stream of historically repressed anarchism and has brought forth a wide rejection of grand narratives in various intellectual and political forums. Fueled by this postmodern spirit, the now flourishing "identity politics" seeks to secure a niche identity for each minority social group and accuses any political act that attempts to "universalize" or "naturalize" of reinforcing existing power relationships. Here, overarching concepts, such as the Universal or the Natural, are considered as merely ideological tools that ought to be abandoned by political activists who seek social change.

Another polemic force, however, stands against this postmodern current and tries to reclaim the political value of the Universal. This group of thinkers, represented by Laclau and Žižek, criticize postmodern "identity politics" for promoting partisan interest and believe that true politics employs the power of the Universal to build political alliance among different interest groups. They propose a paradigm for minority politics that subverts the existing social order by articulating the Universal with the particular interests of excluded groups.

The film *Brokeback Mountain* is an excellent case through which we can gauge the efficacy of the latter kind of political strategy. First, one of the most prominent questions concerning this movie is: Is *Brokeback* a political polemic for the gay rights movement? This essay contends that the answer is yes. Actually, the fact that this question is even asked demonstrates the political effectiveness of this movie. This essay argues that, although appearing to be apolitical and even "ahistorical," *Brokeback* appropriates the grand ideology of Nature to *naturalize* and *universalize* homosexual relationships and is, therefore, a highly charged political endeavor which coheres with the agenda of the gay rights movement. The essay also points out that the effectiveness of this kind of naturalizing strategy is shown exactly through its own effacement.

Homosexuality: A Life Against "Nature"?

Ideology critics usually accept the assumption that one of the main ways oppressive ideology functions is by *naturalizing* existing social relationships. However, there is one question often ignored: Why is naturalization oppressive? Or, why naturalize at all? If we look under this assumption, we can find what is taken for granted to be the underlying logic: that which is natural is assumed to be normal, that which is natural is assumed to be good, that which is natural is what can stand uncontested. This unspoken logic of ideology critics, then, places *naturalism* as the fundamental ideology of criticism, one against which all others are measured: what is natural is that which is normal, good, and legitimate.[1] Striving to monopolize the symbolic assets of "naturalness," dominant groups exclude other social groups that are considered as "unnatural" and thereby exert oppression on them.

If we suppose that the level of "naturalness" of a minority group is inversely proportional to the level of exclusion it receives from the mainstream society, then homosexuals are probably the high-profile minority that suffers the most from this exclusion. The reason is simply because the popular conception of homosexuals is the least compatible with the concept of "naturalness." Since homosexuals have been historically regarded as cases of perversion or mental disease, they have always been kept outside the mainstream of the society. Jack Babuscion represents the oppressive dominant ideology in the following binary: "heterosexuality = normal, natural, healthy behavior; homosexuality = abnormal, unnatural, sick behavior."[2] Even after the 1970s when homosexuality was no longer regarded as pathological by the medical profession, socially homosexuals still remained excluded. Babuscion explains the reason, "Gayness is seen as a sort of collective denial of the moral and social order of things. Our very lifestyle indicates a rejection of that most cherished cultural assumption which says that masculinity (including sexual dominance over women) is 'natural' and appropriate for men, and femininity (including sexual submissiveness towards men) is 'natural' and appropriate for women."[3] The homosexual group's unique relationship with the concept of "naturalness" distinguishes them from other types of minorities: While other traditional racial and ethnic minorities are all (believed to be) more or less grounded in "natural" biological settings, homosexuals are considered as people who live "against nature." That is why Larry Gross aligns them with political minorities: "In both cases [sexual minorities and political minorities] their members typically are self-identified at some point in their lives, usually in adolescence or later, and they are not necessarily easily identifiable by others. These two groups also constitute by their very existence a presumed threat to the 'natural' (sexual and/or political) order of things...."[4]

Although homosexuals are always excluded from normality and "naturalness," they conceptualize their status of exclusion as a unique vantage point from which they can contemplate social reality with an alternative insight. As Cohen and Dyer write, "It made me feel myself as "outside" the mainstream in fundamental ways — and this does give you a kind of knowledge of the mainstream you cannot have if you are immersed in it ... it denaturalizes normality."[5] While the price of being "inside" the mainstream is to be blinded from some simple truths (the basic rationale for ideology criticism), the detached insight of an "outsider" may be viewed as compensation for being excluded from the mainstream. In *Brokeback*, this outsider/insider dichotomy is strengthened by the traditional nature/culture dichotomy in order to invert the homosexuals' position in the dominant heterosexual ideological binary.

Nature vs. Culture: The Sublime vs. the Banal

The reason why "nature" takes on such a significant political value is primarily because of its linguistic advantage: it is a polysemantic word with multiple meanings and each of them has its own ideological functions. In addition to the above-mentioned "nature" as normality or "naturalness," the word "nature" could also refer to pristine wilderness which is always opposed against human culture and civilization.

This nature/culture dichotomy has long standing in Western tradition as well as in other cultures. On the one hand, it poses an opposition between pristine nature and the industrialized and urbanized human world; on the other hand, it believes that humans originally were a harmonious part of the nature but were severed from it by industrialization and urbanization. This type of rhetoric always carries a nostalgic pathos and suggests one go back to nature in order to find true freedom of mind.

Such a depiction of nature has remained one of the few overarching ideologies of our times. In a study of Watkins' landscape photographs of the Yosemite Valley, Deluca and Demo (2000) have shown how this ideology of naturalism appropriates the power of aesthetics to achieve political purpose.[6] Based on an analysis of the visual rhetoric of Watkins' photographs, they argue that pristine wilderness, as a popular icon that stands for "nature," has been constructed by environmental politics as a *sublime* object for the purpose of public preservation. In reviewing the history of the sublime in Western thought, they examine three terms used by nature romanticism to describe different types of landscape portraits: "beautiful," "picturesque," "sublime." While the beautiful and the picturesque require human presence or artistry, the sublime is the representation of nature with the least human involvement. As Demars points out in *The Tourist in Yosemite, 1855–1985:* "'Sublime' was used increasingly to refer to the 'wild' in nature, and rather than focus on some work of man that gave meaning to the scene, romanticists tended to perceive a sublime landscape as a nondirect expression of God Himself. Again, the matter of scale was important, as well as the greater element of mystery, of supernatural manifestation that engendered a more reverential perception of the natural scene.[7] According to Demars, the sublime produces an aesthetic experience for the observer that resembles a religious experience. It usually occurs during one's encounter with vast and enormous objects and often comes with a mix of mystery and awe. Subjecting the audience to an enormous but unknown power, the sublime captivates the observer with a sense of reverence and spares them from making rational, ethical judgments. *Brokeback* later uses this sublime power of nature to suspend the moral judgments imposed on the homosexual group and to induce emotional identification with them.

The Politics of Brokeback: *From "Nature" to "Natural"*

Without direct reference to any gay rights issue, *Brokeback Mountain* is different from many other movies that deal with gay politics. It does not seem to be political like *Philadelphia* or *Angels in America* that deal with popular gay controversies such as AIDS; it does not seem very historical either because "the romance takes places in a vacuum, with no reference to anything outside the relationship," Andrew Holleran notes.[8] So, is *Brokeback* an apolitical and ahistorical movie? The forthcoming analysis will show that the answer is no. Wielding the power of visual rhetoric, *Brokeback* demonstrates a sophisticated political strategy that transcends the traditional idea of politics and radically subverts the traditional ideological binary that oppresses the homosexual group.

The plot of *Brokeback Mountain* is very simple and can be explained in a short paragraph. It tells the story of two cowboys, Ennis and Jack, who fall in love with each other while herding sheep on Brokeback Mountain in Wyoming during the summer of 1963. Due to the cultural constraints of the time (both externally and internally), they separate and marry. However, after reuniting four years later, they find their passion still as fresh and strong as before and start a twenty-year secret affair that lasts until Jack dies in 1983.

Despite the lack of twists in the plot, this 2 hours and 15 minute movie manages to capture the audience from the beginning to the end: it is the power of images that it wields to grab one's attention. The overall visual style of *Brokeback* is very slow-paced, without drastic camera movements and blatant actions. In fact, many of its shots lack movement to such an extent that they become still portraits. The trump card that this movie plays is the sublime object that it portrays: nature. Employing a massive number of shots of the Wyoming landscape (actually shot in Canada), *Brokeback* constructs the wildness of the American West as a Sublime which it uses to suspend the audience's ethical judgment on homosexual behavior in order to universalize the gay experience.

The movie begins with a long distance panoramic shot of a mountain in the twilight. The shot is so still that it almost looks like a landscape portrait, until the eye is drawn to a truck moving at the foot of the mountain. The far away shot of the truck is followed by a medium-long shot of the truck, followed by a medium shot of Ennis getting off the truck. This set of shots captures the vastness of the nature and captivates the audience with a sublime feeling and a sense of reverence. It humbles them, dethrones them from a predetermined judgmental stance, and thus conditions them to an emotional rather than a rational state with which to perceive the subsequent homosexual love story.

The early scenes of the movie are devoted to depicting Ennis and Jack's life camping, herding sheep, riding horses, and hunting wild animals during which their affection for each other grows. Continuing to evoke the feeling of the sublime, the camera captures varying-scaled shots of the mountain landscapes closely interwoven with the activities of the protagonists in the woods, along the brook, at camp, or outside the tent, giving the audience a sense of rustic beauty. Interspersed with these distant mountain landscape shots are medium shots of the protagonists encompassed by the gorgeous mountains in the background. This type of visual composition is referred to by Deluca and Demo as "bifurcated landscapes, with beautiful foregrounds that both point to and are overshadowed by sublime backgrounds."[9] These various ways of temporally and spatially intermingling the portrait of nature and the portrait of the human subjects work to aestheticize, naturalize, and thus, justify the actions and the relationships of the subjects. After watching the movie, the audience is expected to say, "This is so natural. In such beautiful natural surroundings how could they not fall in love with each other?"

Strong evidence for this movie's naturalizing strategy can be found on the tagline marked on the bottom of a *Brokeback* movie release poster: "Love is a force of nature." This declaration makes the message of the movie very explicit: Jack and Ennis fall in love not because they are perverts or moral reprobates, but because they are driven to do so by the irresistible power of *nature* (note the double meaning of this word: nature as pristine wilderness and nature as human nature or normality). Another piece of evidence is a famous line of Jack's in the movie: "I wish I knew how to quit you." This line implies a sense of fatalism and helplessness about the nature of this relationship, and takes the moral blame off the back of the protagonists: there is nothing you can do about "love," because it *just* happens — just like in a typical, traditional heterosexual romance!

In the second half of the movie, Jack and Ennis separately marry and, at their reunion four years later, renew their relationship for another fifteen years. There are two visual threads in this half: one is the depiction of the family and social life of both protagonists; the other is, consistent with the first half of the movie, the sublime representation of nature which reoccurs every time Jack and Ennis retreat from their families and social lives to Brokeback Mountain. These two distinct visual styles form a sharp contrast but are woven together: on the one hand is human society — bleak, banal, depressive, full of worries and inhibitions; on the other is nature — beautiful, nonjudgmental, liberating so one can embrace one's true emotions and desires. This comparison resorts to the traditional nature/culture dichotomy that considers nature as human's spiritual and emotional root and culture as the artificial environment that cuts our umbilical cord with Mother Nature. Since the movie already conditions us to equate "being *in* nature" with "being natural," and "being in society" with "being banal," situating a homosexual relationship *in* nature — while putting several heterosexual relationships in society — certainly helps to *naturalize* the actions of the former. By doing so, *Brokeback* subverts the traditional "gay=unnatural / straight=natural" binary and establishes a new binary: "gay=natural, emotional, truthful / straight= unnatural, instrumental, and banal."

Universalizing Gay Love

One may object that the new binary is just a semiotic inversion of the old binary instead of a truly radical subversion. Such an inversion often seems to take place in partisan politics; it is as if several children are quarrelling with each other by shouting back and forth: "You're a coward," "No, you're a coward," "You are!" "YOU are!!" The argument can keep going on and on without actually achieving resolution as each party hurls accusations at the others but is not able to win without any acquiescence from the others. The truly subversive political act is not achieved by simply role-switching within the old power structure; rather it must displace the previous binary and provide the possibility for transcendence. *Brokeback* is an instance of a truly subversive political act. While it does invert the "gay=unnatural / straight=natural" binary, it also promotes an identification of homosexual culture with a wide variety of social interest groups (including the dominant heterosexual group). This *universal identification* makes *Brokeback*'s political efficacy far greater than just an angry cry back from the homosexual group: "You straight people are unnatural!"

To probe the concept of "universal identification," one can start from its literal meaning: to make anyone in the *universe* able to *identify*. Universal identification entails the appropriation of overarching, universal concepts (namely, ideologies) to enable identification from a wide range of social interest groups. *Nature* is the very first ideology *Brokeback* uses to enable this type of "universal identification." By portraying a sublime nature and opposing it with a banal social life, the movie echoes the popular conception of nature as a sacred space free of instrumentality and artificiality and appeals to a desire widely shared by many urban-dwellers — the desire to escape from the city and be close to Mother Nature. This desire, generated from a mix of nostalgia, romance, self-actualization, and escapism, provides motivation for the increasing consumption in mass media of natural scenery. In *Brokeback*, the very tension between the characters' fictional life and the real life of the audience creates the attraction. The attraction is universal because it appeals to a common desire shared by many audience members regardless of their political or ethical values on gay rights issue.

Brokeback also promotes universal identification with the important ideology of *love*. Although this movie indeed closely depicts a homosexual relationship, it is first of all advertised as a *"love"* story and not a *"gay"* story. "Love is a force of nature" — that tagline from the poster — is a declaration of love and not a declaration of sexual orientation. Furthermore, this movie portrays a gay life far from what gays are commonly thought to be living. Jack and Ennis's affection for each other is built less upon sex than upon companionship (or say, "friendship," as in the Willie Nelson song heard during the ending credits of the movie, "He Was a Friend of Mine," which plays with the ambiguity between friendship and Eros). This representation of a gay relationship is not exactly consistent with the stereotypes of the modern urban gay relationship that is built primarily upon sexual attractions. Holleran also notices the mismatch between the movie characters' life and the actual life of modern gay men: "most gay stories, critics have pointed out, are urban, and it is ironic that a story about two men who marry, have kids, and ride horses for a living should have such an impact on gay men who have done none of these things."[10] How does identification take place when what is represented in the movie is so different from what our immediate "reality" is?

It is love, or to be more specific, unobtained love, that enables the universal identification of *Brokeback*. Holleran writes, "[W]hy *Brokeback* is so moving ... has something to do with its being what McMurtry called it: 'a tragedy of emotional deprivation.' This is surely a *universal* experience, but at a certain point in life most gay men seem to conclude that it's the *particular* fate of being gay [emphasis added]."[11] Everybody has desires that she/he has never fulfilled, be it a lover, a dream, or an ambition. The feeling of loss is a universal experience and by appealing to that experience *Brokeback* easily wins sympathy from a broad range of audience. However there is a strange dialectical relationship between universality and particularity here. In *Brokeback*, the *universal* experience of loss is embodied in the *particular* experience of being gay. As Roger Ebert puts it, "Strange but true: The more specific a film is, the more universal, because the more it understands individual characters, the more it applies to everyone."[12] *Brokeback* is a story about a particular gay couple in a particular historical situation, but at the same time, it seeks to universalize.

Realizing the universalizing function of this movie helps us see the following stance in a different light: The *Brokeback* film creative team strongly rejected the label of "the gay cowboy movie" that was bestowed upon it by the mass media after its release. They claim that *Brokeback* is a movie about love, but it is *"not* about being gay." Even the movie characters, after a sexual encounter, do not recognize themselves as gay: "You know I ain't queer," Ennis tells Jack after their first night together. "Me, neither," Jack says (SP 20). While traditional ideological critique might interpret this as a sign of internalized homophobia or as a lack of political awareness, we see that within the political context of the movie denying the "gay" label that society would impose on them is in fact the first step to true politics — universal identification. In contrast, the attempt of labeling it as a "gay story" (what postmodern "identity politics" would suggest) will only undo the universalizing effect of such an act.

Excremental Identification: "We're All Homosexuals!"

If gay men claiming "we're not gay" is the beginning of true politics, how about straight men crying "we're not straight"? How about Hispanics crying "we're not Hispanics"? How about alcoholics crying "we're not alcoholics" and homophobes crying "we're not homophobes"?[13] Would these be totally absurd? Indeed, if everyone renounces her/his own identity, the universalizing effect of this strategy cannot be achieved. There is a certain economy in the usage of the universalizing strategy and, to put it simply, not everyone can use it. Thus, it is necessary for us to distinguish the universal identification used by minority groups to induce social change from other pseudo-universal claims used by dominant groups to preserve the *status quo*. Laclau's theory about the "empty signifier" and Žižek's theory about the "excremental identification" may shed some light on the matter.

In his book *Emancipation(s)*, Ernesto Laclau uses modern semiotics and postmodern deconstructionism to complicate the model of hegemony.[14] As introduced by Antonio Gramsci, hegemony refers to political domination based upon cultural leadership and the winning of consent from other social groups (as opposed to domination by coercive force). Laclau describes how hegemonic consensus is produced as a discursive practice that binds universal concepts with the particular interests of a certain social group. He poses the concept of an *"empty signifier,"* a signifier that "does not have a concrete content of its own (which would close it on itself)" and argues that *the Universal* (another word for ideology) is an empty signifier waiting to be joined with a particular signified at a particular time.[15] This act of joining is called "articulation." Take as an example human rights, one of the most universal ideologies of our time. The phrase "human rights" is an empty signifier which has no direct reference to any particular case in immediate reality. It only makes sense when it is placed in a particular context and associated with a particular content, such as the right to survive, to practice religion, to vote, to express one's thoughts, and so on. Pro-choice advocates would argue from the perspective of the pregnant woman and define human rights as the rights to have control over one's own body; pro-life proponents would argue for the unborn child and define human rights as the rights to survive; pro-choice advocates would then rebut that a fetus cannot be counted as a human and thus cannot have "human rights." As each side struggles to fill this empty phrase with different particular contents in order to enhance its cause, the meaning of "human rights" will undergo constant redefinition and will never be pinned down. This is what Laclau means by *hegemonic democracy*: different groups struggle to win consent from other groups by articulating their particularity with the empty Universal. However, while every group strives to represent the Universal, a truly subversive political act takes place only when the empty Universal is articulated with the particular interest of the exclusion of the society. In Laclau's words, when the empty signifier becomes "the signifier of the excluded," the process of signification is subverted and true politics dawns.[16]

Laclau goes on to criticize contemporary multiculturalism, a proposition that is driven by the same postmodern spirit as "identity politics" and upholds a system in which different cultures exist with equal status. He argues that although multiculturalism seeks to assert the particular identity of minority social groups, it in fact severs them from political power: "the more particular a group is, the less it will be able to control the global communication terrain within which it operates, and the more universally grounded will have to be the justification of its claims."[17] Contrary to our usual assumptions, Laclau suggests that difference (as in multiculturalism) is a tool for preserving the status quo, while sameness (as in hegemonic democracy) is a tool for producing social change.

Based on the theoretical edifice of Laclau and other theorists (Lacan, Badiou, Balibar, Ranciere), Slavoj Žižek advances his theory of political subjectivization in *The Ticklish Subject*. What Laclau calls the "empty universal," Žižek calls the "split" Universal, the Universal that is constituted by what it excludes. The exclusion which sustains the Universal is called *constitutive exception*.[18] Homosexuals are an example of the constitutive exception — their exclusion serves a necessary condition that sustains the unity of the society. That is to say, homosexuality defines what a healthy, normal, moral, love life is not; without them, the dominant notions of normality, morality, and love cannot hold together. Since constitutive exceptions do not have any proper place within the system, they are practically the "excrement" of the society. According to Žižek, a true political act is the universal identification with the very "excrement" of the society: the "excrement" cries: "We are the true Universal [the People, Society, Nation...!]" and the public exclaims "We are all *them* [homosexuals, women, blacks...]!"[19]

Žižek then specifically distinguishes "excremental identification" from postmodern "identity politics" which he despises. While the latter posits that all identities are formed in particular social historical situations and that each social group should assert the particularity identity of its own, it suggests minority groups resist any generalizing or universalizing claim about who they *are*. This kind of universalization, however, is what "excremental identification" passionately embraces. A movie addressing gay rights issues in the spirit of postmodern "identity politics," for example, would probably deliver messages such as: homosexuals are a particular group shaped by their unique experiences and we should show more tolerance for their difference. However, according to Žižek, the postmodern attempt to secure a niche identity for homosexuals in the multicultural world would only lead to the "deadlock of gay politics" — that the homosexual group "loses its specificity when [...] acknowledged by the public discourse." The choice that contemporary gay community faces is, as Žižek puts it, "Do you want *equal* rights or *specific* rights to safeguard your particular way of life?"[20] *Brokeback* chooses *specific* rights over *equal* rights. It evokes the power of the Universal and subverts the structure of signification by putting homosexuals, the constitutive exception of the system, in the very position that stands for the Universal. For once, homosexuals become the particularity that represents the universal notion of love and nature; for once, homosexuals are no longer homosexuals but are "everybody" and everybody becomes a "homosexual" because everybody faces loss and sacrifice in her/his life. As the aura of love and nature is transferred to the homosexual group, the existing social hierarchy is radically subverted.

Aesthetics as Meta-politics

Laclau and Žižek both uphold the political act that invokes universal identification with excluded social groups. However, there is a crucial distinction between Laclau's "hegemonic democracy" and Žižek's "excremental identification:" while Laclau's political struggle remains within the symbolic realm, Žižek's politics takes place in the material realm as well. For Žižek, "excremental identification" is not merely the symbolic attempt to make the excluded group the stand-in for the Universal. It makes "*impossible* demands," which are "made to be rejected." Its logic is, "in demanding that you do this, I am actually demanding that you do not do it, because *that's* not it."[21] For instance, instead of making particular requests such as "Abolish that new tax! Justice for the imprisoned!" one exclaims: "We want justice! Equality for all!" The dominant group cannot take specific actions to fulfill these general demands without jeopardizing its own dominant position. When the "impossible" demands are rejected, Žižek argues, "the only way to articulate this universality [to break free from the dominating ideological closure] consists, then, in its apparent opposite, in the thoroughly 'irrational' excessive outburst of violence."[22] Here Žižek slides back to a crude Marxian model in which violence lies at the root of proletariat revolution because symbolic actions simply would not work.

By making "impossible" demands, Žižek's "excremental identification" becomes more of a provocation for violence than an actual hegemonic negotiation. He believes that any Leftist political action necessitates and justifies the use of violence. For him, politics is meta-ethics and it calls for "a kind of *political suspension of the Ethical*" as soon as it clashes with traditional ethics and morals.[23] Nevertheless, the radical political impact of *Brokeback Mountain* shows how a truly subversive politic act does not necessarily entail violence. By subjecting the audience to the aesthetic power of nature, *Brokeback* (re)forms the dominant ethical criteria and (re)structures the existing social hierarchy *without being recognized as such*—thus demonstrating that the ultimate form of politics, instead of calling for a suspension of ethics (as proposed by Žižek), reestablishes the norms of ethics by the power of aesthetics. Compared to other forms of politics, an aesthetic-political act works in a "peaceful" but powerful way: on the one hand, it subverts the existing power structure on a symbolic level rather than a material level (like violence); on the other hand, it works in a self-effacing manner because it operates on the level of the unconscious and induces social changes before it comes into the realm of the public conscious. The current debate on whether *Brokeback* should be considered as a gay polemic is the very sign of its success.

Notes

1. The basic definition for *naturalism* given here — what is natural is that which is normal, good and legitimate — can be derived from other popular usage of the word, such as in social naturalism and ethical naturalism: Because the natural world and the human social world are governed by similar principles (as in social naturalism), natural phenomena can be used to explain human ethical phenomena (as in ethical naturalism); therefore, human values and actions which are deemed to be natural can also be judged as ethical and legitimate.

2. Jack Babuscio, "Camp and Gay Sensibility," in *Gays and Film*, ed. Richard Dyer (New York: Zoetrope, 1984), 40.

3. Ibid., 45.

4. Larry Gross, "Out of the Mainstream: Sexual Minorities and the Mass Media," in *Gay People, Sex and the Media*, ed. Michelle A. Wolf and Alfred P. Kielwasser (New York: Harrington Park, 1991), 20.

5. Derek Cohen and Richard Dyer, "The Politics of Gay Culture," in *Homosexuality: Power and Politics*, ed. Gay Left Collective (London and New York: Allison & Busby, 1980), 177–178.

6. Kevin Michael DeLuca and Anne Teresa Demo, "Imaging Nature: Watkins, Yosemite, and the Birth of Environmentalism," *Critical Studies in Media Communication* 17, no. 3 (Sept. 2000): 241–261.

7. Standford Demars, *The Tourist in Yosemite: 1855–1985* (Salt Lake City: University of Utah Press, 1991), 12–13.

8. Andrew Holleran, "The Magic Mountain," *Gay and Lesbian Review Worldwide* 13, no. 2 (Mar./Apr. 2006): 13.

9. Deluca and Demo, 248.

10. Holleran, 14.

11. Ibid., 15.

12. Roger Ebert, review of *Brokeback Mountain*, *Chicago Sun Times*, Dec. 16, 2005, <http://rogerebert.suntimes.com/apps/pbcs.dll/article?AID=/20051215/REVIEWS/51019006/10 23>, 2005 (accessed Sept. 20, 2006).

13. There is a very funny video called "I'm NOT gay" online which shows exactly the same story at the following link: <http://www.youtube.com/watch?v=sEj7JmwwLe0&search= I%27m%20not%20gay> (accessed Sept. 19, 2006).

14. Ernesto Laclau, *Emancipation(s)* (London and New York: Verso, 1996).

15. Ibid., 34.

16. Ibid., 38.

17. Ibid., 48.

18. Slavoj Žižek, *The Ticklish Subject: The Absent Centre of Political Ontology* (London and New York: Verso, 1999).

19. Ibid., 229, 231.

20. Ibid., 230

21. Ibid., 230.

22. Ibid., 204.

23. Ibid., 223.

ACKNOWLEDGMENTS: *The author would like to thank Aaron Breneman for his selfless help in correcting the grammar mistakes and enhancing the general readability of this essay. She also thanks Jim Stacy and the readers of the* Brokeback *anthology who provided her with so much precious feedback for the revision of this essay.* — Xinghua Li

9

Broke(n)back Faggots: Hollywood Gives Queers a Hobson's Choice

by W. C. Harris

Brokeback Mountain has allowed legions of well-meaning Americans to wax rhapsodic over how moving this story of "universal" love is, or even to empathize with the tragedy of gay love banned from speaking its name in a benighted time and place. Daniel Mendelsohn's careful analysis of the film's marketing and reviews lays bare the extent to which claims that *Brokeback* tells a universal story in fact marginalize or closet the narrative's experiential gay core — presumably out of a "desire that [it] not be seen as something for a 'niche' market but as a story with broad appeal."[1] Critics have routinely hailed the film as "a human story" where the "two lovers just happen to be men": generic, euphemistic diction which obscures or seeks to excuse a possibly discomfiting divergence from the master narrative of heterosexuality.[2] Similar critical acts of erasure are ubiquitous. "This slow and stoic movie, hailed as a gay Western," writes Anthony Lane in the *New Yorker*, "feels neither gay nor especially Western: it is a study of love under siege."[3] Richard Alleva holds that *Brokeback* is "not a gay movie. This superb work of art is about the tragedy of emotional apartheid, and none of us, no matter our sexual orientation, is ever safe from the way life conspires to make us put our hearts on ice."[4]

Ignoring the fact that the crux of *Brokeback* is that sexual orientation *does* matter, even reader letters, such as the following one from *Commonweal*, take up the mantra of universality: "the themes of love, loss, and regret are universal and transcend mere sexual orientation. This is why the film has such broad appeal. As a gay man, I can watch a film of *Romeo and Juliet* and cry just as much as I did watching *Brokeback Mountain*. Love is love, heartbreak is heartbreak.... That ... the star-crossed lovers are both men is secondary."[5] Jack and Ennis are *not* Romeo and Juliet. They are two *men*, not a man and a woman. Ranking Ennis and Jack with canonical figures such as Shakespeare's young lovers obscures the disparate origin, weight, and breadth of the interdict each couple faces: opprobrium from potentially every member of one's culture versus simply from one's family.[6] As Mendelsohn puts it,

> The real achievement of [the film] is not that it tells a universal love story that happens to have gay characters in it, but that it tells a distinctively gay story that happens to be so well told that any feeling person can be moved by it. If you insist, as so many have, that the story of Jack and Ennis is OK to watch and sympathize with because they're not really homosexual — that they're more like the heart of America than like "gay people" — you're pushing them back into the closet whose narrow and suffocating confines Ang Lee and his collaborators have so beautifully and harrowingly exposed.[7]

Jack and Ennis may bear little resemblance to gay characters American mainstream film has given us to date — witty sidekicks, AIDS victims, serial killers — but bracketing them with the Capulets and the Montagues brackets *off* homosexuality as incidental, when what precipitates *Brokeback*'s primary conflict is Jack and Ennis's homosexuality.[8]

Of the multitude who have weighed in on *Brokeback*, Roger Ebert travels furthest toward a gay vanishing point. Jack and Ennis's "tragedy is universal," Ebert writes in the *Chicago Sun-Times*. "It could be about two women, or lovers from different religious or ethnic groups — any 'forbidden love.'"[9] As Mendelsohn points out, Ebert's analogy is "seriously misguided."[10] Lovers from different religious or ethnic groups may be hated or persecuted, but, unlike queers, they have not been taught "beginning in childhood" to "despise *themselves*" as "unhealthy, hateful, and deadly."[11] Interracial or interfaith couples may still find themselves subject to violence, intimidation, and prejudice (though, in many parts of the country, arguably less so than in the past), but that violence comes from without not within: "[B]ecause they learn to hate homosexuality so early on, young people with homosexual impulses more often than not grow up hating themselves: they believe there's something wrong with themselves long before they can understand that there's something wrong with society."[12] Asserting that Jack and Ennis could be "two *women*" or any other culturally sundered lovers might seem to scotch the erasure accomplished by "any 'forbidden love.'" Yet inclusion is, in this case, not really inclusion; the universal category ("'any ... love'") trumps and subsumes the specific (gay love).

Refusing to see difference, politically correct as the intent may be, can be a more benign form of closeting. As Vito Russo trenchantly wrote two decades ago in *The Celluloid Closet,* queer art that attempts to be or is described as "universal" might be better characterized as pandering and/or inauthentic:

> The Hollywood trap is that the success of a film is judged by whether or not it reaches a mass audience. The gay activist trap is that a film is judged by whether or not it succeeds in persuading that audience to accept homosexuals. Neither of these barometers is valid or important. Both encourage the making of films in which acceptance of homosexuals is based on the notion that they are just like everyone else.... Yet this is a false premise that never works. You can't plead tolerance for gays by saying that they're just like everyone else. Tolerance is something we should extend to people who are not like everyone else. If gays weren't different, there wouldn't be a problem, and there certainly is a problem.[13]

It's *crucial* that the lovers in this case are homosexual. Effacing difference does away with the need for tolerance, begging the question of why Ennis and Jack feel out of step with almost everyone except one another. Andrew Holleran, author of the iconic gay novel *Dancer from the Dance* (1978), who admits *Brokeback*'s kinship with straight classics of American literature likewise concerned with "the dream we fail to realize," nonetheless ends his review of the film on a note of specificity: "I'm not sure why *Brokeback* is so moving.... I think it has something to do with its being what [screenwriter Larry] McMurtry called it: a 'tragedy of emotional deprivation.' This is surely a universal experience, but at a certain point in life most gay men seem to conclude that it's the particular fate of being gay."[14] McMurtry's words resonate with queer experience because the "particular fate of being gay" involves much more than *emotional* deprivation. Being queer in America, especially in recent years, involves being simultaneously included and excluded — made more visible and treated more humanely by enough organizations and individuals to make the stark, invidious political and economic inequities still endured by queers and the continuing debate about the threat queers constitute to marriage, children, and American (religious) values that much more demoralizing. If *Brokeback* is to have substantive value for American viewers, it seems vital — though oddly forgotten by most reviewers — not to forget that it is a story about *gay* Americans.[15]

An Ambivalent Polemic

Of greater concern, however, is an equally rankling aspect of the film's apotheosis, one that seems to have gone unremarked. *Brokeback* is an irreducibly ambivalent work. From one angle, it reads as an antihomophobic polemic against the deforming and stunting impact of homophobia, which the film subtly implies may be endemic to heterosexuality rather than sadly anomalous. Yet it takes minimal effort to see *Brokeback*'s potential to serve also as an *antigay* polemic, a cautionary tale about homosexuality not homo-phobia. (This is not to accuse author Annie Proulx, screenwriters Larry McMurtry and Diana Ossana, or director Ang Lee of *conscious* or intentional homophobia. Part of this argument touches on the extent to which homo-phobia courses throughout the most carefully antihomophobic discourse.) *Brokeback* stands as an antigay polemic inasmuch as it depicts, albeit in the tragic register, the deleterious effects of violent homophobia as well as het-eronormative imperatives to marry, to perform one's gender and sexuality in prescribed ways. While *Brokeback*'s tragic register is meant to elicit our sym-pathy, and while its content may deserve sympathy, none of this should dis-tract from the brutal nonfictionality of the story: victimized, marginalized, and disenfranchised queers populate America's present as well as its past. Like-wise, we should be careful to distinguish the brutality of Jack's death (imag-ined by Ennis as a gay bashing), a brutality necessary to Ennis's terrified vision of the world, from the *unnecessary* brutality of Proulx's decision, as the writer, to kill off Jack, when Ennis's emotional and erotic isolation is long complete, and complete without such a price being paid. Determining the film's status as polemic requires elaboration in order to clarify both how necessary *and* how otiose and *unnecessary* its doubly tragic ending is. Whatever the antiho-mophobic intent of Lee's film or Proulx's original story, or to whatever extent viewers have generously read in them an antihomophobic intent *to the exclu-sion* of other, rebarbative messages, we should not blind ourselves to the homo-phobic energies circulating in these texts and the culture that produced them.

Ang Lee has delivered a sad film, but one which is finally all the sadder for its eliciting pity rather empathy, tears rather than anger. On some level, empathy is what a film about gay life can *never* elicit from a straight audi-ence. But one can fault *Brokeback* insofar as its tone remains elegiac, uncon-scious that its tragic conclusion is not inevitable. Indeed, the film's setting — the West, the 1960s and 70s — is unfamiliar to contemporary urban and suburban audiences, thus reifying the distancing potential of tragedies about minority populations, further hollowing out the catharsis the film has provided for so many. As media contretemps over dubbing *Brokeback* "the gay cowboy movie" have shown, the resonances produced by a slippery text risk undermining, if not overwhelming, its potential as a gay-*positive* polemic.

Fit to Be Tied

Brokeback is, in fact, eerily descriptive of the present state of gay Ameri-cans. What seems troublingly apropos is Ennis del Mar's sense that, outside of the open spaces "up on Brokeback," there is no place in the world he knows for him and Jack Twist to love one another — no place that is not inimical, hostile, murderous. Proulx's choice of temporal setting seems hardly accidental: the love story spans two decades, from pre–Stonewall 1963 to 1982 — the dawn of AIDS and an era of governmental indifference to treatment and research. As Proulx comments, "Although there are many places in Wyoming where gay men did and do live together in harmony with the community, it should not be foregotten that a year after this story was published Matthew Shepard was tied to a buck fence outside the most enlightened town in the state, Laramie, home of the University of Wyoming."[16] Although less extreme but in the same vein, gay men are still vilified by the culture — if not outright, then by the bare fact that, regardless of not everyone's taking it seriously, pundits and policymakers are still debating whether or not gays and lesbians deserve the human rights accorded to the republic's other citizens. If queer Americans are included in significant ways that they patently were not twenty years ago — ranging from media visibility to tolerance and spotty legal victories — they are fundamentally still *ex*cluded as Americans, denied basic equity of treatment and rights of property.

Ennis himself *constitutes* the closet, that deforming nexus of homophobia and heteronormativity as learned, felt, and enforced by queers and the alien culture into which they are born (and alien homes as well, unless they are raised by same-sex parents). Coming out, then, involves not so much overcoming that nexus — homophobia and heteronormativity seem too deeply imbricated to escape by one act or by one person's repeated acts of coming out — as much as reorienting oneself *toward* it, disengaging at least from the psychologically and emotionally oppressive effects of its force. According to Andrew Holleran, *Brokeback* "indicts both kinds of homophobia: the external and internal. As awful as the homophobes are who litter the film ... it's equally about gay men's self-censorship, their internalization of what is expected of a man."[17] What a number of critics read in Ennis as not just internalized homophobia[18] but the fatalism of classical tragedy[19] seems more problematic than simply either. It's true that Ennis fears homophobic retaliation, but the words conveying his fear — " I doubt there's much we *can* do. I'm stuck with what I got here" (SP 49) — also relay the cognitive poverty that comes from not being able to conceive of an alternative to the heteronormative rubric, much less to articulate his thoughts or desires in recognized cultural discourse. Unable to conceive of "two guys livin' together," merely of stealing infrequent, furtive moments "in the back of nowhere," Ennis rejects Jack's proposal of "a little ranch together somewhere" (SP 52–53). It is not merely a dearth of (non-virulent) models for same-sex love that has obliterated for him the possibility of "some sweet life" (SP 52). When he was a boy, his father took him to see the genitally mutilated and battered corpse of a gay rancher who dared live openly with his lover and business partner. Recounting the sight to Jack ("they'd took a tire iron to him ... drug him around by his dick till it pulled off"), Ennis recites the lesson clearly intended by the rancher's assailants (one of whom may have been Ennis's father): "this thing grabs on to us again in the wrong place, we'll be dead" (SP 52). *That* likelihood seems to be what Ennis means by the laconic line, "If you can't fix it ... you gotta stand it," for that violence, along with Ennis's surety, is what stands between them (SP 54).

Few scenes in recent literature or cinema have as potently shown the function of fag bashing. Like lynching, fag bashing is terrorist violence,[20] visited at random on one individual less to justify than to naturalize the inferior social or political status of all members of the victim's sexual (or, in the case of lynching or other hate crimes, ethnic or religious) cohort. But the leverage wielded by fag bashing is importantly, structurally dissimilar to the impact of hate crimes against others groups, specifically in the effect on spectators *not* belonging to the victim's group, in this case, on non-homosexuals. While non-African-Americans may have been repulsed by lynchings, it's doubtful that any feared for their own safety (on the contrary, quite the opposite). And, instances of passing aside, whites never fear that their blackness may be discovered; they certainly are not culturally coached to live in fear that they *might* be black. Yet this is precisely the wide net cast here, since homophobia implants in every Western male the fear, lived with for shorter or longer periods depending on the individual, that he might be gay. As defined so acutely by Eve Sedgwick, that fear is "homosexual panic," the "structural residue of terrorist potential ... of Western maleness," the "most private, psychologized form in which many western men experience their vulnerability to the social pressure of homophobic blackmail."[21] Ennis lives in quiet panic, fearing that at any moment his homosexuality will be detected, if for no other reason than it is something that *must* be detected, a state of being so antithetical to collective society that it can only exist in hiding.

Equally striking, though, is Jack's *lack* of fear. One might say that, by comparison, Jack Twist represents a "pure" (unrealistic or advanced?) gay consciousness inasmuch as he seems not to have internalized any of the guilt heterosexual discourse teaches us all, if somewhat more quietly than in the past, to associate with homosexuality. Ennis speaks as the inscribed subject, unquestioningly mouthing the dogma with which he has been inculcated, the *law of the father.* Gay happiness cannot exist because men like Ennis's father will kill it. Ennis's fear of meeting a fate like Earl's is palpable and realistic. At the same time, Ennis's vision typifies the violence with which the dominant discourse refuses to afford homosexuals any unsubjugated place. What Ennis presents as the pragmatic implausibility of gay love is also a fair reflection of its cognitive impossibility — at least on its own terms, terms that are not dictated by a phobic, pathologizing discourse. The question is whether or not, Jack's bravado and self-acceptance aside, Ennis speaks to the power of a discourse largely beyond either man's control.

When Coming Out Is Hard to Do

As queer theorist David Halperin suggests, and as day-to-day queer experience corroborates, coming out is not only an always unfinished, differential experience but also one that fails to live up to its pop-psychological reputation as an act of *self*-empowerment:

> [I]f there is something self-affirming or *liberating* about coming *out* of the closet, that is not because coming out enables one to emerge from a state of servitude into a state of untrammeled liberty. On the contrary: to come out is precisely to expose oneself to a different set of dangers and constraints, to make oneself a convenient screen onto which straight people can project all the fantasies they routinely entertain about gay people, and to suffer one's every gesture, statement, expression, and opinion to be totally and irrevocably marked by the overwhelmingly social significance of one's openly acknowledged homosexual identity. If to come out is to release oneself from a state of unfreedom, that is not because coming out constitutes an escape from the reach of power to a place outside of power: rather, coming out puts into play a different set of power relations and alters the dynamic of personal and political struggle.[22]

Being out or being visible (arguably quite different) does not obviate the fact that many queers cannot see a place in the culture, in the republic, where they're unequivocally brooked. Media visibility can be a valuable PR tool for education, but inclusion of fictional characters is not tangible, is neither political voice nor economic equity. From Ennis's point of view, he and Jack face the immediate possibility of being harassed or killed for, as one critic put it, "liv[ing] life on their own terms."[23] And even though queers' lives are still devalued, threatened, and taken, queer viewers of *Brokeback* can't help but wonder: in 2005, after decades of incremental but demonstrable progress in representations of homosexuality, are *these* the characters we get? In their mournful, tight-lipped, doe-eyed (and admittedly affecting) pain, Ennis and Jack feel reminiscent of pre-Stonewall characters, loving conflictedly (like Beth in Ann Bannon's *Odd Girl Out* or Charlie in Gordon Merrick's *The Lord Won't Mind*) or flatly refusing to acknowledge their love (like Marcher in Henry James's "The Beast in the Jungle"). Halperin's Foucauldian perspective explains the backward-looking affect of the film's protagonists more reassuringly — as a mark of the "different set of dangers and constraints" queers face now. This essay reads Ennis and Jack as a reactionary response to lesbians and gays' increasing visibility and our continued, sometimes heeded demands for rights and dignity — an atavistic projection of "straight fantasies about gay people" onto a queer public body that has become increasingly salient and human, defying and galvanizing the dissemination of phobic images (by anti-gay marriage and adoption organizations, for example).

Like fellow queer theorists Lee Edelman and Michael Warner, Halperin counters that being "release[d] ... from a state of unfreedom" yet not beyond "the reach of power" is hardly a hopeless situation.[24] It can actually be a productive one, provided we adopt an honest, efficacious stance: "The most radical reversal of homophobic discourses consists not in asserting, with the Gay Liberation Front of 1968, that 'gay is good' ... but in assuming and empowering a marginal positionality — not in rehabilitating an already demarcated, if devalued, identity but in taking advantage of the purely oppositional location homosexuality has been made to occupy by the logic and the supplement and by the fantasmatic character of homophobic discourse."[25] It's this latter oppositional stance which the film and most critics fail to adopt, instead taking as given, at least not questioning, the tragic, marginal vein in which *Brokeback* depicts gay desire. Eliciting pity and regret, far from "empower[ing]" gay marginality, simply enervates it. The tonal grandeur and cathartic timbre that Lee's film lends to Ennis's tragic journey may solidify that marginality, but Ennis's failure to challenge the homophobic pressures inculcated in him *generate* it. To *that* extent, he is responsible for his own misery. This last point may seem belligerent without good cause, since reviewers including Mendelsohn, Grundmann, Holleran, and Lane have acknowledged Ennis's impossible fight against a barrage of negative cultural messages. Yet because most critics accept the inexorability of Ennis's *losing* that struggle, their responses translate too easily into an affirmation of the normative, phobic idea that there's something tragic, if noble, at the core of gay identity. What is the value of— and worse, what is the damage inflicted by— sportraying queer liminality and oppression as a predicament one "can't fix," as Ennis declares, and therefore has "gotta stand"?

An Unnecessary Death

Positioning tragedy in *Brokeback* within a classical context seems inappropriate if for no other reason than its singular focus (Ennis as tragic hero). What gets lost in such a reading is the more mundane tragedy of Jack's death. Lureen, Jack's wife, relays the details of his death to Ennis over the phone: Jack was inflating a flat tire when it blew up, knocking the tire rim into his face, breaking his nose, and leaving him unconscious, on his back, to choke on his own blood. Proulx and Lee both juxtapose this story with the image of Jack being beaten to death by tire iron–wielding homophobes, an attack

Mendelsohn refers to as "clearly represented, in a flashback."[26] Yet, in handling Jack's death, McMurtry and Ossana's script, as well as Lee's realization of it, is faithful to Proulx's story: this image is marked as Ennis's *imagination* of what really happened.[27] After Lureen's lines describing Jack's death, Ennis "wonders ... if it was the tire iron":

> SHARP CUT TO
> ENNIS'S POV...
> A FLASH ... ENNIS and WE SEE, in the evening shadows, a MAN being beaten unmercifully by THREE ASSAILANTS, one of whom uses a tire iron.
> SHARP CUT BACK TO
> ...ENNIS [who] doesn't know which way it was, the tire iron — or a real accident, blood choking down JACK'S throat and nobody to turn him over [McMurtry/Ossana, 87–88].

On film Lee clarifies that the beating image originates from Ennis by cutting to it and back to Lureen *during* her lines. Although the circumstances of Jack's death may seem unusual, neither Proulx, the screenwriters, nor Lee gives us any reason to believe Lureen is lying.[28] To be fair, it's true that Lureen's version of events is a reconstruction after the fact, and thus open to doubt (we're told that Jack's body was found after he'd died). In Proulx's original story, hearing Lureen's description of the death, Ennis is even more emphatic about the veracity of his own interpretation of events than he is in the screenplay: Proulx writes, in a one-sentence paragraph:

> No, he thought, they got him with the tire-iron [SS 23].

The later statement that, hearing from John Twist about Jack's new lover, Ennis "now ... knew it had been the tire iron" (SS 25) is not any more conclusive. Ennis's certainty is no more factually based than Lureen's. One might even argue that it is *less* so: whatever scenario Ennis was confronted with, he could not interpret it as anything *other* than a fag bashing. He must square it with the way he has been taught the world treats queers, a way he must confirm at every turn if he's to make his denial of Jack and himself palatable. Aside from the fact that the death-by-beating seems to emanate from Ennis's fear-driven mind (Proulx's story is written in limited third person, focused mostly on Ennis), this scene serves as an obvious bookend to the film's first flashback of homophobic violence (the mutilated gay rancher), one of only three flashbacks in the entire movie, two of which belong to Ennis.[29]

Regardless of the plausibility of Jack's death as Ennis imagines it, *how* Jack dies is not only unknowable or speculative but, finally, immaterial. That he dies *at all* is the point. To call the circumstances of Jack's death "immaterial" might seem insensitive or at least inappropriate; there's certainly a material difference between being killed in a freak accident and being killed because one is queer. But "immaterial" is the appropriate word inasmuch as Ennis can read Jack's death, however it occurs, *only* as the result of homophobia. The bashing scene is most instructive for what it reveals about Ennis: in a sense, he needs to have Jack die that way for verification of his own father's warning. In death Jack serves as a substitute for Ennis, who, never having shed the power of the father, believes he deserves to die.

The discussion thus far raises the matter of whether *Brokeback* is not so much a gay polemic as it is a cautionary tale — not necessarily a conscious warning but, equally culpable, one passed on by writers and filmmakers unconsciously transmitting ubiquitous homophobic cultural energies. Deliberately or not, Jack's death (much more so than Ennis's self-imposed exile) exposes a belief that undergirds *Brokeback,* a notion that, despite the honest, vehement demur of many an individual, seems nearly everywhere woven into heteronormative culture: gay happiness is unimaginable. As Christian Draz writes, "It's as if, for all their good will, [the filmmakers] were unable to understand these two gay characters as anything *other* than tragic."[30] Peter Swaab's enlightening reference to Willa Cather disputes the inevitability of Proulx's ending: "Proulx's mountain reminds me of the New Mexican mesa where Tom Outland and Roddy Blake live amorously in Willa Cather's novel *The Professor's House* (1925). Cather's fictions imagine a real if compromised place for all sorts of outsiders, racial and sexual, in pioneering America; but in *Brokeback Mountain* there is simply no place for Jack and Ennis to continue their love, in the Wyoming of their time."[31] Swaab, like others, seems too prompt to add the "simply" to "there is no place for ... their love," too ready to accept that that is "simply" the way things are. This is not to petulantly insist that stories must end happily just because they *can*. But, given the definitional "double bind" that imbricates hetero- and homosexuality, queer love is rarely, if ever, "*simply*" impossible, at least not inherently, on its own. All manner of dicta, traditions, and circumstances — warnings and threats both adventitious and witting, transmitted and perceived by the lovers and by the larger culture — impact its expression and survival. Further, as pointed out by Matt Foreman, a "native Westerner whose parents have ranched in Wyoming" and currently executive director of the National Gay and Lesbian Task Force, Jack's proposal is not beyond the realm of possibilities, even in 1967 Wyoming.[32] More lamentable is our willingness to cheer a depiction of queer life as backward as that Cather imagined eighty years ago. Since when is "no place" *better* than a "real if compromised place" where one can "live amorously"?

While a number of happy queer films have emerged fairly recently (such as *The Broken Hearts Club, The Ski Trip, Connie & Carla,* and *Another Gay Movie*), one should note that these are all comedies or at least seriocomic works. It's an old saw that serious art rarely features happy endings because happiness lacks conflict and without conflict narrative is banal. And part of the argument of this essay, admittedly, is that unhappy endings for queer characters may more accurately reflect literally and/or symbolically the continued legal and cultural marginalization of American queers. Yet none of these qualifications can dissipate the lingering feeling that, after a handful of mainstream gay films in the past two decades (*Philadelphia* being the most prominent of these), happy endings for queers lie beyond the compass of the American mind. Roy Grundmann, writing for *Cineaste*, finds it "petty to fault [the film] for its reticence on the availability of alternative sexual venues for its lovers," and one must concede that the paucity of queer stories puts an undue amount of pressure on each new work of art to be representative and/or satisfying.[33] But that's not what galls here. The 1980s saw a number of queer films hailed rightly or wrongly as "groundbreaking," including *Personal Best, My Beautiful Laundrette, Desert Hearts, Parting Glances,* and *Prick Up Your Ears.*[34] Even a movie such as *Making Love*— not without its flaws but starring established straight actors Harry Hamlin, Michael Ontkean, and Kate Jackson — is worthier of the "groundbreaking" label than *Brokeback.* The gay characters played by Ontkean and Hamlin don't end up together, but neither one dies: one "play[s] the field" while the other "finds himself a rich architect and marries the guy."[35] What's galling about *Brokeback* is that Proulx first — and then McMurtry and Ossana, who chose to remain faithful to Proulx's original vision in this detail — envisioned an ending for Jack but chose to extinguish it. Regardless of the realities of rural life in 1960s Wyoming, or the continuing menace of homophobia and violence, choosing to tell *this* story at *this* moment feels oddly incognizant of the last twenty years in gay art and history. David Ansen's *Newsweek* review exemplifies this disquieting link between progress and loss: "the reason [*Brokeback*] feels like a breakthrough is that Lee has made it for the right reasons: he recognizes a heartbreaking love story when he sees one."[36] By this dubious logic, queer tragedy is a narrative "breakthrough." "[H]eartbreaking" gay stories are the "right" ones to film, while implicitly heartwarming ones are the *wrong* ones. While Grundmann is right that the "paradox of all great romances" is "the promise of a happily-ever-after and the mandate that this must never come to pass," a doomed *gay* romance, especially one recounted by straight storytellers, risks carrying a valuative, if not also proscriptive, charge absent from heterosexual romance.[37] The latter, though subject to individual instances of failure, never faces the charge that it categorically cannot or ought not to be.

What makes calling *Brokeback* the "right" gay story more perturbing is that Jack *has* a happy ending — or *almost* does. After Jack's death, Ennis learns from Jack's father, John, that Jack had recently found "another fella" willing to move to Lightning Flat with him and begin the life together Ennis had rejected as incapable of realization without fatal consequences (SP 90). Although the idea may run counter to a slavish habituation to generic convention (doomed romance) and to enduring (gay and straight) acculturation to queer inferiority, *Jack's death is not necessary*. Jack's finding someone else to live with, even if only as a substitute for Ennis, is sufficient to produce the unhappy ending that Ennis's claustrophobically constricted mentality demands. Jack's sullen father snips that, "like most a Jack's ideas," leaving his wife and working the family ranch with another man "never come to pass" (SP 90). But this is fallacious reasoning on John Twist's part. Neither his pessimism nor Jack's own admission of his historic bad luck expunges the fact that *this* plan, as far as we can tell, *was about to* "come to pass." This reading might seem baselessly optimistic, but it's worth noting that we're given no reason, other than John's cynicism, to think that Jack's notion of setting up house with another man was *not* going to be realized. McMurtry and Ossana lend substance to the possibility of this plan's actualization by inserting a scene in which Randall Malone — presumably the "ranch neighbor ... from down in Texas" Jack had asked to live with him — makes a pass at Jack (SP 90, 76). If Jack were to live, much less live happily, such an ending (Jack finds love; Ennis knows only paralysis) would punish Ennis sufficiently to convey the oppressiveness and the personal cost of homophobia. At minimum, happiness is possible for Jack in a way it cannot be for Ennis. That Jack would find someone other than Ennis to love is a reasonable assumption, if only because he seeks it, because he, unlike Ennis, can envision it.

That Proulx could envision a happy ending for Jack Twist but could not envision him *realizing* that ending is perhaps the most saddening dimension of the narrative — because it renders Jack's death entirely gratuitous. In regard to the ending, Proulx writes, "While I was working on this story, I was occasionally close to tears. I felt guilty that their lives were so difficult, yet *there was nothing I could do about it. It couldn't end any other way.*"[38] Proulx's reflection is patently a statement of bad faith, however heartfelt. Brushing aside the facile suggestion that stories write themselves, we're faced with the bald admission that Proulx cannot visualize, let alone write, another ending — just as Ennis cannot visualize it. In effect, we're being told that Ennis functions as Proulx's mouthpiece in the text, that Proulx is incapable of inhabiting Jack Twist, seeing the world from his point of view. The narrative circumstances of Jack's death, in which a future is imagined and then cancelled out (apparently by irrevocable Fate, not authorial volition), undermine Proulx's otherwise apparently *anti*homophobic motives. Cultural antipathy to homosexuals is so deeply and sometimes covertly ingrained that the numbing fatalism of "it couldn't end any other way" passes for an inexorable aesthetic law rather than the inflection of the old phobic aphorism that it is: gay life is solitary and sad — and there's nothing anyone can do about it.[39] Rather than merely a tale, as Proulx puts it, of "destructive rural homophobia," her story and Lee's film both embody, if unwittingly, the appalling extent to which homophobia imbues even the willfully most antihomophobic context.[40] Although many of them have joined the rush to lionize Annie Proulx for her courage, sympathy, or insight, queers should intuit more easily than anyone how unenterprising, formulaic, and orthodox her conception of gay life is. It is deracinated, joyless, fugitive, clichéd; without hope of outlet, fulfillment, articulation, or sanctuary.

Always the Bridesmaid

One of the film's most significant additions to the original story, the final scene between Ennis and his daughter, Alma Jr., likewise comes off as less heartwarming than intended. Alma Jr. visits her hermit-like father in his solitary trailer home to invite him to her upcoming wedding. After gruffly claiming he can't get time off work, Ennis thaws toward his daughter and agrees to attend. Once she drives off, Jack notices she's forgotten her sweater. Opening his locker to store it, he sees the hanger with his old flannel shirt (which Jack had secretly stolen after their first summer on the mountain) and a shirt of Jack's layered beneath it. To signal both Ennis's closeted sexuality and his deeply internalized love for Jack, Ennis has reversed the layering of the shirts as he initially found them in Jack's closet at the Twist home (Ennis's shirt inside Jack's). Looking at the shirts, along with the postcard of Brokeback Mountain pinned on the locker door, Ennis starts to tear up and delivers the film's truncated last line, "Jack, I swear..." (SP 97). Roy Grundmann shrewdly diagnoses this scene's "political instrumentality."[41] Ennis's "I swear," juxtaposed with talk of his daughter's impending wedding, evokes marital vows ("And do you take this man...?" "I do.") — a token, for Grundmann, of the screenwriters' "liberal-minded nod to gay mainstream politics" in "legitmiz[ing] the gay marriage that would have been by linking it to the straight wedding that will be."[42] No other critic seems to have made the connection between Alma Jr.'s marriage and the partnership Ennis will never have, or to have remarked in this context on gay marriage's less desirable implications: inducting gays and lesbians into the institution of marriage grants equality only to those who choose to marry; the married are still rewarded and valued in ways that the unmarried are not.[43] He also correctly attributes any political freight in the scene to the screenwriters. While Proulx ends the source story with the image of the two shirts, the scene between Ennis and his daughter is the invention of McMurtry and Ossana. But it's possible to read this added scene even more cynically — and truthfully. Proulx allows the two lovers (Ennis remembering Jack) to close the story. In the screenplay, by contrast, heterosexuality and the society Ennis has avoided so long intrude into his last private space (the closet within which his locker doubly closets his love for Jack), coaxing him back into the straight fold with the proverbial ties that bind (parent-child affection and duty), requiring his presence at heterosexuality's central sacralizing, promulgating event (marriage).

At the same time, a happy ending for Ennis and Jack might seem *inappropriate* at present. Queers are outsiders in America. (Michael Warner would suggest that oppositionality is the proper, perhaps the only authentic, way for queer culture to survive — which makes *Brokeback* a wrongly mournful account of exclusion, as if there can be no newly made culture, no contentment outside heteronormativity.) Obviously much has changed over the past forty-odd years. Yet whatever the material circumstances or political gains of the past decade (most prominently, the Supreme Court decision in *Lawrence v. Texas*), queers remain the symbolic and — to judge from the number of state-level laws and amendments against gay marriage, civil unions, and domestic partner benefits — also the material pariahs of heteronormativity. It's in this vein, in the historically familiar stereotype of *scary* (or toxic) gay, that *Brokeback* presents gay men: as a corrosive agent undermining the family, eroding it from within and without. Finally confronting Ennis with her knowledge of his affair with Jack, Alma hisses, "Jack Twist? ... Jack Nasty," identifying Jack as the "nast[iness]" that wormed its way into the Del Mar domestic sanctum, destroying their marriage. Ennis, having become nasty himself, is enraged with Alma for discovering his secret, wrenches her arm, and must be expelled: "Get out of my house, Ennis del Mar!" (SP 68–69). The fact that Alma is pregnant with a third child, her first with second husband Monroe, renders the expulsion of Ennis, of "nast[iness]," doubly vital, not merely to domestic tranquility but to fetal life, to the future of (straight) hearth and civilization. Like Ennis in Alma's view, in rhetoric and images that not everyone promotes and many find offensive but that continues to resonate, queers still stand poised to destroy civilization.[44]

That Old, Familiar (Tragic) Feeling

The era of good feeling inaugurated by *Brokeback*'s success is unwise for queers and unfortunate for straights. In neither group does the film incite anger at current discrimination, violence, or exclusion. The film's somber affect and painterly eye, along with its status as a genre and period piece, encourages — or at the very least *permits*—distance. We're invited to regret that it didn't work out for Ennis and Jack and how sad it was *back then*. If a common first reaction is "how sad," this is uncomfortably close to that common phobic refrain that being gay is a hard life (as if it were a choice; no one says such things about being a person of color or female precisely because that would nonsensically imply one has a choice in such matters). Richard Schneider, editor of *Gay and Lesbian Worldview*, falls victim to a tantalizing yet falsely content sense of progress by virtue of cultural distance from "back then" when he writes, "Proulx ... create[s] the worst possible environment to be gay, reducing that struggle to a stark choice between living a lie and risking one's life. There but for the grace of God, one can't help thinking, but for the fact that times have changed. *Brokeback Mountain* reminds us of the progress we've made, and the film's very existence is a case in point."[45] Faced with the excluded middle Proulx constructs, either alternative ("risking one's life" by living openly like Jack or "living a lie" like Ennis) is a strong contestant for a *pis aller*. Schneider may have hit upon *Brokeback*'s catch-22: Jack's death at once upbraids *and* vindicates Ennis for staying in the closet. Queers understandably welcome the advent of the gay blockbuster, but might wonder whether it has to be *tragic* gay? For all its beauty, or partly because of it, *Brokeback* is fundamentally reactionary, both on paper and film, reinscribing homosexuality within conventional, all too familiar parameters. The most hopeful note in *Brokeback* may be found, surprisingly, in Ennis's enigmatic, final words: "Jack, I swear...." If one interprets Ennis to be swearing regret at not having acted more courageously, at denying himself and Jack both what the latter was so ready to grasp, then screenwriters and directors might learn from Ennis's and *Brokeback*'s shortcomings and dare, next time, to conceive of and dramatize gay happiness, to redeem it from its historically and continued chimeric status in the national imaginary.

Notes

1. Daniel Mendelsohn, "An Affair to Remember," *New York Review of Books*, Feb. 23, 2006, <http://www.nybooks.com/articles/18712> (accessed Apr. 6, 2006), par. 2.
2. Quoted in ibid., par. 2.
3. Anthony Lane, "New Frontiers," *New Yorker*, Dec. 12, 2005, *Academic Search Premier*, EBSCOhost, Shippensburg University (accessed Apr. 6, 2006), par. 5.
4. Richard Alleva, "Emotional Apartheid," *Commonweal*, Feb. 10, 2006, *Academic Search Premier*, EBSCOhost, Shippensburg University (accessed Apr. 6, 2006), par. 10.
5. Chuck Anziulewicz, "A Love Story," *Commonweal*, Mar. 10, 2006, *Academic Search Premier*, EBSCOhost, Shippensburg University (accessed Apr. 6, 2006).
6. Nathan Lee remarks on this ambivalence: "On the one hand [the film] isn't very queer.... On the other hand, the one that's lubed up with saliva, could *Brokeback Mountain* be any queerer? ... [W]e don't actually see Ennis ... bareback Jack ... [but] *the many millions of 'mos on the planet* [have] *just been given* ... the epic romantic tragedy straight people have taken for granted all their lives." Lee's admirably queer take is compromised by the price he seems willing to pay (not expecting "pedigree[d]" heterosexuals to play graphic sexuality) for getting to be play tragic just like straights (*"Brokeback Mountain," Film Comment* 42, no. 1 [Jan./Feb. 2006], 42).

7. Mendelsohn, par. 15.

8. See Eve Sedgwick on the "void[ing]" effect of "universalizing" readings in *Epistemology of the Closet* (Berkeley: University of California Press, 1990), 165.

9. Roger Ebert, "*Brokeback Mountain*," *Chicago Sun-Times*, Dec.16, 2005, http://roger ebert.suntimes.com/apps/pbcs.dll/article?AID=/20051215/REVIEWS/51019006/1023 (accessed July 30, 2006), par. 3.

10. Mendelsohn, par. 8.

11. Ibid., par. 8.

12. Ibid., par. 9.

13. Vito Russo, *The Celluloid Closet* (1981; rev. ed, New York: Harper & Row, 1987), 271–272.

14. Andrew Holleran, "The Magic Mountain," *Gay and Lesbian Review Worldwide* 13, no. 2 (Mar. 2006): 12, 15.

15. *Brokeback* "universalists"—including Lane, Alleva, Ebert, and Lee Harris ("Misunderstanding *Brokeback Mountain*," *TCS Daily,* Jan.17, 2006, http://www.tcsdaily.com/article.aspx?id=011606D [accessed May, 11 2006])—typically argue that Jack and Ennis are not "'really' gay" (Mendelsohn, par. 13). The thinnest version of this argument turns on the pair's scarcely credulous "morning after" dialogue ("I ain't queer," "Me neither"—SP 20) (Proulx's original first line was "I'm not no queer," SS 7.) Not wanting Jack and Ennis to *be* gay and wanting them to be seen as more than *just* gay both amount to wanting gayness out of the picture. While some might object that reading Ennis and Jack as gay collapses alternative alignments of identity, sexuality, and gender among rural Americans into a more familiar urban-centric model, it seems possible both to discuss what *Brokeback* offers or is read as offering to all queer Americans about their cultural liminality (in a discourse that seldom differentiates between those who identify as queer and those perceived as such) without ignoring Judith Halberstam's insight into the urbanist prejudice of models of gay identity ("The Brandon Archive," in *In a Queer Time and Place: Transgender Bodies, Subcultural Lives* [New York: NYU Press, 2005], 22–46).

16. Annie Proulx, "Getting Movied," in *Brokeback Mountain: Story to Screenplay* (New York: Scribner, 2005), 130.

17. Holleran, 14.

18. Christian Draz, "Lost in Adaptation," *Gay and Lesbian Review Worldwide* 13, no. 2 (Mar. 2006): 12.

19. Holleran, 14.

20. Dan Gorton, "The Hate Crime," *Gay and Lesbian Review Worldwide* 13.2 (March 2006): 14.

21. Eve Kosofsky Sedgwick, *Between Men: English Literature and Male Homosocial Desire* (New York: Columbia University Press, 1985), 89. Ennis's identificatory crisis suggests that, *pace* Sedgwick, gay men may *not* be categorically "exempt" from the "wasting rigors" of homosexual panic (Sedgwick, *Epistemology*, 188).

22. David M. Halperin, *Saint Foucault: Toward a Gay Hagiography* (New York: Oxford University Press, 1995), 30. See also Sedgwick, *Epistemology*, 67–70, 78–86.

23. David Ansen, "The Heart Is a Lonely Hunter," *Newsweek* Dec. 19, 2005, *Academic Search Premier*, EBSCOhost, Shippensburg University (accessed Apr. 6, 2006), par. 3.

24. Halperin, 30. For Lee Edelman, see *No Future: Queer Theory and the Death Drive* (Durham, N.C.: Duke University Press, 2004), 1–31; for Michael Warner, see *The Trouble with Normal: Sex, Politics, and the Ethics of Queer Life* (New York: Free Press, 1999), 33–40, 61–80, and *Publics and Counterpublics* (New York: Zone Books, 2002), 7–63, 187–223.

25. Halperin, 61.

26. Mendelsohn, par. 7.

27. Roy Grundmann observes that although "[e]asily misinterpreted as omniscient narration, these fleeting pictures" of Jack's death by gay bashing are, "in fact, Ennis's imagination"—Grundmann, "*Brokeback Mountain*," *Cineaste* 31.2 (Spring 2006), *Academic Search Premier,* EBSCOhost, Shippensburg University (accessed May 11, 2006), par. 17.

28. Distrusting Lureen's version of Jack's death as a cover story requires reading the fag-

bashing images as emanating from *her* consciousness — which would make little sense since the film grants her no other flashbacks.

29. The exception is Jack's memory of his and Ennis's "dozy embrace" by the campfire their first summer on the mountain (SS 22). This is Jack's only moment of interiority or flashback in Proulx's story — an odd exception to the text's overall structure, which is framed as one extended flashback by Ennis. Lee retains this quiet moment as Jack's: the embrace by the campfire in 1963 cuts directly back to Jack's face as he watches Ennis drive away in 1981.

30. Draz, 13.

31. Peter Swaab, "Homo on the Range," *New Statesman*, Dec., 12, 2005, 42.

32. Adam B. Vary, "The *Brokeback Mountain* Effect," *The Advocate*, Feb. 28, 2006, *Academic Search Premier*, EBSCOhost, Shippensburg University (accessed May 11, 2006), par. 22. See also Grundmann, par. 20.

33. Grundmann, par. 15.

34. See Vary, pars. 19, 12; Russo, 248–323.

35. Russo, 272.

36. Ansen, par. 2.

37. Grundmann, par. 10.

38. Quoted in Sean Smith, "Forbidden Territory," *Newsweek*, Nov. 21, 2005, *Academic Search Premier*, EBSCOhost, Shippensburg University (accessed May 11, 2006), par. 3 [emphasis added].

39. Following Sedgwick, one might go further and read in Jack's death a "fantasy trajectory toward a life *after the homosexual*," "a culture's desire that gay people *not be*" (*Epistemology*, 127, 43).

40. Proulx, 130.

41. Grundmann, par. 16.

42. Ibid., pars., 16, 17.

43. Although he does not cite Michael Warner, Grundmann's discussion of gay marriage seems indebted to Warner's in *The Trouble with Normal* (81–147); see also Judith Butler, *Undoing Gender* (New York: Routledge, 2004), 105–112.

44. Edelman, *No Future*, 2–7, 13–17.

45. Richard Schneider, Jr., "Not Quitting *Brokeback*," *Gay and Lesbian Review Worldwide* 13.2 (Mar. 2006), 10.

ACKNOWLEDGMENTS: *Karl Woelz deserves thanks for, again, listening more carefully than any; Dawn Vernooy-Epp, for vetting successive drafts. Generous, precise feedback from Jim Stacy and the essay's anonymous readers led to substantial improvements.* — W. C. Harris

10

Brokeback Mountain at the Oscars

by Charles Eliot Mehler

On Sunday evening, March 5, 2006, Jack Nicholson remarked on the situation with a simple, understated "Whoa!" as he revealed to viewers what might have been the greatest upset in the history of the Academy of Motion Picture Arts and Sciences: Paul Haggis's *Crash* had bested the overwhelming front-runner, *Brokeback Mountain*, for the Best Picture Oscar. It would be easy to attribute this *Brokeback* snub to simple homophobia.[1] Yet besides engendering what one might consider a homophobic reaction on the social right, *Brokeback* perhaps also might have evoked a reaction bordering on antipathy on the part of many who identify with the social left: urban homosexuals[2] and those who identify as "queer theorists" and postmodernists in academia. At contention is the idea that *Brokeback Mountain* posed a threat to both the right and left ends of the spectrum of sociopolitical thought concerning homosexual issues, and that this combination proved too formidable a force for *Brokeback* to overcome at the Oscars.

In the end, the motion picture academy denied ultimate recognition to a genuinely groundbreaking film. In an industry that prides itself on its social conscience, denial such as this can be seen by the Hollywood outsider as severe, ironic embarrassment.

Simple and Not-So-Simple Homophobia

Film critic Kenneth Turan theorized in the *Los Angeles Times* on the morning after the 2006 Oscar telecast, "[F]or people who were discomfited by *Brokeback Mountain* but wanted to be able to look themselves in the mirror and feel like they were good, productive liberals, *Crash* provided the perfect *safe harbor*" [emphasis added].[3] No one could prove that there was a well organized "conspiracy" against *Brokeback* for the Oscar, yet evidence suggests that in fact a significant element of homophobia entered into the minds of Hollywood's elite as individual members voted for the Best Picture Oscar.

As early as New Year's Day 2006, an opinion piece written by television writer/actor Larry David appeared in the *New York Times*. Intended humorously, this piece describes David as intransigent against being party to viewing *Brokeback Mountain*. David writes, "I haven't seen *Brokeback Mountain*, nor do I have any intention of seeing it. In fact, cowboys would have to lasso me, drag me into the theater and tie me to the seat, and even then I would make every effort to close my eyes and cover my ears.... I don't want to watch two straight men, alone on the prairie, fall in love and kiss and hug and hold hands and whatnot."[4] What may strike many as absurd here is David's reference to *Brokeback* protagonists Ennis and Jack as "straight men." It is as if someone suddenly defined wearing cowboy attire as tantamount to being heterosexual. Nowhere in David's opinion piece does he refer to the sexual orientation of actors Heath Ledger and Jake Gyllenhaal, each of whom is an acknowledged heterosexual. Thus, any attempt for Larry David to claim that he was referring to the orientation of the actors involved is disingenuous. As we shall see with queer theorists, David would seem to subscribe to the idea that if it *looks* straight, it must *be* straight, or might as well be straight.

David himself raises the question as to whether his decision *not* to view *Brokeback Mountain* is borne of fear of homosexuality. He continues,

> If two cowboys, male icons who are 100 percent all-man, can succumb, what chance to do I have...? I'm a very susceptible person, easily influenced, a natural-born follower with no sales resistance.... So who's to say I won't become enamored with the whole gay business? ... I just know if I saw that movie, the voice inside my head that delights in torturing me would have a field day. "You like those cowboys, don't you? They're kind of cute. Go ahead, admit it, they're cute. You can't fool me, gay man. Go ahead, stop fighting it. You're gay! You're gay!" Not that there's anything wrong with it.[5]

Here, David offers the idea that homosexuality is to be treated as something infectious, something to which two "he-man cowboys" can "succumb." In addition, David also implies, albeit humorously, that such an infection is something to be avoided. Thus, in Larry David World, homosexuality becomes a disease concept, at least in terms of its contagion and its lack of desirability. Yet as David himself quips, "Not that there's anything wrong with it." This quote refers to an episode of the *Seinfeld* television program for which David was part of the creative team. In this episode, the characters Jerry and his best friend George are mistakenly identified as a homosexual couple. The quip becomes a running gag as characters Jerry and George, two heterosexual men, deal with the misidentification among friends, parents, and sundry passers-by. The phrase "not that there's anything wrong with it" is repeated so often that the viewer stops believing it, ultimately acquiescing in the idea that the characters Jerry and George *do* have a problem with homosexuality. In the *Seinfeld* episode, "not that there's anything wrong with it" emerges as Gertrude's "lady" who "protests too much," and David's *Times* opinion piece would seem to suggest a similar "protest." For in the *Times* article, David turns his homophobia — literally the fear of becoming homosexual — into what must be seen as a callous, repetitive joke. At the heart of David's "not that there's anything wrong with it" quip lies the essence of homophobia: a belief that there is something at least minimally wrong, perhaps even unsavory, with being homosexual or engaging in homosexual activity. If that were not the case, why would David show concern over his lack of "sales resistance?"

Larry David was not alone among the Hollywood elite to avoid viewing *Brokeback Mountain* for homophobic reasons. While being interviewed before the Oscar telecast, veteran screen actor Tony Curtis also admitted that he hadn't seen the film. As Mark Salamon reports, "During the run-up to the Academy Awards Tony Curtis told Fox News that he hadn't yet seen *Brokeback Mountain* and had no intention of doing so. He claimed he wasn't alone in the sentiment.... Furthermore, Curtis contended, his contemporaries no longer alive to speak for themselves wouldn't have cared for the highly acclaimed Best Picture nominee either. "Howard Hughes and John Wayne wouldn't like it," Curtis said in an interview."[1] Not only does Curtis refuse to view the film. Not only does Curtis invoke the demigod spirits of the likes of Howard Hughes and John Wayne to demonize *Brokeback*. By his own admission, Curtis is not alone in his refusal to view this critically acclaimed masterpiece. This is especially curious, given Curtis's history concerning issues of homosexuality and gender alignment. In 1959, Curtis performed with Jack Lemmon in *Some Like It Hot*, a film in which the two actors donned standard female attire. In 1960, Curtis appeared in *Spartacus*, which included Curtis's performance in a steamy, male-on-male bathing scene. Most importantly, in 1994, Curtis acknowledged his own homosexual dalliances in a magazine interview.[7]

Homophobic reaction to *Brokeback* was not limited to certain celebrities' refusal to view the film. In the aftermath of the *Brokeback* Oscar snub, news analyst David Carr of *The New York Times* reported that many Oscar voters could not see "why a story that was essentially a tale of two men cheating on their wives ... should be chosen to represent Hollywood's best effort of the year."[8] One can only imagine the legitimate reaction of disgust among the lion's share of women and feminist sympathizers had *Thelma and Louise* been reduced in description to a film about "cops chasing criminals." Conceivably, it is possible to view Carr's observation as equally insulting and shallow. The characters Thelma and Louise broke the law in reaction to mistreatment of and violence against women. Analogously, *Brokeback* protagonists Ennis and Jack entered into sham heterosexual marriages as a result of the forces of heterosexual supremacy. This supremacy continues to be enforced well after the timeline of *Brokeback Mountain*, both in the legal sense — after all, private, consensual homosexual relations in America were not fully decriminalized until the *Lawrence v. Texas* Supreme Court decision in 2003[9] — and as a result of the mistreatment and violence homosexuals experience at the hand of heterosexually-identified members of society. Taking this idea to its logical if ridiculous extreme, one has to wonder if Carr would regard the Jew who defied the Spanish Inquisition by practicing her/his religion in private as "cheating" on the Catholic Church.

Salamon continues his comments by creating an imaginary scenario in which a film about cross-racial intermarriage has had the same overwhelming effect on the culture in a pre-civil-rights-era venue as *Brokeback* has had in ours. Like *Brokeback*, this mixed-marriage film becomes the butt of bigoted humor on the part of pundits and television comedians, and racist celebrities refuse to view it, much in the way Larry David and Tony Curtis refused to view *Brokeback*. This mixed-marriage film goes on to win nearly every award imaginable in the pre-Oscar season and is the odds-on favorite to win the Oscar for Best Picture. On Oscar night, this *Brokeback* stand-in loses to a film that was released much earlier in the year to tepid critical reaction. "This example," argues Salamon, "is *not* an overstatement of the abuse that has been hurled at *Brokeback Mountain*, nor have its accolades been exaggerated. Merely substitute 'gay male relationship' into the analogy ... and you will have an accurate picture of the scathing climate *Brokeback Mountain* has had to endure."[10]

To bolster Salamon's qualitative argument, Michael Jensen offers a quantitative study of the *Brokeback* Oscar snub. Jensen describes the exhaustingly long list of pre–Oscar awards with which *Brokeback Mountain* was honored: "[*Brokeback*] had more Best Picture and Director wins than previous Oscar winners *Schindler's List* and *Titanic* combined," notes Jensen[11] — and compares this to the relative paucity of awards with which *Crash* was honored. "[O]f the major awards," notes Jensen, "*Crash* managed to win only the [Screen Actors Guild] Award, the Chicago Critics award, and an Image Award. And *Crash* won the Chicago honor mostly because Chicago-area film critic Roger Ebert relentlessly pushed it."[12]

Chicago Sun-Times film critic Roger Ebert's reaction to the *Brokeback/Crash* controversy presents an interesting twist on homophobic reaction to

Brokeback Mountain. In contrast to Turan's "safe harbor" comment, Ebert declared, "I was not 'discomfited' by *Brokeback Mountain.* I chose *Crash* as the best film of the year not because it promoted one agenda and not another."[13] Furthermore, Ebert argued that each of the five best picture nominees presented its own share of controversy, reserving special notice for the controversy surrounding Steven Spielberg's *Munich* which, according to Ebert, "afforded *Steven Spielberg* the unique [and perhaps bizarre] experience of being denounced as anti-Semitic."[14] Thus, in comparison to those who support any conspiracy theory concerning the *Brokeback* Oscar snub, Roger Ebert attempted to present the motion picture academy's choice of *Crash* over *Brokeback* as a relatively fair artistic contest, free of any predisposition against controversy, tainted by the sinister specter of outside-issue politics.

This assessment of a fair artistic contest on Ebert's part begs a challenge. One need not even consider the quasi-censorial decisions by the management personnel of numerous movie theatres in rural venues *not* to screen *Brokeback Mountain,*[15] an issue which makes Ebert's argument of equal controversy among the five nominated films seem unreasonable. More importantly, Ebert would seem to infer that some unreasonable, unfair political agenda lies at the heart of the pro-*Brokeback* argument, and that his choice of *Crash* over *Brokeback* was based on aesthetic consideration alone. The two issues of political concern here, homophobia and racism, come to the fore when one examines Ebert's original reviews of *Brokeback* and *Crash*. Specifically, Ebert concluded his review of *Crash* by saying, "Not many films have the possibility of making their audiences better people. I don't expect *Crash* to work any miracles, but I believe anyone seeing it is likely to be moved to have a little more sympathy for people not like themselves."[16] Let us take particular notice of Ebert's use of the phrase "making audiences better people." Though stated in pleasant, innocuous terms, this phrase displayed a political agenda. Certainly, the agenda itself, one of promoting racial harmony, is a noble one. Yet no matter how Ebert might demur, his description of *Crash* was nevertheless no less a political agenda than any which might be attributed to supporters of *Brokeback Mountain*. In very stark comparison, Ebert spent much of his review of *Brokeback* displaying what would seem an inordinate, overwhelmingly self-conscious need to prove that the film had universal appeal, something he seemed to have taken for granted in his review of *Crash*. Early on, Ebert noted, "*Brokeback Mountain* has been described as 'a gay cowboy movie,' which is a cruel simplification."[17] The words "a," "cowboy," and "movie" certainly cannot be considered a source of cruelty. Clearly, Ebert found use of the word "gay" *cruel* in this context. If Ebert were truly neutral on outside issues, then the simple act of calling something or someone "gay" could *not* be seen as cruel. Ebert saw a need for *Brokeback* to justify its agenda in a way that the assumedly ennobling *Crash* need not have done. For Ebert then to attempt to defend the academy's choice of *Crash* over *Brokeback* by accusing *Brokeback* enthusiasts of some sort of unreasonable political agenda is thus, as playwright Mart Crowley remarked in his groundbreaking *The Boys in the Band*, "the pot calling the kettle beige."[18]

To bolster his quantitative argument concerning *Brokeback*, Michael Jensen continues by taking particular note of a "trifecta" of commercial film awards that *Brokeback* won. "Before [the] upset," writes Jensen, "no film that had won the Writer's Guild, Director's Guild, and Producer's Guild awards did not go on to win the Academy Award for Best Picture."[19] In addition, *Brokeback Mountain* won the 2006 Best Picture (Drama) Golden Globe, an award for which *Crash* was *not even nominated*.[20] Since 1955, when the current system of five nominees each for best picture in the classifications of comedy/musical or drama or its equivalent came into place, only three films not nominated for a Golden Globe in a "Best Picture" category have gone on to win the Best Picture Oscar: *Ghandi* (1982), *Chariots of Fire* (1981), and *The Sting* (1973). Reviews by, for example, Roger Ebert indicate that these three films were released very late in the year, either past or perilously close to the Golden Globes deadline. Again in stark contrast, Ebert's *Crash* review appeared on May 5, 2005. Thus, unlike the three other films that won the Best Picture Oscar without winning a Golden Globe for Best Picture, Golden Globe voters had plenty of opportunity to develop a passion for *Crash*. They did not.

Jensen also notes *Brokeback* garnered the most Oscar nominations for films made in 2005. Jensen believes that each of these instances of *Brokeback* success — especially the Golden Globe for Best Drama and the most Oscar nominations — represents, under normal circumstances for the painfully traditional motion picture academy, a strong indicator of a film's chances to win the Best Picture Oscar.[21] Jensen heaps more evidence on the quantitative "conspiracy theory" pile by noting that in addition to being the highest grossing film among the nominees for Best Picture Oscar, *Brokeback* was the favorite of the critics. Jensen adds, "Every year, both *Premiere Magazine* and *Entertainment Weekly* rank the year's movies according to the reviews they received. *Brokeback* came in first on both lists. Three other Best Picture nominees — *Good Night, and Good Luck*, *Capote*, and *Munich*—also placed in the Top Ten on both lists. Meanwhile, *Crash* ranked number thirty-six on *Premiere*'s list, and down in the fifties on *EW*'s. A half-dozen critics even gave it outright pans, saying it was a movie to be avoided."[22]

Thus, when taking into account the mass of evidence presented by Jensen, Salamon, and Turan, *and* the off-handed homophobia of Larry David, *and* the more overt homophobia of Tony Curtis, *and* the disingenuous political agenda of Roger Ebert, it becomes reasonable to conclude that something highly out of the ordinary, likely the result of this very homophobia, happened to prevent *Brokeback* from winning the Best Picture Oscar. Yet as we shall see, other factors that would be difficult to be described as "simply homophobic" played into the Oscar snub of *Brokeback Mountain*.

Don Roos and Urban Homosexual Reaction *to* Brokeback Mountain

Not all pro-homosexual, presumably anti-homophobic, reaction to *Brokeback* was positive. "I was so irritated by those stupid, stupid cowboys [in *Brokeback Mountain*]," said writer/director Don Roos. "I felt like saying, 'Guys, get a map. Go to New York. Go to L.A. Your problems will be over if you just get a map!'"[23] In this comment, Roos showed that it was possible to fashion a response to *Brokeback* that criticized the film yet showed no evidence of active homophobia.

Roos raises two important issues with this reaction. First is the implied question of the time-line writer Annie Proulx, upon whose work the film is based, chose when creating *Brokeback*. One must consider that Ennis and Jack's story happens, substantially, in the mid-to-late 1970s and beyond. Thus, much of Ennis and Jack's story happens after the Stonewall Rebellion of 1969[24] that ushered in the latter day homosexual rights movement, after Phyllis' brother had come out of the closet on the *Mary Tyler Moore* television comedy program,[25] and contemporary with Anita Bryant's anti-homosexual referendum campaign in Miami-Dade County, Florida.[26] Thus, if one simply owned a television set, one could not by this time avoid the topic of homosexuality entirely.

Both the film and short story featured a near-complete ignorance of a sociopolitical context involving homosexual issues as part of the common culture. Thus, the *Brokeback* story might have made more sense to some in an earlier time frame, and Roos would seem to have made a valid point. The dramatic tension that made the storytelling in *Brokeback* so compelling resulted, at least in part, from the ability of its creative team to muster a sense of stifling, unrelenting claustrophobia in terms of homosexual issues. The timeline chosen by Proulx served at least minimally as an obstacle to the creation of such claustrophobia, and might have served somewhat to take the reader or viewer out of the moment. Don Roos's suggestion of possible ahistoricism in *Brokeback*, that there were already safe havens for homosexuals by this time, thus could be acknowledged as a fair criticism.

The other issue raised by Roos's comment is more troublesome. Roos would seem to assume that the only way for people like Ennis and Jack to live happily homosexual lives is to move to the "walk-in closet" of a large city, an assumption that would seem as coercive as if someone actually were to lasso Larry David and force him to, in fact, watch *Brokeback Mountain*. Roos's solution fails to address the raw bigotry Ennis and Jack faced. The physical and emotional cruelty people in Ennis and Jack's position faced in rural Wyoming is well exemplified in the story Ennis tells of being taken by his father as a child to see the corpse of a castrated homosexual, in whose murder Ennis's father may have had a hand.[27] Yet the solution Roos offers is to reward the bullies.

Nevertheless, Roos's "get a map" comment begs the idea that perhaps *Brokeback* is *not* the perfect piece of art its most ardent supporters claim it to be. Furthermore, Roos was part of the creative team that put together *The Opposite of Sex*, a film about a homophobic and otherwise dysfunctional young woman who learns to deal with her elder brother's homosexuality in a rural environment. It is clear that Roos's credentials as a critic of a film like *Brokeback* cannot be discounted.

On the other hand, Roos's idea to have Ennis and Jack haul off to a big city presents a more difficult conundrum and causes Roos to lose any points he may have gained for pointing out, if back-handedly, any ahistoricism in *Brokeback*. Roos's assertion that homosexuals need to abandon their rural roots fails to take into account the strong literary/cinematic motif of the Wild West as spiritual home to Ennis and Jack. For as much as this film and the short story upon which it is based present a love story about the two men Ennis and Jack, *Brokeback Mountain* is also a love letter to the American West. Philip French lays down the ground rules of this love affair with the Wild West of American cinema. "There are two things that every schoolboy knows about the [western film] genre. First, that the western is a commercial formula with rules as fixed and immutable as the Kabuki Theatre. Second, that the events depicted have little to do with the real nineteenth-century American frontier life.... Rather like, in fact, the Neverland of Barrie's *Peter Pan*, populated by children who refuse to grow up, fugitives from the urban nursery, marauding Indians, and menacing bands of pirates."[28] These ground rules would seem no longer to be sacrosanct in contemporary Hollywood, especially as concerns the Oscars. Recent deconstructions of the Western genre, like *Dances with Wolves* and *Unforgiven*, have appealed to members of the motion picture academy's voting sensibilities. What distinguishes *Brokeback Mountain* is its acceptance, perhaps even its attempted *re*construction, of French's rules of the West. Certainly, *Brokeback* depicts the hard lives that Ennis and Jack led in the real American West. Nevertheless, *Brokeback* offers a fascination with the great American frontier that perhaps shows greater affection toward the cowboy lifestyle than anything offered since the golden age of the Western film, circa 1945 to 1965. Neither Ennis nor Jack is willing to compromise his love of this Western style of life. Ennis remains the unrequited lover of the Western lifestyle even when it fails him financially. Though Jack sells out to his wife's family's more bourgeois way of life, the "rootin' tootin' rodeo cowboy" in his essence remains stolid, especially when he rebels against the wife's father. Even in discussing their dreams, the idea of going to a big city like Denver is out of the question for our "gay cowboys." Ennis and Jack's dream involves something inherent and stunningly simple in their souls — a no-frills ranch spread where they can lead a "sweet life" with each other, raising cattle in peace and harmony with their beloved, if romanticized, lone prairie.

The values and ambiance of this lone prairie, as we have already discovered, would seem to evade the likes of the blasé urbanite like Don Roos. As well, the cowboy ethos, especially among non-gender-realigning homosexual men, evades the postmodernist and the queer theorist.

"*I'm Not No Queer!*": Brokeback Mountain and Postmodernism

In "Quo Vadis: Literary Theory Beyond Postmodernism," Jens Zimmerman hails the apparent end of the paradigm that followed eighteenth- and nineteenth-century positivism in the wake of the atrocities of the twentieth century: both world wars, the atom bomb, racial strife, the assassinations of the 1960s. Postmodernism, declares Zimmerman, can hear the fat lady warming up. "Finally, we can say out loud," Zimmerman observes, "what a growing number of books admit: postmodernism as a movement of renewal has run its course."[29] Zimmerman's essay focuses on prose fiction in his deconstruction (as it were) of postmodernism. Yet his argument, that postmodernism has in many ways expired, could be applied to the *Brokeback Mountain* phenomenon. Specifically, postmodernism and its love child, queer theory, more often than not fail to take into account the kind of persecution the homosexual, as homosexual, faces in venues like the rural Wyoming of *Brokeback Mountain*.

To understand how postmodernism has failed the homosexual in this regard, it is helpful to examine the "bear" phenomenon among homosexual males. "Bear" is a colloquial term used to describe the male homosexual who might be any combination of large, overweight, hairy, or indelicate.[30] Bear culture often revolves around the portly, hirsute appearance of its adherents. Nevertheless, there exists at least a passive polemic agenda among bears, one that displays a radical defiance of the effeminate,[31] narcissistic, *exotic* stereotype of the male homosexual. Former *New Republic* editor Andrew Sullivan describes this defiance, arguing that for bears, "there is no contradiction between being a gay man and being a man as traditionally understood. And if that includes cracking open a six-pack and watching the game; or developing a beer-and-nachos belly; or working in a blue-collar job; or having the clothes sense of the average check-out guy; or preferring the company of men to women, then so be it."[32] It is the bear prototype that has been ignored, until *Brokeback Mountain*, by a Hollywood establishment that is relatively comfortable with, if not enthusiastic about, the homosexual-as-exotic stereotype.

When casting *Brokeback*, Ang Lee and company may have erred to the side of Hollywood "pretty boy" aesthetics in choosing actors like Heath Ledger and Jake Gyllenhaal, probably having more to do with box-office economics than any issue, positive or negative, with bear culture. Thus, Ledger and Gyllenhaal may not quite have *looked* the part, perhaps deceiving the naïve viewer into believing that they fail to come off as bears. To support this possible deception, one only need to look at the change in appearance late in the film when actor Jake Gyllenhaal, playing Jack Twist, makes a somewhat feeble attempt to grow a moustache. Gyllenhaal's attempt comes off as more '70s disco-bunny than bear. Nevertheless, the symbol of Jack's new moustache may belie a prognostication of the future of the couple's physical appearance. Given the chance to age to maturity in an atmosphere of simple safety — an opportunity tragically withheld from Jack — it is not too hard to imagine these two men as fat, hairy, and still happy with each other on their small cattle spread, casually developing their "beer-and-nachos" bellies. So to what many, if not most, Americans view as an overabundance of effeminacy and narcissism among homosexual men, Ennis and Jack would eventually present a surprisingly polar, un-exotic opposite — two normal looking guys whom you would see at a Wal-Mart on the weekend checking out the heavy lawn equipment and camping gear and who are also homosexual. Thus, even in consideration of the actors' standard surface good looks, Ennis and Jack, as portrayed by Ledger and Gyllenhaal, nevertheless ultimately serve as poster children for the bear phenomenon. The beer and chilidogs they might consume in the present tense of the film and short story could eventually make way for the rounded bellies of the future, possibly making them too lethargic and laid-back to shave.

Sullivan discusses the political consequences of the bear phenomenon, tentatively quoting gender-theory journalist Camille Paglia. Paglia states, "In [his] defiant hirsutism, ... [t]he gay bear is simultaneously animalistic and nurturing, a romp in the wild followed by naptime on a comfy cushion,"[33] and comes to the conclusion that bear culture presents traditional features of both masculinity and femininity: the nasty looking male animal on the exterior, the female nurturer on the interior. However, as discussed above, Paglia's observations seem mostly concerned with surface-appearance aspects of the "gay bear." Picking up on this and in contrast, Sullivan contradicts Paglia's conclusion, asserting,

> Paglia underestimates ... a rebellion among many gay men against both the feminizing impulses of the broader culture on the right and left and against prevailing norms in gay culture as a whole. In recent years, after all, men have come under withering attack — not just from the [politically correct, postmodern] left which tends to view all forms of unabashed maleness as oppressive but also from the nannying right which views men as socially irresponsible sexual miscreants. Bears are simply saying that they're men first and unashamed of it. More, in fact. What they're saying is that central to the gay male experience is an actual love of men. And men are not "boys," they're not feminized, hairless, fat-less icons on a dance floor. They're grumpy and kind and responsible and also happy to be themselves....[34]

Actors Ledger and Gyllenhaal may have appeared relatively hairless and fat-less as compared to *uber*-bears like James Gandolfini and Bob Hoskins, younger versions of whom as Ennis and Jack might have made an interesting and challenging casting choice for Ang Lee. However, even the most severe observer would have a hard time classifying these characters and their film characterizations as realized by Ledger and Gyllenhaal as even vaguely "feminized." As Sullivan so eloquently asserts, Ennis and Jack are "grumpy, and [essentially] kind and responsible and also happy to be themselves," at least in terms of their cowboy lifestyles–in short, bear-like.

Much like the bears that Andrew Sullivan describes, Ennis and Jack are males whose only difference from the larger society is that they engage in consensual homosexual activity. To say that Ennis and Jack were persecuted in *Brokeback* for this difference should be self-evident. Nevertheless, the basis of queer theory advocacy would seem to be that non-gender-realigning homosexuals, like Ennis and Jack, are somehow not in touch with their true "queerness" unless they are willing to explore the blurring of gender role distinctions. What the queer theorist fails to realize is that this is something the typical bear is, almost by definition, reticent to do. Like bears, men such as Ennis and Jack are as constitutionally incapable of tossing aside their gender role and appearance as Bree/Stanley, the Felicity Huffman male-to-female transsexual character in *Transamerica*. Cowboy boots and flannel shirts are as natural to Ennis and Jack as a shocking-pink if conservative-in-appearance woman's business suit is to Bree/Stanley.

Avoidance on the part of queer theorists to the persecution of the Ennises and Jacks of the world seems to lie at the heart of its advocacy. As evidence, one only need look at Judith Halberstam's early queer theory treatise, "F2M:

The Making of Female Masculinity." In celebrating the most out-of-the-ordinary examples of non-heterosexual culture, Halbestam chooses to focus on the ethnic drag underworld in New York City: "One recent film, Jenny Livingston's *Paris is Burning*, shocked white gay and straight audiences with its representations of an underexposed subculture of the African-American and Latino gay world in New York. The shock value of this film lay in is ability to confront audiences with subcultural practices that the audience thought they knew already....[35] What is shock value for one, however, is fairly ordinary fodder for the popular culture machine for another. Outrageous drag and gender alignment, with its ethnic variations, has been a mainstay of popular culture since the no-longer-recent advent of pop-singers like Lou Reed, Boy George, and Ru Paul. Additionally, Halberstam displays her penchant for portraying the homosexual as exotic in her list of "queer identities": "guys with pussies, dykes with dicks, queer butches, drag kings, pomo afro homos, bulldaggers, women who fuck boys, women who fuck like boys, dyke mommies, transsexual lesbians, male lesbians."[36] Here, the quoted author is writing mostly about lesbians who are chromosomally female, yet one could easily apply this narrow description of "queer identities" to a homosexual male situation. It would be difficult to imagine the typical queer theorist invoking a category such as "guys who look like guys who like guys who look like guys," or even the chromosomally female counterpart, as a "queer identity." Insisting that homosexuality can be expressed *only* in an atmosphere of the blurring of gender roles, queer theorists severely limit inclusion. No one would argue against the queer theory precept that there exists an analog continuum of performative gender roles. What is at stake here is the idea in evidence among queer theorists that sexual orientation must *always* be considered at the most liminal (i.e., at the borderline of binary categories like "homo-/heterosexual" and "female/male") and least essential (i.e., treated as pure social construct rather than something inherent), in a way that race and gender simply are not. Defining "queering" as the blurring of binary distinctions like black/white, male/female, and homosexual/heterosexual, if there has to be a GLBTQ in order to be inclusive of the gender-role/orientation spectrum, one has to wonder why there is no BIQ (black, interracial, queer) or WIQ (women, intersexual, queer) available to handle all the ambiguities of race and chromosomal sex. Such alphabet-soup categorizations as forced on the homosexual, especially the homosexual male, by queer culture display an inherent lack of consideration for what should be evident and obvious: the millennia-long oppression of homosexuals *as* homosexuals. As Andrew Sullivan implies, the adherent to queer theory, via its parent theory postmodernism, has difficulty dealing with the more sexually assertive aspects of male homosexuality. What easier, more clever way could there be for the queer theorist to get rid of binary homosexuality that accepts these aspects of sexuality comfortably than to wish it out of existence by blurring distinctions? Sadly and perhaps offensively, this effort fails to take care of the crying needs of homosexual men in tragic situations like Ennis and Jack. For the average homosexual, queer theory has failed.

In this failure, queer theory would seem to be in league with the prevailing attitude on homosexuality in Hollywood. For the one thing that these two seemingly disparate points of view, Hollywood values and queer theory, have in common is an apparent need to have their homosexuals be flamboyant, thus entertaining and capable of success at the box office. A movie about two "gay cowboys" could not be, in the standard Hollywood (or queer theory) take on the subject, as entertaining or interesting as a broadly farcical comedy about a drag queen and her/his daddy-ish looking lover. No one need deny that the gender-realigning antics of films such as *La Cage Aux Folles* and *To Wong Foo* ... are entertaining. Yet the image presented in films that focus on gender realignment as an expression of homosexuality is one of a sort of *faux* heterosexuality that presents one homosexual partner as playing the "girl" and one playing the "boy." Even when gender-alignment issues are taken more seriously, as in *Kiss of the Spider Woman* and *Transamerica*, this face-value *faux* heterosexual image presents itself: *la femme* Molina and his/her big, bad, butch revolutionary, male-to-female transsexual Bree/Stanley and *her* big, bad, butch (if slightly more sensitive) Native American cavalier, respectively. Such recent films that have dealt with homosexuality by presenting it as *faux* heterosexuality have not faced the kind of uproar and attempts at suppression that *Brokeback* has endured. There is a simple reason for this: *Brokeback* presents homosexuality, warts and all, with no apology, with no postmodern, queer-theory explanation, *with no way to avoid the sight of two normal looking guys fucking.* Films about the gender-liminal allow both extremes of the culture wars, the fundamentalist Christian and the postmodernist, some distance to avoid dealing with the nastiness of two ordinary looking men seriously and intimately involved with each other. *Brokeback Mountain* offers no such comfort, and is thus more revolutionary than the antics of the most outrageous drag queen in *Paris Is Burning.*

Soon after their first intimate encounter, Ennis del Mar looks at Jack Twist and says "I'm not no queer!" Jack replies, "Me neither!" (SS 7). These casual remarks offer a two-fold interpretation. On the surface, they indicate Ennis and Jack as in deep denial of their powerful sexual attraction for one another, through the use of what *must* be interpreted as a slur word. More deeply, in what might be seen as an unintended overlay interpretation, these remarks make what is perhaps the most astute political observation of the film: that there is nothing liminal, nothing postmodern, nothing exotic or sensationalistic about Ennis and Jack's involvement with each other.

LIVERPOOL JOHN MOORES UNIVERSITY
LEARNING SERVICES

Only the most virulently homophobic among critics of *Brokeback Mountain* might have even come close do describing the film as sensationalistic or as depicting anything exotic. *Brokeback,* in fact, is noteworthy for its depiction of the ordinary. But the unwritten code of the Hollywood heterosexual hegemony (and seemingly the queer-culture hegemony as well) encourages viewing the homosexual as sensationalistic, the homosexual as exotic, *the homosexual at a safe distance.* By failing to conform to this code, *Brokeback Mountain* posed a threat to both the Hollywood heterosexual power structure *and* queer theory. Its commercial and critical success created a juggernaut that needed to be stopped by these seemingly nonaligned forces. The juggernaut stopped on Oscar night when Jack Nicholson presciently and quietly exclaimed, "Whoa!"

But Crash *Won...*

With *Brokeback Mountain,* Ang Lee and company attempted to fulfill Hollywood's historic role as a provocateur in social issues, much in the way that in an earlier era Hollywood led the way in dealing with issues of race and ethnicity with such films as *Gentleman's Agreement* and *Pinky.* Thus, *Brokeback Mountain* was part of a deep, proud tradition of social conscience in even commercially oriented Hollywood. In this regard, one must consider the speech George Clooney delivered upon winning the Best Supporting Actor Oscar during the *Brokeback/Crash* Oscar telecast:

> We are a little bit out of touch in Hollywood every once in a while. I think that's probably a good thing.... This Academy, this group of people gave Hattie McDaniel an Oscar in 1939 [for *Gone with the Wind*] when blacks were still sitting in the backs of theaters. I'm proud to be part of this Academy, proud to be part of this community and proud to be out of touch.[37]

Brokeback Mountain, by all reasonable standards the most honored film of the 2005 film year, failed to win the Best Picture Oscar. This snub would seem to have been the result of *both* homophobia *and* the postmodern, queer-theory effort to diminish the concerns of non-gender-liminal homosexuals. A *Brokeback* victory indeed could have been a "Hattie McDaniel" moment, a juncture in which society takes a good hard look in the mirror and begins to sort out the injustices it has heaped unfairly upon those outside the mainstream. The *Crash* victory, as aided by the forces of homophobia and postmodernism, prevented this moment from happening. For many concerned with the fair and just treatment of homosexuals, this either saddens the heart or begs cynicism.

Crash won the Best Picture Oscar because it was the anti–*Brokeback.*

Crash won because it didn't have two hand-holding, tongue-kissing cowboys as main characters. *Crash* won because it did not violate the first rule of the code of the heterosexual hegemony *and* queer theory, that the homosexual male must be portrayed as flamboyant and exotic in order to appeal to commercial interests and to keep the unpleasant aspects of male homosexuality at a safe distance. *Crash* won because it did not attempt to reconstruct the hallowed "code of the West" in a homosexual venue. *Crash* won because it did not offend the social-left precept that the non-gender-liminal homosexual no longer faces real oppression.

Another *Brokeback Mountain*, another critically well-received, commercially successful film that pulls no punches in dealing directly with homosexual concerns, may well come along within the next few decades and actually *win* the Best Picture Oscar. In order for this yet-to-be-made film to achieve this success, it will have to overcome the three-fold conspiracy of contemporary queer theory and postmodernism, the enforced urbanization of the homosexual, and any lingering sense of heterosexual supremacy. Time may make the securing of a Best Picture Oscar for such a film a less formidable task to accomplish than it is today. Yet as compared to what any of the three aforementioned contemporary hegemonies have to offer, such an achievement presents a truly revolutionary possibility for the homosexual.

Notes

1. "Homophobia" is the term coined by clinical psychologist George Weinberg to describe anti-homosexual xenophobia. For a broader discussion, see Weinberg's *Society and the Healthy Homosexual* (New York: St. Martin's Press, 1972).

2. In response to what this author believes to be mistaken attempts to reclaim the word "queer" in serious discourse by the academic community, this essay will attempt a similar, positive reclamation. The word "homosexual" will be used in most cases. When necessary, the word "gay" will be used when appropriate colloquially. Because of the nature of the film *Brokeback Mountain* itself, this article will use the word "homosexual" almost exclusively to refer to male-on-male sexual activity. The phrases "queer theory" and "queer culture" will be used to indicate an area of academic inquest and its collective adherents.

3. Kenneth Turan, "Breaking No Ground: Why *Crash* Won, Why *Brokeback* Lost, and How the Academy Chose to Play It Safe," *Los Angeles Times,* Mar. 5, 2006.

4. Larry David, "Cowboys Are My Weakness," *New York Times,* Jan. 1, 2006, <http://www.nytimes.com/2006/01/01/opinion/01david.html?ei=5088&en=911bb046b77cbb2d&ex=1293771600&partner=rssnyt&emc=rss&pagewanted=print> (accessed Sept. 17, 2006).

5. Ibid.

6. Mark Salamon, "A Harrowing Affair: Commentary from a *Brokeback Mountain* Fan," March 13, 2006, http://www.afterelton.com/movies/2006/3/affair.html (accessed Aug. 10, 2006).

7. "Tony Curtis," Wikipedia, <http://en.wikipedia.org/wiki/Tony_Curtis> (accessed Aug. 10, 2006).

8. David Carr, "Los Angeles Retains Custody of Oscar," *New York Times,* Mar. 7, 2006.

9. For a full transcript of this Supreme Court decision, please see <http://supct.law.cornell.edu/supct/html/02–102.ZO.html> (accessed Aug. 10, 2006).

10. Salamon.

11. Michael Jensen, "The *Brokeback Mountain* Oscar Snub," Mar. 7, 2006, <http://www.afterelton.com/movies/2006/3/snub.html> (accessed Aug. 10, 2006).

12. Ibid.

13. Roger Ebert, "The Fury of *Crash*-lash," *Chicago Sun-Times*, Mar. 6, 2006, <http://rogerebert.suntimes.com/apps/pbcs.dll/article?AID=/20060306/OSCARS/603070301> (accessed Sept. 17, 2006).

14. Ibid. In *Munich,* screenwriter Tony Kushner implicitly criticizes the state of Israel for its role in prosecuting terrorists as a result of the massacre at the 1972 Summer Olympics.

15. See "Utah Cinema Boots *Brokeback*" on the Canadian Broadcasting Company's news website as reported on Jan. 8, 2006, for a discussion of "Red State" quasi-censorship of *Brokeback Mountain*. <http://www.cbc.ca/story/arts/national/2006/01/08/utah-brokeback.html?ref=rss> (accessed Aug. 10, 2006).

16. Roger Ebert, Review of *Crash, Chicago Sun-Times,* May 5, 2005.

17. Roger Ebert, Review of *Brokeback Mountain, Chicago Sun-Times,* Dec.16, 2005.

18. Mart Crowley, *The Band Plays:* The Boys in the Band *and Its Sequel* The Men from the Boys (Los Angeles: Alyson, 2003), 104

19. Jensen.

20. Information at <http://www.hfpa.org/nominations/index.html> confirms the snub of *Crash* at the Golden Globes (accessed Aug. 10, 2006).

21. Jensen.

22. Ibid.

23. Roos's comment appeared in the "Quote Unquote" column of syndicated gay journalist Rex Wockner in the week following the Mar. 5, 2006, Oscar telecast.

24. In 1969, patrons of the gay Stonewall Inn in New York City's Greenwich Village rioted when police attempted to raid the bar. The Stonewall riots are often seen as the birth of the contemporary gay liberation movement.

25. In this episode, Mary's best friend Rhoda tells landlady and busybody Phyllis that she cannot date Phyllis's brother. Phyllis asks why, implying that Rhoda (for whom Phyllis bears a mild dislike) thinks Phyllis's brother is not good enough for her. When Rhoda responds, "He's gay," Phyllis blurts out, "Thank God!" This episode, "My Brother's Keeper," aired on the CBS television network on Jan.13, 1973. For more information, please see www.mtmshow.com.

26. For a short, succinct discussion of the life and career of Anita Bryant, please see <http://www.nndb.com/people/177/000024105/> (accessed Aug. 10, 2006).

27. Roger Ebert's original review of *Brokeback* on Dec. 16, 2005, features the opening paragraph, "Ennis tells Jack about something he saw as a boy. 'There were two old guys shacked up together. They were the joke of the town, even though they were pretty tough old birds.' One day one of them was found beaten to death. Ennis says, 'My dad made sure me and my brother saw it. For all I know, he did it'" (SP 53).

28. Philip French, *Westerns: Aspects of a Movie Genre* (Manchester, UK: Carcanet, 1973) and *Westerns Revisited* (Manchester, UK: Carcanet, 2005) (same volume), 5.

29. Jens Zimmerman, "Quo: Vadis? Literary Theory beyond Postmodernism," *Christianity and Literature* 53, no. 4 (summer 2004): 495

30. A parallel phenomenon, the "lipstick lesbian," exists among homosexual women.

31. Recently, I sat on a panel for homosexual playwrights. In having to describe the phenomenon of stereotypical homosexual behavior, I stammered and was awkward. Another playwright on the panel looked at me and said, with glorious simplicity, "We know what you mean!" Using "effeminate" to describe the exaggerated performance of the stereotypical homosexual male is probably an inaccurate comparison to the average chromosomal female. Let us understand and accept that, and allow ourselves to use this word "effeminate" (as well as "normal" for the polar opposite) for simplicity and clarity, so that everyone "knows what I mean."

32. Andrew Sullivan, "Da Bears: Behind a Hairy sub-subculture," <http://www.andrewsullivan.com/main_article.php?artnum=20030802> (accessed Sept. 17, 2006). Special thanks go to journalist Rex Wockner for featuring snippets from this article in his regular "Quote Unquote" feature the first week of August, 2003.

33. Camille Paglia, quoted in Sullivan, *Da Bears.*

34. Sullivan.

35. Judith Halberstam, "F2M: The Making of Female Masculinity," in *Literary Theory: An Anthology,* ed. Julie Rivkin and Michael Ryan (Malden, MA: Blackwell, 1998), 759–760

36. Ibid., 760.

37. Quoted in *Hollywood Reporter,* <http://www.hollywoodreporter.com /thr/film/article_display.jsp?vnu_content_ id=1002116228> (accessed Aug. 10, 2006).

11

Whiteness of a Different Kind of Love: Letting Race and Sexuality Talk

by Long T. Bui

It is ironic that *Crash,* a film about tense race relations in Los Angeles, bested *Brokeback Mountain,* a film about two men who fall in love during the Stonewall era, for the 2006 Best Picture Academy Award. The former may be seen as an attempt at salving the lingering enmities of the 1992 L.A. riots while the latter offers a paean to the old Westerns of the past situated within a homoerotic fantasy. In 2005, both works were top contenders for top film prizes in a "maverick" year of political filmmaking that also included *Syriana, Munich, The Constant Gardener, North Country,* and *Good Night, and Good Luck.* Unfortunately, the two films were counterposed in opposition to each other based on "different" subject matter (since one apparently deals with racism while the other homosexuality), and so popular media missed how race and sexuality were central issues in *both* films. Specifically for *Brokeback Mountain,* it contains its own racial motif in the form of whiteness, but this aspect was obscured by the many television junkets, talk show comedians, and weekly magazines that referred to the film as the "gay cowboy movie."

In taking the pastoral life of cowboys as the setting for a gay drama, *Brokeback Mountain* forces a reevaluation of commonplace notions of cowboys. Because the movie is *about* cowboys, it is nearly impossible to ignore precedents Billy the Kid, Wild Bill Hickok, Roy Rogers, Gene Autry, and the Lone Ranger — definitive icons in history and film that solidified the cowboy as a white archetype. Even if it tries to break away from the stereotypical mold of the cowboy by giving it a gay twist, *Brokeback* invokes the standard racial cast of this all–American male hero as white. Indeed, the cowboy as masculine idol speaks to the mythology of American rugged individualism and "pioneering spirit" as well as the larger historical narrative of Anglo-Saxon conquest. As such, films about cowboys, rather than reflecting historic accuracy, serve as popular mediums and vehicles for crystallizing norms about race.[1] In other words, cowboys in popular culture serve to define core American culture and values, to characterize its heroes and villains, and to represent what types of people are central to the U.S. nation-state and what types are not. A popular figure for patriotic heroism, the cowboy is consolidated as "pure white identity."[2] Thus, most do not think of cowboys as Spanish vaqueros (the original cowboys) but as Anglos such as John Wayne and Clint Eastwood, legendary definitive figures in the Western genre.

While racialized as white, cowboys are also gendered and sexualized. According to feminist film theorist Laura Mulvey, films generally position spectators in a "masculine subject position" so as to identify with male characters while the role of women is largely reduced.[3] Western cowboys are part and parcel of a larger male-centered industry that predominately subordinates the presence of women to the omnipotence of men protagonists. For films like *Brokeback Mountain*, the minor role of women in the film plot, production, and promotion allows for a particularly masculinist articulation.[4] Thus, the relegation of women and racial minorities to the sidelines allows for the expression of dominant sociocultural conventions around race, gender, and sexuality.

In line with academic scholarship and criticism on "white studies," "whiteness" refers to that unmarked racial category for a homogeneous Anglo identity.[5] Whiteness in short is a *social* construction that stands for a system of racial power and inequality. As an ideological construct, whiteness places whites at the center of American consciousness through "racializing projects" while minorities are posited at the margins.[6] In this paradigm, blacks, Latinos, Asians, Arabs, and other groups are regarded as having "race" or an "ethnicity" but not whites who are seen as having no racial identity when in fact they actually do — an oversight owing to the inconspicuousness of groups in power. Consequently, the transparency of whiteness inhibits an awareness of "white" as a racial category. Recognizing whiteness entails an understanding of not only racial operations but also sexuality because ascribed racial identities are *always* sexualized and gendered (e.g., the effeminate Asian, the misogynistic Arab). In regards to *Brokeback Mountain*, it does not come off at first as a film about race but, behind its homosexual premise, there is an important message about the symbolic power of whiteness in America as well as a message about oppression of minorities in general. Yet, the popular misreading of *Brokeback Mountain* as solely a "gay thing" keeps in place an epistemological gap between race and homosexuality — two classifications usually seen as totally unrelated. Such a misinterpretation divorces the issue of race from any grounded discussion of sexuality as it renders the existence of white identity inconsequential.

The Whiteness of Queerness

Examining *Brokeback Mountain* through the lens of whiteness, the film can be seen as part of a larger history where whiteness is institutionalized through social representation. In the post–World War II period, television featured cowboy shows like *Bonanza* in conjunction with family sitcoms such as *Leave It to Beaver* to reinforce a view of American culture as monolithically WASPish. In many ways, *Brokeback Mountain* has both a contemporary and nostalgic "feel" to it. The film harks back to the suburban innocence of the baby-boom era and to the Western settlement frontiers fantasized by historian Frederick Jackson Turner. Through cowboy iconography, films like *Brokeback Mountain* retain their function as what Jane Hill calls "white public space"—a "morally significant site for the practices of a racializing hegemony, in which whites are invisibly normal and in which racialized populations are visibly marginal."[7]

At the same time as *Brokeback Mountain* evokes an imagined past for "things that never were," it merges with the current commercialism of gay mass culture.[8] Whereas the fictional story is set during the Stonewall period — a formative period for the coming-of-age consciousness for U.S.-based lesbians, gays, transgenders, and queers — the *Brokeback Mountain* film itself explodes onto a gay scene entrenched within an age of global capitalism. According to Donald Morton, "If in the moment of Stonewall the closet was a set of life-limiting material conditions, in the Reagan years ... it became a space of post-materialist desire, when coming out moved up the social ladder, a moment extending throughout the decade of the 1980's and into the early 1990s." Morton elucidates here the transition from early modes of queer liberation where "coming out" meant joining "a political movement in recognition of the reality of social injustice"[9] to the present-day moment concentrated on the conspicuous consumption and "class habitus" of a gay community seen largely as gentrified and middle-class.[10]

Commodification of queer identity is most visible in U.S. pop culture wherein gays are encoded as privileged whites (an encoding that belies the social complexity and stratification of queer culture). Indeed, the media's celebration of *Brokeback Mountain* follows in the wake of a gay cultural revolution that began in the 1990s marked by the advent of TV shows such as *Will and Grace* and *Queer as Folk*. The currency of those programs made gay cultural products trendy and hip and posed the gay community as having "made it," often at the expense of ignoring the ongoing political battles waged by the LGBT community. Put another way, current representations of "diversity" do not reveal the complex processes of social oppression. Thus according to Sarah Banet-Weiser, "As much as *Brokeback Mountain* (partly) subverts the myth of the cowboy through the inclusion of gay identity, other commercial forms such as advertising and souvenirs offer an opportunity to reflect on how the boundaries of consumer culture are policed and monitored in terms of sexuality."[11] This perspective on gay identity hinders a comprehension of social factors (such as homophobia) which created that identity in the first place and discounts the difficulties of openly gay actors to procure leading roles in Hollywood. The contradictory practice of championing minority groups while continuing to marginalize them continues today so that in the "year of the gay Oscars," many LGBT-related offerings such as *Transamerica* and *Capote* effaced queer people of color at the same time they disavowed real-life struggling *gay* actors in their preference for decidedly heterosexual ones. Historically, none of the Academy Awards given for LGBT roles were played by self-identified queers, including recently Charlize Theron for *Monster*, Philip Seymour Hoffman for *Capote*, Hilary Swank for *Boys Don't Cry*, Tom Hanks for *Philadelphia*, and Liza Minnelli for *Cabaret*.[12]

To be sure, Hollywood yields to the dictates of the milieu in which it is working as much as it militates against social norms. Considering the pervasiveness of homophobia in the U.S., it is not surprising that marketers for *Brokeback Mountain* avoided hyping it explicitly as a gay film (even though that was exactly what it was). Advertisements brokered the movie as "a love story" to a mainstream audience not accustomed to seeing gay cowboys but familiar with seeing white cowboys (all the more reason why a black country music star like Cowboy Troy is such a novelty).

Does Homophobia Beat Out Racism?

Despite this country's ethnic diversity, multicultural ideals run up against the historic image of a white "America" (the land of the Pilgrims). This reality is evident when comparing director Ang Lee's gay cowboy opus to his previous gay drama, *The Wedding Banquet* (*Hsi yen*). Such a comparison shows how race plays disparate functions in demarcating different minority subjects. Whereas *Brokeback*'s white-on-white love evinces a domestic (as in American) love affair, *Banquet*'s white-and-Asian romance projects an "international" liaison if only for the fact that Asian Americans are still usually thought of as "perpetual foreigners" despite having lived in the U.S. for many generations.[13] *The Wedding Banquet* garnered attention as a "foreign film" although most of the dialogue is in English and all of the action takes place entirely in New York City. Even if the 1993 film *Wedding Banquet* was not technically classified as a "foreign" film, it would still be seen as one only because most American audiences do not see a Chinese male protagonist as an "all–American" hero with whom to identify.[14] Gay romances are typically about whites loving whites but if there is an interracial relationship involving an Asian, he/she must have a white lover. It is not unreasonable then to suggest that one potential source for the film's marketability to North American audiences is stereotypes about "rice-potato" (Asian-white) romances — despite all that the film actually presents in contradiction to those assumption. Simply put, *Banquet's* interracial theme acted as the overarching "cultural" lens through which audiences could watch two men in love in which one of them is not your average GWM (gay white male).

In Hollywood, differential markings of race manifest themselves most clearly in casting. Despite the few well-known faces that have supposedly "made it," actors of color (especially those who are not the requisite African American) continue to occupy a peripheral role in the film industry. This marginalization accounts for the tokenism of colored people in film and the frequent charges of racial discrimination by civil rights groups like the NAACP. Given the fact that the leading and featured actors in *Brokeback Mountain* are all white,[15] its racial homogeneity creates what is called *homophily*— the tendency for people to identify affectively with someone who resembles them or appears to have a common ancestry with them (this is opposite to psychological *dissonance* from encountering someone who appears "different"). If the basis for identifying with *Brokeback*'s characters through sexual orientation is not feasible (since not all of the audience are queer or even comfortable with gay simulated sex), the film's whiteness enables the essential homophilia for white viewers to identify with the characters. (Minorities have received the movie in variegated ways.) Whereas *The Wedding Banquet's* popular appeal was tempered by its "foreignness" (and low budget), *Brokeback Mountain's* depiction of a tale of love between two regular white guys who happen to be "gay Americans" made it more receptive to mainstream viewers. Incidentally, the overt addition of an *interracial* element in *Brokeback* would have worked against it as the contentious issue of race would have conflicted with the simple commercial sell of a gay film. Adding race then might possibly fracture its cogent marketing strategy and imbue it with too much perplexity for mass consumption, *even though race was there all along* under the specter of whiteness.

Needless to say, the subject of race doesn't even come up in media discussions about Ang Lee's film since the overarching singular topic of homosexuality hides the work's oblique racial dimensions. This obliviousness conforms to what Morton calls "the Age of Difference" where public attention ... has canceled any sense of the 'common' [for] utterly incommensurate differences."[16] Difference, rather than something that unifies communities, appears to isolate them from one another; thus resulting in the misunderstanding of gay politics as *disparate* from the struggles of racial minorities, especially since race and sexuality are generally strangers in public discourse. Additionally, current gay civil right demands are generally seen as *superceding* racial politics, and this erroneous conception makes it difficult to talk about race in the context of gay rights as the "New Civil Rights" battle.[17]

In the very same year that "It's Hard Out Here for a Pimp" the hip-hop theme song to *Hustle & Flow* won for Best Song, Hollywood producers didn't even consider the radical alternative of making a story about two gay pimps in love — notwithstanding the cliché and stereotype of the pimp. Thus, while *Brokeback Mountain* destroyed the illusion of the macho and always heterosexual cowboy (not a difficult enterprise since the cowboy is already loaded with homosocial possibility), the black male pimp was excluded from the queer treatment because of deeply engrained, stereotypical perceptions about black hyper-heterosexuality (that is, the black stud, the promiscuous black woman). Moreover, homosexual expression in the black community is impeded by social denigration of black same-gender love and the media scrutiny of the "Down-Low" (which in popular culture refers to black men who have both male and female sex partners but keep their sex lives secret).[18] Such impediments restrict a positive gay black identity from surfacing in social consciousness, according to Gary Younge. However, Younge is quick to point out the relevance of *Brokeback* to the black community because it is "a film that sensitively illustrated how even our most intimate human relationships are framed and shaped in no small part by the power, prejudices and conventions of the world around us."[19] Overcoming insurmountable odds, especially those stacked against people who are unable to love whoever they want, remains the universal message of the "gay cowboy" movie. Still, this generative point is not able to insert itself within the ideological trappings of public debate, particularly the one that ensued after *Crash*'s victory over *Brokeback* in the Academy Awards, the fallout from which included highly-charged accusations of homophobia in the film industry that passed over smaller gay triumphs.[20] For many working in the entertainment sector *Crash* provided the "perfect safe harbor" for which the Academy members "could vote for it in good conscience ... and not feel that there was any stain on their liberal credentials for shunning what '*Brokeback*' had to offer." Thus, Hollywood's "liberal" moment in dishonoring racism served as an expedient "cop-out" from supporting homosexuality. Such a view however overlooks the rooted presence of racism in Hollywood and how *Crash* was *also* about *socially unsanctioned* forms of sexual desire (for example, the white cop molests the black woman, the white housewife fears rape around the Latino repairman resembling a gang banger). Likewise, *Brokeback Mountain* is political not just because it is about homosexuality *ipso facto*, but because it disrupts the heterosexual normalcy of *whiteness* in conservative "red" states — a heteronormativity that is implicitly racist because it is antagonistic toward *any* form of diversity. In that regard, the suggestion that racism is a "safe harbor" from homophobia forgets their imbrications: how the two actually overlap.

This overlap is evident when looking at *Crash*, a film which needs to employ racial (and thus sexualized) stereotypes to navigate its mosaic of interracial conflict: black male criminals; bigoted white male cop; shrill, middle-class white suburban housewife; tough, cool-headed city black police chief; successful, light-skinned mulatto couple; diffident, sassy black female bureaucrat officer (her name is Shaniqua!); and the list of trite representations goes on. Ultimately, *Crash's* narration of racial identity (and racism) is able to appear "culturally authentic" only by speaking through gender and sexual stereotypes. Summarily, racial identities are atomized, reduced to caricatures, bounded and fixed.

In this configuration, Los Angeles epitomizes the racialized heterosexism of urban blight inasmuch as Wyoming and Texas (the settings for *Brokeback Mountain*) symbolize idyllic places for unperturbed whiteness. Consequently, the sexual orientation of the black car thieves in *Crash* is not questioned just as the racial identities of *Brokeback's* cowboys are not. Following through with this line of thinking: What if those two carjacking buddies in *Crash* were gay? It's hard to imagine a film about two queer black thugs since media representations of gay African Americans in general are so few and far in between. Moreover, the black homo-thug remains implausible because black men are commonly depicted as *innately* heterosexual. This bears similarity to the manner in which the imagery of the cowboy is wrapped up in its own whiteness. In cultural representation, for cowboys to be gay, those cowboys must somehow *also* be white since in the U.S. gays and cowboys are usually envisaged as white. A gay Anglo cowboy then follows the racial scripts of whiteness even if it breaks from *sexual* scripts for gays (seen as wimpy) and cowboys (seen as hetero)!

Because it examines dominant norms of social behavior, cultural "scripting" is an important concept to consider here. Indeed, a comprehensive apprehension of *Brokeback Mountain's* cultural impact must extend beyond the immediate frame of homosexuality and unearth the role of whiteness and heterosexism in defining social templates. Biased cultural representations makes race incommensurable to homosexuality; when in fact racism suffuses homophobia and heterosexism (the presumption that everyone is or has to be heterosexual). For many racial minorities, their constant struggles against social oppression sometimes forces an acceptance of heterosexism so much so that the admittance of homosexuality as a gay person of color amounts to a betrayal of one's racial community as well as a rejection of ethnic identity. As Cathy Cohen writes, "We have to recognize that a gay sexual identity has been seen in black communities as mitigating one's racial identity and deflating one's community standing."[21] The supposed boundary between gay and ethnic identity stands so firmly that an endorsement of one appears as a negation or disavowal of the other. It is for this reason a gay *black* cowboy film cannot happen because it goes against certain racial scripts (the whiteness of the cowboy figure) as well as sexual scripts (the presumed heterosexuality of African-American identity). Yet, as Cohen observes, this choosing one-or-the-other option is not viable or realistic because racial and sexual identities are not so easily disentangled. They are sometimes one and the same; therefore *cross-cutting* linkages are required to wrestle with this ontological dilemma of self-identity. Moreover, just as people have "multiple identities" across racial, religious, and sexual lines, films possess multiple, sometimes conflicting connotations as clearly shown in *Brokeback* as cinema and as cultural phenomenon. In both its story and its broader impact, the film is so much more than a "gay thing" since it relates to other social conditions such as classism, sexism, familial paternalism, racism, and religious intolerance, but until those conditions are brought to light in public consciousness, the film remains encased in the boundaries of gay whiteness.

Bridging the Race and Sexuality Divide

In summary, the media's presentation of *Brokeback Mountain* as a "gay cowboy film" and *Crash* as a film about racism created barriers to intersectional dialogue on issues of race and homosexuality. This impasse also stems from debates about which movie was "better" — a proxy for the bigger debate on which movie was more *politically* significant in terms of addressing contentious social issues like racism and homophobia. Absent from all the brouhaha was a discussion of what is hidden from our field of vision, what we are all not seeing as a result of just focusing on the movies' *main* themes. Such focus explains the increasing use of *Crash* for teaching about "racism" on college campuses and the utilization of *Brokeback* for gay-related seminars, even though more fruitful discussions and creative insights may be garnered by switching the two so that students of race will look at *Crash* through a queer perspective and *Brokeback* from the vantage point of race and ethnicity. Limiting the broader social meanings of those films — since the former portrays only "racism" while the latter illustrates homophobia — reduces social relations to a superficial level (after all, racism oftentimes bears elements of homophobia and vice versa). The juxtaposition of racism and homophobia as equally similar controversies fails to distinguish among various levels of oppression (for example, discussing racism may be controversial but it is no longer taboo whereas for many, homosexuality still is). All of this then impels a reassessment of public discourse and its social terrains.

If the megalopolis in *Crash* allows us to picture "racialized sexualities" in an urban environ, the mountains of *Brokeback* provide the natural setting for a movie about the alienation of white gays. Racial minorities are metaphorically encased in the segregated enclaves of a Balkanized city like Los Angeles, where they embattle one another in a kind of Southern Californian Yugoslavia; whereas gays find solace and sanctuary and vistas of the outback. Unfortunately, because whiteness in *Brokeback Mountain* and heterosexism in *Crash* go unnoticed, the coterminous relationship between race and sexuality remains indiscernible. Once those dormant things are exposed, however, it is possible to entertain the idea of *Brokeback Mountain* as a film about the racial isolation of whites living in the American hinterlands and *Crash* as a story about racialized sexuality. In the imaginary division between race and homosexuality however these social constructs are cancelled out by one another because of our inattention to people of color as *sexualized* beings and whites as *racialized* subjects. In that regard, the year of *Brokeback Mountain* was not a "breakout" year in "queer film" just as the year when Halle Berry and Denzel Washington received lead statuettes for their respective portrayals of a single-mother super-freak and a shady cop did not "open the door" or create a watershed moment for African Americans in the film industry. Indeed, the very act of declaring "breakout" moments for these two groups ignores a rich history of black influence on queer life as well as queerness on black arts/politics — a history not openly acknowledged because of the way we departmentalize and think of identity.[22] Until there is a critical interrogation of racial minorities as sexualized "queer" subjects and an exploration of the whiteness that shores up Anglo performance (in film, TV, and other media), intersectional understandings of race and sexuality are foreclosed. Despite their admirable critiques of racism and homophobia, *Crash's* heterosexism and *Brokeback's* whiteness are still left unexplored in popular media and discourse. And despite proclamations that these films opened up public dialogue on race and sexuality, many believe that we have not begun to talk about these things through more nuanced angles. So let's give them something to talk about ... how about black thug love?

Notes

1. R. Philip Loy, *Westerns and American Culture, 1930–1955* (Jefferson, N.C.: McFarland, 2001); Andrew Brodie Smith, *Shooting Cowboys and Indians: Silent Western Films, American Culture, and the Birth of Hollywood* (Boulder: University Press of Colorado, 2003); Scott Simmon,

The Invention of the Western Film: A Cultural History of the Genre's First Half-Century (Cambridge, UK: Cambridge University Press, 2003); Dan Moos, *Outside America: Race, Ethnicity, and the Role of the American West in National Belonging* (Hanover, N.H.: Dartmouth College Press, 2005); Arnoldo De León, *Racial Frontiers: Africans, Chinese, and Mexicans in Western America, 1848–1890* (Albuquerque: University of New Mexico Press, 2002).

2. Quoted in Shirley Geok-lin Lim, "Gender Transformation in Asian/American Representations," in *Gender and Culture in Literature and Film East and West: Issues of Perception and Interpretation*, ed. Nitaya Masavisut, George Simson, and Larry E. Smith (Honolulu: University of Hawaii Press, 1994), 77. See original in Alexander Saxton, "The Racial Trajectory of the Western Hero" *Amerasia Journal* 2, no. 11 (Fall-Winter 1984): 67–79.

3. Laura Mulvey, "Visual Pleasure and Narrative Cinema," *Screen* 16, no. 3 (1975): 6–13.

4. Once the film hit mainstream attention, however, the promotional campaign began to utilize its female actresses more and more in posters and photos in order to attract a wider audience.

5. Matthew Frye Jacobson, *Whiteness of a Different Color: European Immigrants and the Alchemy of Race* (Cambridge, Mass: Harvard University Press, 1998); Noel Ignatiev, *How the Irish Became White: Race and the Making of the American Working Class* (New York: Routledge, 1995); George Lipsitz, *The Possessive Investment in Whiteness: How White People Profit from Identity Politics* (Temple University Press, 1998); David R. Roediger, *The Wages of Whiteness: Race and the Making of the American Working Class* (New York: Verso, 1991).

6. Racial formation is defined as "the sociohistorical process by which racial categories are created, inhabited, transformed, and destroyed ... a process of historically situated projects in which human bodies and social structures are represented and organized." Altogether, racial projects are those institutional and social forces that construct, institute, and promulgate racial categories. See Michael Omi and Howard Winant, *Racial Formation in the United States: From the 1960s to the 1980s* (New York: Routledge, 1994), 55–57.

7. Jane H. Hill, "Language, Race, and White Public Space," *Contemporary Issues Forum, American Anthropologist* 100, no. 3 (1998): 682.

8. Arjun Appadurai, *Modernity at Large: Cultural Dimensions of Globalization* (Minneapolis: University of Minnesota Press: 1996), 77.

9. Donald Morton, "Pataphysics of the Closet," in *Marxism, Queer Theory, Gender*, ed. M. Zavarzadeh, Theresa L. Ebert, and Donald Morton (Red Factory: New York, 2001), 15–17. These days what sometimes passes as civil rights victories come in the form of commercial benefits, social concessions, and advertising products from major companies who merely target gays and lesbians as a viable and lucrative consumer market.

10. Pierre Bourdieu defines habitus as the "system of acquired dispositions" that function as principles of organizing action, in which embodied practices are sedimented onto the individual from cultural institutions and social conditions; see Bourdieu, *The Logic of Practice* (Cambridge, UK: Polity, 1990), 58. Class habitus then is the particular adopted and embodied modes of taste, preference, sensibility, and body language corresponding to the historically contingent expectations, adaptations, and operationalized social rules of a class. Bourdieu's discussion of "social classes" of course does not neatly align with the specificity of American queer/racial culture but there are generative insights to be gained from Bourdieu's work on domination, capital, culture, and aesthetics. See also Bourdieu, *Distinction: A Social Critique of the Judgment of Taste* (Cambridge, Mass.: Harvard University Press, 1984).

11. Sarah Banet-Weiser, "The Business of Representing," *American Quarterly* 58, no. 2 (2006): 496.

12. Sir Ian McKellan, possibly the most famous gay actor in the world, says, "It is very, very, very difficult for an American actor who wants a film career to be open about his sexuality ... and even more difficult for a woman if she's lesbian. It's very distressing to me that that should be the case." See "Hollywood Resists Gay US actors," *BBCnews.com*, Feb. 12, 2006, <http://news.bbc.co.uk/2/hi/entertainment/4706092.stm> (accessed Aug. 18, 2006).

13. Ronald T. Takaki, *A Different Mirror: A History of Multicultural America* (Boston: Little, Brown, 1993).

14. Well-known "Asian American" male actors like Russell Wong are of mixed ancestry

with Caucasian features, and Asia-imported actors like Jackie Chan and Jet Li obviously fill America's narrow niche for Kung-Fu action, but in general, these actors are not seen as sexually appealing for American audiences.

15. In *Brokeback Mountain* the only speaking non-white characters in the film are the Basque servant who delivers supplies and the Mexican street hustler — two stereotypical roles for racial minorities.

16. Morton, 14.

17. The advent of the modern gay movement dates back to the time of Black Power during the late 1960s and continues to draw inspiration from it. In this regard, the fight for gay rights is not a new civil rights movement but because the issue of same-sex marriage is a contemporary hot topic that appears in the post–civil rights era, many people, especially in the conservative parts of the African American community, feel gays are inappropriately appropriating the struggles for equality for blacks. See *Daisy Hernandez*, "Gaily Ever After: Is gay marriage the new civil rights struggle or has it co-opted a legacy?" *Colorlines Magazine: Race, Action, Culture (Fall 2004)*.

18. "Down-low" men do not identify with a gay identity and might instead call themselves bisexual, sometimes out of internalized homophobia. Gary Younge however expands the semantic meaning of "down-low" by describing *Brokeback Mountain* as a film about "the down-low up high in the hills." See Younge, "Why There Will Never Be a Black Brokeback Mountain," *The Guardian*, Jan. 23, 2006, <http://film.guardian.co.uk/features/featurepages/0..1692 946,00.html> (accessed Aug. 18, 2006).

19. Ibid.

20. There was of course Logo, the first gay cable station on TV. For the Academy Awards, there is no consensus on why underdog *Crash* beat out forerunner *Brokeback Mountain* for Best Picture, especially in various awards shows leading up to the Academy Awards. Many observers, including Annie Proulx herself, have cited the generally conservative character and age of the Academy's voters or general homophobia in Hollywood but there are still too many conspiracy theories around this issue to reach a firm conclusion. Roger Ebert points out that the single-minded battle over best picture may be more about ideology than genuine sentiment as few people talked about the implications of Felicity Huffman's loss for lead actress (when she won for that same role in the Golden Globes) or Philip Seymour Hoffman's win. His contention that *Crash* is a better movie than *Brokeback* however is questionable and underestimates the level of homophobia extant in society. See Ebert, "The Fury of the 'Crash'-lash," *Chicago Sun-Times*, Mar. 6, 2006.

21. Cathy Cohen, *The Boundaries of Blackness: AIDS and the Breakdown of Black Politics* (Chicago: University of Chicago Press, 1999), 14.

22. Examples of cross-influence between the gay movement and the civil rights movement are too numerous to list fully but some major leading figures of this interaction include James Baldwin, Bayard Rustin, Alice Walker, Robert Mapplethorpe, Audre Lorde, Barbara Smith, Little Richard, Grace Jones, Billie Holiday, and Bessie Smith.

ACKNOWLEDGMENTS: *The author would like to thank Ana Celia Zentella for ideas generated in this paper and Carol Vu and Viet Le for proofreading this paper and offering helpful comments as well as Jim Stacy and the anonymous readers who read this piece.*— Long T. Bui

12

The Queerness of Country: *Brokeback*'s Soundscape

by Noah Tsika

In a movie largely responsive to the complexity of the queer experience, no song encourages the survival of same-sex, socially objectionable romantic relationships quite like "A Love That Will Never Grow Old," by Gustavo Santaolalla and Bernie Taupin. Sung in the film by a prominent recording artist, Emmylou Harris, who gives a female (though not necessarily straight) voice to the lyrics, the song can seem, like a number of others in *Brokeback Mountain*, to effectively "side" with one of the film's pair of male homosexual lovers. On the face of it, "A Love That Will Never Grow Old" would seem to speak for Jack Twist (Jake Gyllenhaal), the poignantly optimistic ex-rodeo rider in love with the largely fearful, chronically reticent Ennis del Mar (Heath Ledger). But on reflection the song, uniquely among the majority of ballads on the movie's soundtrack, works to affirm, on the one hand, the youthful optimism of Jack Twist while pointing toward another, intractable and adamantine response to social prejudice — a brave response neither man shares: who gives a toss about bigotry? When we're together, we're free.

If the movie is a romance, so is the song. It speaks more for the spectator, living presumably safely in the early years of the "enlightened" twenty-first century, than it does for either of the film's paired men (though Jack in all his blind yearning is more readily accommodating an "heir" of the song than Ennis, who infrequently speaks; for the record, neither says "love"). "A Love That Will Never Grow Old" is not *their* song, but the spectator's. One of the fascinating aspects of *Brokeback*'s song track is that it creates — verbally determines — an atmosphere of classical romance around these boys (and eventual men) who cannot, for a whole host of reasons — and quite literally — speak the language of love. "A Love That Will Never Grow Old," one of five songs written expressly for the film, works doggedly to prove love *can* overcome social obstacles, provided both lovers maintain faith in one another and in the basic nature of romantic attachment. So is it ironic, incongruous? In the context of Ennis del Mar's not unfounded paranoia and Jack Twist's paradoxical wordy inability to impart (the more he speaks, the less Ennis listens), it *is* a peculiar, if not quite mocking, song. And yet, watching the film, the spectator can scarcely hear it.

Brokeback's bestselling soundtrack album is thus the outstanding showcase for "A Love That Will Never Grow Old." On its own terms, the song was not a "hit" by industry standards and was not released as a single. It gained little if any radio play and won its only major award (Best Original Song) at the 2006 Golden Globes. Very much standing as an addendum to the movie, the song "corrects" the hopelessness of the movie's leading men and seeks perhaps to erase the loss they suffer, that of enduring love (its most observable achievement being, in fact, the adding-on of that single word — *love*). It is steadfast, an unwavering recounting of perilous romance; its heartening espousal of pure love gains ironic significance from being so inaudible a part of the movie's soundtrack and story world. It is a classically decisive love song, important for having been written in response to a queer text; that it doesn't figure prominently is cause for, not alarm, but bewilderment. Establishing trust as the foundation for any relationship and suggesting that a *Walden*-esque social isolation is preferable to city living, the lyrics advocate a somewhat simplistic, though hardly flippant, denial of extensive intolerance: if you and I can find one another, what's wrong with the world? This is precisely the viewpoint Ennis eschews while Jack only feebly argues the case. Both understand their country to be a nasty place where queer-killers abound, but it is questionable whether the self-loathing Ennis recognizes this as a bad thing — he wants only to avoid it, his own murder; Jack's encounter with a hateful crowd at a Texas pool hall is another reminder, that men are cruel and can betray their own. Hardly apolitical, "A Love" offers a politics of hatred of the discriminatory wider world.

The song suggests both Jack's tender hope of a better tomorrow as well as a more defiant reaction to social pressure that both men see as impossible to achieve, Ennis for being at the mercy of prevailing structures of western capitalism and Jack for being subordinate to the anxious Ennis. Significantly, "A Love That Will Never Grow Old," which Santaolalla wrote expressly for *Brokeback Mountain* and which Focus Features, the film's distributor, isolated for Oscar consideration as Best Original Song, does not figure prominently in the film. Scarcely audible, the song exists within the diegetic "story world" of *Brokeback Mountain*, linked as it is to the visualized source of a car radio: a faint, vaguely sad anthem that accompanies Jack's tearful ride away from

Ennis and to Mexico and other men. The somewhat veiled presentation of this lyrically, queerly complex song, coupled with its realistic or vérité use within the film, indicates the significance of the soundscape of *Brokeback Mountain*. Complicating or extending the function of compiled scores in such "new wave" American movies as *Five Easy Pieces* (Bob Rafelson, 1970), *The Last Picture Show* (Peter Bogdanovich, 1971), and *Nashville* (Robert Altman, 1975), *Brokeback Mountain* performs an acoustic juggling act, giving equal thematic weight to the "leitmotif" of Santaolalla's traditional through-score and the pop familiarity of roughly a dozen country, folk, and rock songs.

One Sings, the Other Doesn't

This essay examines the significance of popular music to the specifically queer task of *Brokeback Mountain*, suggesting the innately queer-receptive nature of its compiled score. Roger Miller's hymn to hobo freedom, "King of the Road," celebrates Jack's itinerant actions, his willingness to drop everything and join Ennis in Wyoming. Contemporary ballads like Rufus Wainwright's "The Maker Makes" reveal the blinkered refusal of the culture at large to acknowledge the plainly romantic nature of Ennis and Jack's relationship: an allegorical ballad about breaking cruelly wrought chains, it acknowledges the "two steps forward, one step back" aspect of any social growth movement. Such songs work not in opposition to Santaolalla's traditional instrumental score but extend through language that score's sometimes celebratory, sometimes cautious or ambivalent response to the queerness of the film's central couple. If both sonic categories are born of and/or comment on the queer experience, both also announce the likelihood of heartbreak and loss, and acknowledge the gradual acceptance of powerlessness that is part of the queer subject's social maturation. Just as the through-score commences with the motivating musical concept of pastoral harmony, of hope, it ends in the heavy, guitar-based sound of defeat. If the male subject of one song is "king of the road," the subject of another—Bob Dylan's "He Was a Friend of Mine"—dies on the road.

Not by chance, both *Brokeback* protagonists demonstrate divergent approaches to sound (the spoken word) and music: Jack plays the harmonica and is convivial, gregarious; Ennis cheers the loss of said harmonica and favors silence.[1] The film itself is alert to the importance of music as not only meaningful commentary but also "filler"—something that is per expectation for any mainstream narrative film but that assumes added significance given the periodic crises of expression of the movie's nervous male lovers. In a 1929 essay for *The Musical Quarterly*, Harry Alan Potamkin argued, "There is no *absolute* justification for the use of music to accompany ... film," but noted, "For the

LIVERPOOL JOHN MOORES UNIVERSITY
LEARNING SERVICES

western audience, accustomed to the music of the organ or the orchestra, the absence of music would ... prove ominous and even terrifying."[2] *Brokeback Mountain*, by periodically containing its protagonists within the remote geographical space of high-elevation Wyoming, distills the human essence of just such an argument. Adapted to country-western dirges and the hymns of the Pentecostal church, Jack, rather than succumb to Ennis' speechlessness, compensates, albeit clumsily, by making music. The film itself compensates, or simply evades ominous silence, with Santaolalla's Oscar-winning musical score, which plays over high-angle shots of the mountain, as a bridge between certain scenes, and during moments of montage.

Some mainstream American films have contrastingly figured the absence of a traditional soundtrack of extra-diegetic music as a way of heightening suspense, as in the nuclear-disaster thriller *The China Syndrome* (James Bridges, 1979). Peter Bogdanovich's *The Last Picture Show*, based on a novel and co-scripted by Larry McMurtry, famously used songs by Hank Williams and Pee Wee Smith, but only as diegetic radio music controlled by the characters. *Brokeback Mountain* partly follows *The Last Picture Show*'s use of diegetic recordings, as "The Devil's Right Hand" (Steve Earle), "No One's Gonna Love You Like Me" (Mary McBride), and "It's So Easy" (Linda Ronstadt) are introduced on saloon jukeboxes, while "A Love That Will Never Grow Old" plays on a car radio. Otherwise the movie makes use of a traditional prevailing music track of string and wind instruments, used to score the natural splendor of the mountain and to reinforce the underlying structure of bathos of queer defeat. But as Daniel Mendelsohn has pointed out, in one of the movie's scenes, silent but for the whispering of the distant wind, the absence of extra-diegetic music emphasizes, as in the suspense narrative of *The China Syndrome*, the suggestion of imminent disaster: Joe Aguirre (Randy Quaid), the boss of the shepherding venture, is using binoculars to spy on Ennis and Jack, and the menacing silence points to the threat of queer exposure, a threat the men will spend the rest of their lives hoping to sidestep.[3] Significantly, though, before the commencement of the love affair, it is Jack who recognizes the ominousness of Ennis's silence and who seeks refuge through melody.[4]

As the men move higher up the mountain to settle on new pastures, the threat of silence seemingly becomes too constant for Jack to bear, as after posing a question he typically receives, from Ennis, little more than a shrug or a grunt. As Potamkin observed: "Profound silence demands too much of the human species, western style."[5] But silence is comfort for Ennis, either the effortless comfort of a naturally taciturn man or the strenuously achieved comfort of a homosexual pining to embody the strong-silent myth of the Western "hero." After pitching a new camp, Jack removes from his pocket a somewhat damaged, rusty old harmonica, and plays the instrument with all the crassness and intensity of a boisterous child in a school solo. Such musical incompetence would seem to exist in opposition to Jack's actual tender feelings for the instrument, which he keeps tucked close to his body, seemingly at all times—a constant promise of safety from silence. The harmonica itself, its musical classification, is significant: A free reed wind instrument, sometimes known as a mouth organ, the harmonica, to make music, requires the verbal silencing of the musician. Jack cannot verbally accompany his own playing of the harmonica (as would potentially be the case with a guitar), and so exchanges his nervous loquaciousness for music poorly played. When Ennis, turned off by the noise, comments that the harmonica "don't sound quite right," Jack explains that it "got kinda flattened" when his mare threw him. Ennis, in response, announces his thorough displeasure over the tenor of Jack's "music," but evokes also the beginnings of romance or attraction: "If I was lucky, that harmonica woulda broke in two." Such a statement, and Ennis' buoyant tone and roguish smile that accompany it, suggest a common courtship routine, the love lyric that often comes enclosed in ridicule.

After a temporal leap foregrounding both the calmness of the mountain and the evening idleness that comes with being a shepherd, Jack, to fill the silence (and perhaps to deflate or deflect some of his amorous energy), howls a Pentecostal hymn, "Water Walking Jesus," with lyrics that evoke Christ, and an unnamed subject who asks to be spared life on this earth for existence in heaven with God.[6] The performing of the song gives way to a touchingly confused discussion of religion, as Jack, to explain "Water Walking Jesus," affirms, "My mama, she believes in the Pentecost." But when asked to elucidate the Pentecost, Jack cannot come up with an answer because "Mama never explained it. I guess it's when the world ends and fellas like you and me march off to hell." If this equivocal belief in hell as the place to which Jack and Ennis belong stands in stark contrast to "Water Walking Jesus" and its promise of an assured route to heaven, it also, and gloomily, signals at least Jack's consciousness of the pair's incipient homosexual desires. Having already, and visibly, lusted after Ennis, Jack has already committed a sin the punishment for which is nothing less than a "march off to hell," according to the stringent edicts of the Pentecostal church. Though Ennis claims he "ain't yet had the opportunity," Jack in predicting a hell-bound path for both men predicts also the fulfillment of Ennis's (assumed) homosexual desires.

Men in Jeopardy: The High Cost of Country Songs

The acceptance of human finitude in the lyrics of "Water Walking Jesus" points to the causal elements of despair—the obsession with death, broken

or crumbling marriages, poor health, and impoverishment — of much of country music. If such "new wave" American films as *Five Easy Pieces* and *Nashville*
approached the perceived "hokum" of country music critically, disdaining its
god-fearing sentimentality and fixation on hardship (Timothy Brown's "blue-
bird," in *Nashville*, has neither money nor kin), then *Brokeback Mountain*
contrastingly reclaims as case-hardened, even objective, the gloom of this
musical tradition, and positions it as queer. Recent leftist films such as Barry
Levinson's *Wag the Dog* (1997) have argued for the falsifying nature of country music, while those films that can seem to celebrate country are typically
biographical movies like James Mangold's *Walk the Line* (2005).[7] *Brokeback
Mountain* is unique (for a non-musical) not merely in diegetically privileging a compiled score of assorted country songs, but in aggressively linking the
fatalism of country music to that of the disconsolate, doubting Ennis del
Mar — which is to say, to an aspect of the collective queer experience.

    If the narrative of the film is open-ended at least in relation to the
offscreen demise of Jack Twist, then it is worth pointing out that his death
may have been achieved through suicide — and a suicidal temperament certainly has a place within country music's framework of despair. A 1983 study
linked gender-role nonconformity to social isolation and suicide, arguing that
closeted gay men were among the most likely to commit the act.[8] Jack, who
dies in 1983, can for some spectators represent but one such case. Annie
Proulx, the author of the original story, explains in her essay "Getting
Movied": "Wyoming has the highest suicide rate in the country, and ... the
preponderance of those people who kill themselves are elderly single men."[9]
It is not the purpose of this essay to "fill in" the narrative gaps of *Brokeback
Mountain* or to argue for the unequivocal cause of Jack's death (mediating,
as it were, the contradictory, perhaps equally apocryphal accounts of Ennis
and Lureen). But the potentially suicidal nature of the film's male protagonists (not to mention Ennis's own fear of the pair "inviting" death through
their queer visibility) emerges as consonant with the self-effacing and heart-
rending force of country music. A 1992 study assessed the link between country music and metropolitan suicide rates, arguing that "the greater the airtime
devoted to country music, the greater the white suicide rate," noting that
"[c]ountry music is hypothesized to nurture a suicidal mood through its concerns with problems common in the suicidal population, such as marital discord, alcohol abuse, and alienation from work."[10]

    Certainly Ennis del Mar is throughout the film engaged in a kind of sui-
cide, the disastrous self-sabotage of denying authentic love. Moreover, he is
a drinker, unhappily and irregularly employed, and the product of a broken
marriage. He seems to find resonance in the music and lyrics of certain country
songs, which have the effect of restating the finer points of his own privation.

Bobby Braddock and Curly Putman's "D-I-V-O-R-C-E," which Ennis pays to hear on a restaurant jukebox, narrates a woman's recognition of the futility of "talking through" her emotional pain. Explicating in plain language her romantic tribulations, she yet has wet cheeks and an aching heart; it doesn't work, such talk — the heart is at best illiterate, untaught of everything the brain in its cleverness can literally spell out. As sung by Tammy Wynette, the song comes to support Ennis del Mar's discretion in not talking about his pain (a marker of his "manliness," his Western authenticity, which counterbalances Jack's comparatively brainy speech), and so works to further disconnect the two men, as two "types." Jack in accusatory disputes with Ennis does spell out his discontent, channeling the whole of his hurt, and represents a more Eastern, certainly a more gender-deviant and loquacious kind of homosexual (the negative stereotype of the fey chatterbox), though he too consents to the Western (and Southwestern) consistency of country music as a repository of heartache.[11]

Significantly, the 1992 study of the effect of country music on suicide, which was published in *Social Forces*, emphasizes "airtime," or the incidence of death-obsessed or simply melancholic recordings on country-based radio playlists. If Jack and Ennis, closeted queers, are already at risk of suicide, then their paying for (via jukeboxes) and tuning to (via car radios) a whole host of largely despondent songs seems especially hazardous. In terms of the larger task of the movie, however, the licensing of a credible "playlist" of diegetic country songs points to an erratic reliance on sonic realism, one that has the added task of denying country music's typical pronouncement of conservative American "values" (within which even marital discord, for simply suggesting the connubial basis for the nuclear family, belongs). For if Jack and Ennis can be counted as fans of country music, then *Brokeback Mountain* has effectively repositioned that music as compellingly resonant with the queer subculture. As their "cowboy" accoutrements — and the fact of their being butch laborers — help Jack and Ennis to queer the icons of the (deceptively) conservative American West, so their trust in country music, in Roger Miller and Tammy Wynette, allows for the queering of (again, deceptively) conservative musical traditions.[12] Just as Jack and Ennis are predictably, not loudly or overtly sexily, dressed, the soundscape of their everyday lives — and the soundscape of the movie in general — is subtle, typically clearly motivated, and meaningful for being so familiar.

The film historian Gerald Mast has observed that, in accordance with an emergent vérité aesthetic, such early-seventies realist films as *Mean Streets* (Martin Scorsese, 1973), *American Graffiti* (George Lucas, 1973), and *Dog Day Afternoon* (Sidney Lumet, 1975) exclusively used recorded music that was "clearly [diegetically] motivated (i.e., playing on a radio or record player nearby)," the better to contain the spectator within a structure of uncompromising realism.[13] *Mean Streets* featured as its characters' jukebox favorites such popular songs as The Marvelettes' "Please Mr. Postman" and The Rolling Stones' "Jumpin' Jack Flash," while *American Graffiti*, a retrospective account of sixties teen culture ("Where were you in '62?"), portrayed characters who happily tune their car dials to a number of period songs, among them The Regents' "Barbara Anne" and Buster Brown's "Fannie Mae." Julie Hubbert has explicitly linked this treatment of music to the policy of "source music only" of such celebrated vérité documentaries as 1969's *Salesman* (Charlotte Zwerin and Albert and David Maysles), as well as the more observably influential pop-rock documentaries *Woodstock* (Mike Wadleigh, 1970) and *Monterey Pop* (D.A. Pennebaker, 1968).[14]

While Bogdanovich researched pop-chart archives in an effort to give *The Last Picture Show* a wholly realistic diegetic soundtrack of 1951's most widely played hits,[15] *Brokeback Mountain* mixes vaguely credible jukebox music only faintly contemporaneous with the setting of certain scenes (Steve Earle's "The Devil's Right Hand," which first appeared on Earle's 1988 album *Copperhead Road*, plays during a scene set in the early eighties) with songs written in 2005 by Gustavo Santaolalla, including "No One's Gonna Love You Like Me," which plays on a jukebox in a scene set in the mid-'60s. This use of contemporary music to underscore period settings is not, however, wholly flagrant for the convincing resonance of some of the lyrics with those of actual period songs ("No One's Gonna Love You Like Me," to take one example, blends the dirge-like musical simplicity of certain of Bob Dylan's early recordings, like 1964's "My Back Pages" and "All I Really Want to Do," with the self-selling lyrical structure of positive avowal of Loretta Lynn's "You Ain't Woman Enough," first recorded in 1966). Importantly, *Brokeback Mountain's* presentation of contemporary songs at least accords with the strict vérité use of "source music only" in some of the movie's tonal antecedents, such as *The Last Picture Show*.

Brokeback Mountain forges a realist aesthetic in part by visualizing the sources of a number of its songs. In addition to the abovementioned juxebox examples, the Spanish-language "Quizás, Quizás, Quizás"[16] ambiguously originates from the Mexican setting of Jack's barrio-brothel of choice, while "King of the Road" plays on Jack's car radio. In the latter case, the contemporary and entirely extra-textual star discourses of Teddy Thompson and Rufus Wainwright, who here perform the song, are partly concealed by Jack's singing along, so that the "star text" of this cover matters less than Jack's echoing the lyrics. Significantly in terms of queer representation, *Brokeback Mountain* employs a compiled score of diegetically motivated popular songs, the better to encase the central gay relationship in a familiar and acceptable musical tradition.

Moreover, it depicts queer characters who authorize the use of pop songs, as Jack gleefully tunes to "King of the Road" while Ennis, gloomily committed to the typically melancholic nature of country music, pays to hear Tammy Wynette sing "D-I-V-O-R-C-E." The exceptions to this sonic structure of realism include, of course, Santaolalla's overlaying orchestral score, but also the closing-credit use of two "sourceless" (and obdurately queer-inflected) contemporary recordings, Willie Nelson's cover of Bob Dylan's "He Was a Friend of Mine," and Rufus Wainwright's "The Maker Makes." *The Last Picture Show* similarly closed with a nondiegetic recoding — a reprise of Hank Williams' "Why Don't You Love Me (Like You Used to Do)," which had earlier played on a car radio — but further complicated or reneged on its promise of strict realism with the use of a Wellesian credit sequence consisting of clips of the actors and their superimposed names.

In *Brokeback Mountain*, the lyrics of both "He Was a Friend of Mine" and "The Maker Makes," partly by virtue of their privileged extra-diegetic presentation, comment on the themes of the movie. The Bob Dylan song reflects both the peripatetic nature of the deceased Jack (the roving subject of the song is dead on the road) as well as the class trappings of Ennis (he's poor, too, and profoundly dissatisfied), just as it helps to position *Brokeback Mountain* as a melodrama by encouraging a tearful response (the remembering "narrator" of the song, always able to recall the dead man, can't help but cry every time). In addition, the song can seem, on the one hand, to support a subtly queer-oppressive approach to the terms of the film, as "friend" in the context of a homosexual love affair can appear a badly chosen word (taking the place of "lover": "He Was a Lover of Mine"), a euphemism to elide the true (sexual) nature of the central romance. On the other it can seem a tacit exposure of the cowardice of just such an approach (in which case it is a deliberately ironic song, one actually *about* the use of euphemism — not unthinkable given that it was written by Bob Dylan). On the simplest of levels, the lyrics of "He Was a Friend of Mine," and the fact of its being sung by a man, work to affirm the affable, compatible basis of the love affair of Ennis and Jack, who begin as friends, without naming as romantic or sexual the social union of two men.

In contrast, "A Love That Will Never Grow Old" makes a bid for the acceptability of queer desire not merely through its lyrics (the "narrating" lover acclaims the other's eyes and laughter) but also by enlisting the singer Emmylou Harris, herself familiar to at least the boomers making up a fraction of the *Brokeback Mountain* audience and recognizable to others as evincing the spirit of country music. Both "A Love" and, to a lesser extent, "The Maker Makes" work to inspire empathy among a diverse audience by extending the popular concept of undying love to include even closeted homosexual men. As the showpiece number singled out for the Academy's Best Original Song category, "A Love That Will Never Grow Old" was initially positioned as the film's representative anthem, and while it was named Best Song at the 2006 Golden Globes ceremony, its muted presence in the film itself ultimately barred "A Love" from Oscar consideration, suggesting a self-sabotaging ambivalence on the part of filmmakers unsure of how to prominently figure a hymn to queer acceptability. Santaolalla's through-score, however, did win the Oscar. Traditional instrumental film scores tend to function with a central and recurring musical concept — typically a short melody suggesting linear continuity — that may be associated with a specific character.[17] In the case of *Brokeback Mountain*, that concept is somber, guitar-based, and largely pessimistic — and thus tied to both leading men. Its deviations, as in brief, one-note piano interludes, are only minimally divergent for growing out of and invariably returning to the ominous nature of the central sonic theme. It is possible to interpret these interludes as the musical equivalent of closeted homosexuality, speaking up for itself only briefly and between bouts of disastrous correspondence with the vastly queer-oppressive larger world. Furthermore, the cross-fading of ominous and cheerful musical strains signifies Ennis and Jack's wavering responses to the experience of anal sex. The film's immediate postcoital scene, which follows a temporal shift from night to morning, is silent: groggy and foggy-eyed, Ennis rises to glimpse the still sleeping Jack, whom he's only recently fucked. Exiting the tent, Ennis awakens Jack, who follows. Both men remain silent, and as Ennis mounts a horse and rides back to the herd of sheep, the ominous underscore, which mixes with the rumbling of distant thunder, gives a sense of what both men are feeling, namely dread at having to face the consequences of anal intercourse.

Brokeback Mountain, a mainstream film, is yet deliberately queer both in terms of its narrative and its style, particularly with respect to its soundscape. If Santaolalla's through-score follows classical Hollywood practice for so aggressively signifying the specific emotional landscape of the movie, it yet works in combination with a number of country and rock songs to convey what is pointedly queer about the depiction of desire in *Brokeback Mountain*. Like the instrumental underscore, these songs are highly attentive to the authentic moods and actual social positions of the principal characters, and work both emotively in relation to Ennis and Jack, and ironically in relation to certain of the film's female characters.

Country Music: Cruel to Women?

Acoustically, *Brokeback Mountain* shifts between hope and heartbreak, hitting very few notes in between: cheerful rock songs ("It's So Easy," "The

Devil's Right Hand") give way to gloomy folk ballads ("He Was a Friend of Mine," "The Maker Makes"), just as the Santaolalla score, largely guitar-based, evokes either menace, the queer's fear of violent reprisal, or romantic comfort, the calm of coupling. Collectively, such compositions form the sound color of Ennis and Jack's queer experience of the American West, and convincingly make a case for the true binary nature of queer everyday life, the queer subject's passing from peril to shelter and back again, or from self-acceptance to self-loathing. *Brokeback Mountain*, by employing both a wide variety of popular songs and a traditional instrumental score, uses its soundtrack to highlight the complicated nature of not only Ennis and Jack's individual responses to queer desire, but also those of the film's straight spousal females, Ennis's wife Alma and Jack's wife Lureen. Along these lines, "No One's Gonna Love You Like Me," a slow song that plays in an early barroom scene, can seem with its very title to speak not only for the emotive Jack, tragically in love with Ennis, but also for Alma and Lureen, both unrequited in their spousal affection, and convinced for a time of the monogamous nature of both marriages.

Sung by Mary McBride (herself the diegetic source of the song), "No One's Gonna Love You Like Me" is introduced by a band playing live at the bar-and-dancehall where Jack and Lureen meet. On stage, a singer (McBride) is crooning in long shot. Below her, on the dance floor, Jack and Lureen have joined for a slow waltz. The opening lyrics affirm what the mutually starry-eyed pair appears to be feeling at this very moment: that they're made for each other. This is Jack and Lureen's first dance, and seemingly the beginning of romance. Both are smiling, she gawking up at him and he gazing steadily down at her, and both move to the beat of the song. While this is initially an excellent example of *Brokeback*'s at times strict vérité use of diegetically motivated music (as in the case of "A Love That Will Never Grow Old"), "No One's Gonna Love You Like Me" actually extends across a cut (to the new lovers driving off in Lureen's 1966 convertible) and becomes nondiegetic. Besides breaking the promise of complete acoustic realism, the effect of this sonic extension, the ballad's playing across two distinct scenes, is to support an "objective" point of view. Since Jack and Lureen are no longer listening to the song (though we in the audience still hear it), the lyrics more ruthlessly comment on the irony of their situation — that of a straight woman blind to the queerness of the man she's "gonna love." This audio/visual dissolve heightens the lyrical involvement of one character (Lureen) at the expense of another (Jack). He knows what she does not: that the lyrics, which argue for the rareness of "the only love that's coming through," are, while true to his own experience of Ennis del Mar, pointedly false to Lureen's initially naïve connection to Jack as his one and only. Significantly, the movie's songs of love work to highlight the exceptional nature of "true love" in relation to Jack and Ennis, but in relation to the female characters the songs can seem laughable. Knowing what we know about Jack's homosexual experience, Lureen's appearing to speak the language of the McBride song ("No One's Gonna Love You Like Me") in the face of the closeted queer object of her desire suggests a somewhat misogynistic, or at least cruelly ironic, approach to the initial lack of awareness of the film's female characters.

While Lureen seems, even at this early stage, capable of loving him passionately, she is not the only such lover for Jack. Having known Ennis sexually and, later, romantically, having internalized the bliss of their quixotic "one-shot thing," Jack's mere presence in this scene makes "No One's Gonna Love You Like Me" seem almost comically misguided as an expression of straight female desire (which, in this case, is bound for ultimate distress and disillusionment). A brief temporal advance depicts the two making love in the backseat of Lureen's car. As if to emphasize the farce of Lureen's reckless sexual eagerness ("You don't think I'm too fast, do you?"), the soundtrack, diminishing the strains of the McBride song, fills at once with the indeterminate and droning language of a Texas talk show to which Lureen's radio is tuned. The cross-fading of "No One's Gonna Love You Like Me," which fades out, and the radio show, which fades in, gives the impression that neither Jack nor Lureen is interested in making this a romantic moment, Jack for still being in love with Ennis and Lureen for seeming so sexually insatiable. Here, both characters occupy queer subject positions, particularly the "too-fast" and unmarried Lureen, who hastily "makes it" in the back seat of her own car, parked in an off-road location to which she herself has driven.

Lureen's almost masculine sexual power (in the car, she's on top) and her willingness to initiate lovemaking have an echo in Cassie Cartwright (Linda Cardellini), who is in numerous ways Lureen's double, her sexually aggressive "man-eating" manner recalling Lureen's desire to have sex before curfew ("What are you waitin' for, cowboy? A matin' call?"). Lureen doesn't wait for Jack to undo her bra — she undoes it herself; Cassie, desiring physical contact, removes her shoes and asks Ennis for a foot rub. But in each case the woman's sexually aggressive, even abrasive manner disguises earnest spousal qualities, the "quiet" care of a supportive wife. The film grants both women the opportunity to resolve or correct the initially dominant sexual impulse, calmly recuperating the importance of pure love and spousal affection. Lureen, overhearing a conversation that takes place in her office, silently rues the abuse visited on her husband by a pair of businessmen who call him a "piss-ant." Cassie, warmly deferring to the man's eldest daughter, asks if Ennis will soon be ready to remarry; she has fallen in love with him, she says, and later adds, as if to deny the weight of her earlier, heated sexual advances: "Girls don't fall in love with fun."

The soundtrack, demonstrating the privileged place of male homosexual romance in the overall film, works to claim Cassie's love as without foundation. Moreover, it ironically comments on her situation, accentuating her blindness to Ennis' queer inner life as well as her apparently easy access to romantic impulses. It is Cassie who, significantly, authorizes the use of a country song ("The Devil's Right Hand") that is (unbeknownst to Cassie) duly ironic in relation to the pair. After happily confirming that, indeed, "It's So Easy to Fall in Love" (to cite the title of the Buddy Holly song to which the woman, spying Ennis and hoping to catch his eye, initially dances), Cassie turns to the jukebox to pay for a second tune, "The Devil's Right Hand." The latter song, about a straight male sex drive at the mercy of an unnamed and devilish female (the devil's right hand), plays a cruel joke on Cassie. Though she seems to understand her own potential complicity in the downfall of men, Cassie does not know that Ennis, the object of her desire, is queer and still enamored of Jack Twist, and that this explains, more than the song's warning scorn of women as dangerous to men, his complete indifference to her display. If she isn't "the devil's right hand" come to tempt his "trigger," then no woman can be.

Recuperation, Reiteration

Recognizing a shift in the "purpose" of country music — from supposedly affirming conservative values to echoing the intricacies of the queer experience — suggests the success of *Brokeback Mountain*'s queer task, its effectively detecting the queerness of both the West where the cowboys roam and the musical and lyrical tenor of that region's most familiar pop tradition. *Brokeback Mountain*'s use of the sonic shorthand of popular music also, in the post-*Saturday Night Fever* age of movie marketing, evinces the commercial drive to package such a collection of songs as a commodity unto itself. By January 2006, the *Brokeback Mountain* soundtrack had sold 26,000 copies in the U.S. alone, making it the bestselling album at both Amazon.com and iTunes Music Store. By February the album had peaked at number 53 on *Billboard*'s "Hot 200" music chart, and shortly thereafter, on Valentine's Day 2006, Willie Nelson premiered a new "tie-in" track titled "Cowboys Are Frequently, Secretly (Fond of Each Other)," which he played on Howard Stern's Sirius Satellite Radio show. Written in 1981 by Ned Sublette, the song, which Nelson recorded in a show of support for his gay male tour manager, confirms the promotional terms of the film ("Love is a force of nature") while at the same time arguing for the commonness of homosexual desire: out West, queer boys abound — and (like Jack and Ennis) understand very little of their own desires, which often surprise them. Apart from citing the specific geographical region of remote West Texas, the song critiques a bigoted rural mentality that sees sex as sin: if Texas (an easy target) doesn't like its cowboys to be queer, and if such seeming anomalies actually exist, the state and its conservative inhabitants can do little to ensure their eradication.

Unlike the songs included on the actual soundtrack to the film, this "bonus" track expresses in undemanding, open language the social hurdles faced by all manner of queers. While none of the "official," diegetic songs name homosexuality by name, each is informed, whether deliberately or not, by the despairing nature of at least some men's queer experience; their mere presence in *Brokeback Mountain* establishes musical and lyrical consonance with facets of the undeniably queer identities of Ennis del Mar and Jack Twist. Apart from commercial considerations and the matter of social realism, the use of both familiar and original country songs points to a keen willingness to queer the sonic details of rural everyday life. *Brokeback Mountain*, with its deliberate placement of a range of popular songs, illuminates what is specifically queer in country. The subtlety and narrative economy of the film make it easy to dismiss as "simple," little more than a story of lasting love — *Back Street* for a modern audience. In truth, the film is committed to a queerly complex task, especially in relation to its soundtrack. Even a song like "The Devil's Right Hand," clearly if not explicitly about sex, is queer for being positioned in relation to Ennis, who is gay, and Cassie, who is, crudely speaking, barking up the wrong tree. Paying close attention to the acoustic space of *Brokeback Mountain* reveals the not only suitable but shrewd and complex union of traditional instrumental and compiled scores. Anticipating a certain audience response that has positioned the film as being about straight male protagonists (who "just happen to fuck"),[18] the movie's soundscape answers to such queer-oppressive claims by consistently affirming as recognizably queer the many facets of Ennis and Jack's mutual desire. Lest anyone forget, Alma's D-I-V-O-R-C-E is from a husband who's Q-U-E-E-R.

Notes

1. Consider also the significance of Ennis's inability to complete the sentence "Jack, I swear...," which closes the film and may seem on the face of it to establish or reestablish Ennis's refusal to speak emotionally. At the same time, the blank latter segment of that sentence constitutes an especially *inviting* silence, and amounts to a recuperation of the stony Ennis as an emotional "good guy": the audience can infer that Ennis — teary eyed at this moment in the film — is suddenly overwhelmed by his feelings for the late Jack Twist; he's only now realizing his love for the deceased man and can scarcely move, let alone speak. Less shaken, he might have said, "Jack, I swear I loved you always" or "Jack, I swear it wasn't my fault but society's," and on and on.

2. Harry Alan Potamkin, "Music and the Movies," *The Musical Quarterly* 15, No. 2 (April 1929): 281.

3. Daniel Mendelsohn, "An Affair to Remember," review of *Brokeback Mountain*, *New York Review of Books* 53, no. 3 (Feb. 23, 2006): 2.

4. In the short story, both men sing. Ennis "had a good raspy voice; a few nights they mangled their way through some songs. Ennis knew the salty words to 'Strawberry Roan.'" In contrast to the film's dividing its queer protagonists between stoic and spirited, the short story even allows Ennis the chance of singing along to Jack playing the harmonica; Ennis, in the story, offers lyrical accompaniment (SS 6).

5. Potamkin, 281.

6. The song, an original, was written for the film by James McMurtry, Stephen Bruton, and Annie Proulx.

7. See *Soundtrack Available: Essays on Film and Popular Music*, ed. Pamela Robertson Wojcik and Arthur Knight (Durham, N.C.: Duke University Press, 2001), 204.

8. Joseph Harry, "Parasuicide, Gender, and Gender Deviance," *Journal of Health and Social Behavior* 124 (December 1983): 350–361.

9. See Annie Proulx, "Getting Movied," in *Brokeback Mountain: Story to Screenplay*, (New York: Scribner, 2005), 131.

10. Jim Gundlach and Steven Stack, "The Effect of Country Music on Suicide," *Social Forces* 71, no. 1 (September 1992): 211–218.

11. David Brackett, in "Banjos, Biopics, and Compilation Scores: The Movies Go Country," argues that country music acts first and foremost as a "repository of white, working-class authenticity." See *American Music* (Fall 2001): 281.

12. Ennis is — mistakenly, perhaps — portrayed as a hick who's confused at Monroe's use of the word *condiments*, and while the intention is probably benevolent enough — to show Ennis as just a confused, uneducated kid — his lack of sophistication can too easily be read as consonant with that of country music's assumed audience. For a discussion of the cultural positioning of country music, see Brackett, 280–282.

13. Gerald Mast, *A Short History of the Movies*, 3d ed. (Chicago: University of Chicago Press, 1971), 420. See also Julie Hubbert, "'Whatever Happened to Great Movie Music?' Cinema Verite and Hollywood Film Music of the Early 1970s,"*American Music* (Summer 2003).

14. Hubbert, 192–193.

15. Ibid., 196.

16. The song also figures — prominently — in Pedro Almodovar's 2004 queer melodrama *Bad Education*.

17. See Richard Davis, *Complete Guide to Film Scoring* (Boston: Berklee Press, 1997), 135.

18. Referring to audience responses collected in a previous paper, "'One Dies, The Other Doesn't': *Brokeback Mountain* and the Queer Spectatorial Experience," by Noah Tsika (forthcoming).

ACKNOWLEDGMENTS: *Thanks to Jim Stacy, Michael Bronski, Robert Sklar, and Moya Luckett.* — Noah Tsika

13

Performing "Lonesome Cowboy" and "Jack Nasty": The Stars' Negotiation of Norms and Desires

by Jessica L. W. Carey

Some of the most compelling implications of the recent success of the film *Brokeback Mountain* concern the emergence of Jake Gyllenhaal and Heath Ledger as confirmed Hollywood stars. Both have drawn accolades and award nominations for their acting talent, and both have quickly gained status as attractive, relatively heteronormative "hunks." In particular, Gyllenhaal becomes known for being both the urban, sophisticated young actor with a penchant for dating starlets, and as "Jack Nasty," the passionate, yet closeted Other Man in a Middle American love tragedy. Likewise, in representational North American pop culture, Heath Ledger is both the brooding, complex young actor from abroad and the quintessential lonesome American cowboy, beginning and ending life as a tough, stoic loner. These paradoxical consequences of stardom install the actors as a compelling illustration of cultural politics and the mechanisms of the star system. Gyllenhaal and Ledger embody a tension arising from their position as stars, each straining to contain conflicting social desires — an embodiment resonating with the theories of Richard Dyer and P. David Marshall.[1] With regard to audience and media reception, this tension exists between two conventional expectations of stars. On one hand, it is evident that the audience and media desire a conflation, or a collapse or complete overlap, of Gyllenhaal and Ledger's newly larger-than-life personalities and their gay characters in the film. On the other hand, there is also a clear desire to gain access to the so-called real heterosexual people behind the acting roles. From the perspective of production, the public performance of the actors themselves with regard to the film and their star status is similarly conflicted. Specifically, the stars must negotiate what it means to embody the public intersection of their own personal, political, and performative desires. For instance, the actors have publicly promoted the universalist political agenda of the filmmakers, while admitting an initial, personal discomfort with playing gay men. Moreover, this particular negotiation is complicated by the fact that there are cracks in both actors' heteronormative narratives of self: both men exhibit characteristics, body language, and verbal assertions that could ultimately undermine their efforts to perform a traditional "straightness." To this end, theories of performativity help to illustrate the provocative implications of the fact that the star system locates its nexus of conflicting desires within actual bodies and persons. Specifically, in their state of perpetual movement and flux, actual bodies and subjectivities are intrinsically susceptible to idiosyncrasy, and the inability to maintain constant adherence to culturally monolithic narratives of identity. Overall, the stars' public negotiation of this paradox and the audience's reception and interpellation of it offer a significant insight into both the inherent friction that permeates the star system, and our culture's still-fraught relationship to queer sexuality and its cultural representations.

Marshall theorizes that one of the defining features of stardom is the audience's desire to see the genuine personality of the actor reflected on screen, noting that "we are more interested in seeing Brando than in seeing Brando transform into someone unrecognizable."[2] This desire for the conflation of role with actor becomes complicated in the case of *Brokeback Mountain*, in that Ledger and Gyllenhaal's characters, Ennis del Mar and Jack Twist, engage in a homosexual relationship on screen. Given that homosexuality remains somewhat of a social taboo in mainstream culture, here the wish for conflation engenders in the media and audience a desire to determine definitively the actors' level of identification with their roles.

Such attention is most apparent in the media. For instance, Ledger's *Rolling Stone* cover inserts his star persona squarely into the content of the film with the headline "The Heart of 'Brokeback Mountain' — Heath Ledger — Lonesome Cowboy." In the article itself, David Lipsky continually draws parallels between Ledger's biography and the character of Ennis, musing, "After all, for years, what had Ledger been doing but Ennis del Mar?"[3] Later, when Lipsky realizes Ledger will not get around to meeting him for a second interview, the collapse becomes complete as he concludes that "I've been Ennis-ed." However, perhaps the most overt instances of the media's compulsive assessment of the level of identification the actors have with Ennis and Jack are the continual questions posed to them about what it was like to film sex scenes with each other. To be sure, love scenes often elicit attention in celebrity culture, indicating a high level of curiosity surrounding this particular aspect of the actor's craft and how it interacts with an actor's "real" life. However, the level of media attention devoted to the love scenes in *Brokeback Mountain* has been undeniably higher and more persistent than average. For instance, Oprah Winfrey spent an entire segment of her show's half-hour feature on *Brokeback* asking the actors "Were you uncomfortable and nervous about it?" and "Did you approach it like any other sex scene?"[4] In fact, virtually every press interview of Ledger and Gyllenhaal regarding *Brokeback Mountain* has posed similar questions, so that by the time of the Oscars in March 2006, Gyllenhaal is noticeably annoyed at having to answer another question on the topic during a red carpet interview. Evidently, while conflations of star with role are a conventional defining feature of stardom, the fact that the actors' characters are gay often seems to heighten the sense of tension surrounding the paradox of star identity.

Audience response to, and participation in, such interrogation of the actors' level of identification with their gay characters has varied. With regard to gay audiences, querying of the actors' sexuality often falls in line with a tradition, outlined by Michael De Angelis, of locating desire in the very ambiguity of the stars' sexuality as it emerges from the combination of homoerotic role and ostensibly straight actor. Here, the inherent availability of fantasy in the realm of stardom "permits spectators and fans to access the star persona emotionally and sexually, on the requisite condition that certain ambiguities in the star's textual and discursive constructions are maintained."[5] In other words, knowing relatively little about a star's private life enables fans to project desired emotional and sexual qualities into the star personality. While anecdotally, many gay men found the movie somewhat boring or unconvincing, there is a thriving internet presence of gay men who are attracted to the film's stars, including one poster to the *Ohnotheydidnt* Livejournal community who claims "I love that man, I can't wait till he comes out the closet."[6] Similarly, the gay blog *Sex and the Second City* asks "who didn't find themselves want[ing] the amazingly beautiful and dream filled Jack Twist played by Jake Gyllenhaal?"[7] Yet another gay blogger writes "Jake was just a joy to behold, every moment he was on screen. He really was. And that was his job — that was his character."[8] That the focus is usually placed upon Gyllenhaal may be related to the fact that both Gyllenhaal and his character convey a higher level of comfort with non-heteronormative sexuality, thus making fantasies of conflation more readily plausible.

Another unique response to the identification of the actors with their roles is evident in segments of the straight female audience that continue to be sexually attracted to Ledger and Gyllenhaal in spite of, or perhaps even aided by, the conclusion that the actors do indeed identify with their gay characters. For example, as if in response to the gay male poster already cited, a woman posts on the *Ohnotheydidnt* Livejournal that "I will love Jake even when he comes out of the closet."[9] This phenomenon may be at least partially explained by Orrin E. Klapp's contention that stars that transgress societal norms become attractive for doing so. He figures this type of transgression in terms of either the seductive hero, who demonstrates that "it is possible, permissible, even admirable, to romp in the forbidden pasture," or the transcendent hero, who has the power to "redefine and recreate standards by which experience is to be judged."[10] Both of these hero types are feasibly applicable to Ledger and Gyllenhaal in *Brokeback Mountain*. Indeed, the excitement involved in transgression is certainly discernable on the Oprah Show, for instance, when a reference to the same-sex kissing in the film is met with hoots and catcalls of desire from the mostly female studio audience.[11]

The relative retreat of homophobia in our society is evident in the fact that the responses to various conclusions yielded from the monitoring of the stars' sexuality are not nearly as overwhelmingly negative as they may have been in past years; however, the fact that such policing still takes place is a testament to the persistence of homosexuality as a mode of identity that has the cultural power to garner special scrutiny and curiosity.

What Are the Stars "Really" Like?

Certainly, those in the media and audience who remain anxious about the conflation of Ledger and Gyllenhaal with their roles can take tenuous and temporary refuge in the second desire invested in stardom: the focus on the actual person apart from the performance, which Dyer characterizes as stemming from the fact that "the whole media construction of stars encourages us to think in terms of 'really.'"[12] We desire to know what stars are "really" like. Indeed, the interest in both Gyllenhaal and Ledger's off-screen heterosexual relationships is indicative of an audience interest in distinguishing them from their *Brokeback* characters. Richard deCordova notes that the extension of attention to the private lives of stars traditionally fosters a focus on "the moral healthiness of the cinema as an institution ... proven largely through reference to the stars' families."[13] The fact that Ledger and his onscreen wife, Michelle Williams, fell in love on the set was reassuring evidence for some that a distinction between the film and the actors could indeed be maintained. Gossip blogs interpreted a producer's comment that it was "a big gift to have two people falling in love in our midst" as proof that the film's "producers are delighted that co-stars Heath Ledger and Michelle Williams fell in love on the set, providing a welcome counterpoint to all the 'gay cowboy movie' talk."[14] Some gay audiences, too, resist the tendency of some of their peers to cast the actors as sexually amorphous, and thus available for identification. Instead, in a gesture inflected by the politically pressing issue of the representation of gay people in culture, critics like Charles Bouley II take the heterosexuality of the stars at face value and ask why gay actors could not have played their roles.[15] To reiterate, however, the conventions of movie stardom ensure that such distinctions between actor and role are to remain largely tenuous and temporary: a clean distinction between gay character and straight actor cannot be rigorously maintained when the competing desire for identification between actor and role remains equally pervasive. Indeed, the conflation of actor and role is such an integral feature of the cultural representation of movie stardom, that it seems continually to inflect attempts to discuss the actors apart from their roles. As Dyer asserts, stars "collapse this distinction between the actor's authenticity and the authentication of the character s/he is playing ... what is interesting about them is not the character they have constructed (the traditional role of the actor) but rather the business of constructing/performing/being (depending on the particular star involved) a 'character.'"[16] Ultimately, then, because the two desires of identification and distinction continually define each other ontologically, they remain in constant tension in the star system.

Turning to the perspective of production, it is clear that the actors' exercise of agency in the star system mirrors the tension that is endemic to their audience and media reception. Both Gyllenhaal and Ledger must continually mediate their political and personal desires while performatively enacting gendered and sexualized bodies that are being doubly scrutinized for the heteronormative hunk qualities expected of male stars, as well as the more queer, spectral traces of Ennis del Mar and Jack Twist.

Politically, both actors are engaged in an attempt to normalize the homosexuality in the film, in concert with the promotional machine that is marketing the film to a mainstream audience. Echoing the film's tagline, "Love is a Force of Nature,"[17] both actors emphasize in the press that *Brokeback Mountain* is simply "a beautiful story" that needed to be told.[18] On one hand, this process of routinization is both typical of star interventions in cultural politics, as Weber argues,[19] and seems to represent Ledger and Gyllenhaal's liberal desire to legitimate gay relationships by asserting that they stem from the same premise that straight ones do. Gyllenhaal invokes this aim in the October 2005 issue of *Out* magazine when he says, "I grew up in a generation, and I grew up in a city, and I grew up with a family where the idea of two men falling in love is not a foreign idea."[20] However, on the other hand, Bouley and others would argue that the actors' normalizing efforts also constitute a certain erasure of homosexuality that is a potentially significant sign of their ongoing, underlying discomfort with being cast as categorically gay men. When asked about what it was like to act in sex scenes with each other, both men repeatedly assert that "it's kissing another human being,"[21] thus effectively universalizing the experience and stripping it of an overtly gay identity politics. Gyllenhaal takes the process even further in an interview in the December 2005 issue of *Details* magazine, stating that he believes Jack and Ennis "are two straight guys who develop this love, this bond."[22] Even after making allowances for the complicated tangle of issues involved in ascertaining gay identity, Gyllenhaal's ascription of a straight identity to Jack Twist seems a stretch. In the film, Jack not only appears comfortable with his desire for Ennis from the beginning of their relationship, but also later has at least one other serious same-sex relationship, as well as multiple casual sexual encounters with men in Mexico and other cities where his business travels took him. In short, if Jack Twist cannot be defined as being at least bisexual, then it is hard to imagine who could be. Perhaps this indeterminate conclusion is a key message of the moviemakers, since sexuality in *Brokeback* is presented as being fairly amorphous and multifaceted. The fact remains, however, that in this interview Gyllenhaal subscribes to essentialized sexuality in his assertion that Jack and Ennis are "straight guys." Such labels, along with the fact that the movie has so often been summed up as "the gay cowboy movie," testify to the lasting valence of fixed sexual identities. While critical and queer theory may tend towards positing sexual identity as fundamentally unlocatable, unstable, or even purely existential, it is clear, given the intense interest in the phenomenon of supposedly straight actors playing evidently gay roles, that much of mainstream culture continues in seeking to discern exactly what may render someone as essentially gay or straight.

Indeed, at the level of personal desire the actors appear to be as conflicted as the audience with respect to the tension between the desire to conflate themselves with their roles and the desire to distinguish themselves from them. Speaking to the desire for identification, Ledger states in an interview with Logo Television that "I always like to try and bare my soul a little bit ... it's therapeutic," while Gyllenhaal claims that he is "always looking for films that go after an emotional journey."[23] However, both actors frame such aspiration for unity with their characters as merely an integral part of the acting process, the discourse of which ultimately serves to separate the actors from their characters. Explaining the love scenes, Ledger asserts "[b]oth Jake and I are very *professional*. It was very important *to the story* that there was a level of intimacy" [emphasis added].[24] Here, any intimacy between the men is placed squarely in the service of their professional work as actors. He reiterates this point more strongly in *Rolling Stone*, stating "[n]ow by no means do I wanna fuck him, we're both very straight and sensible ... But it wasn't ... the butt of a mule; I was kissing a human being with a soul. And part of the magic of acting is, you harness the infinite power of belief."[25] Likewise, Gyllenhaal states, "I was so worried about, like, the love scenes being authentic, trying to do the best I can,"[26] thereby also iterating a narrative of grasping for a sense of authenticity definitively located outside of the self. Furthermore, both actors have also expressed their initial discomfort with playing gay men, admitting nervousness on Oprah and, in Gyllenhaal's case, the fact that he had "heard it was the gay cowboy movie, and I really wanted nothing to do with it."[27] While in the same interview both actors claim that they were able to work through any lingering homophobia by the time they were working on the movie, such anecdotes still contribute towards maintaining the actors' narratives of self as being distinct from their film roles.

Performative Cracks in Heteronormativity

However, in the end the actors' heteronormative narratives of self cannot uniformly conform to the standard of gender and sexuality that they seemingly aim to invoke. Perhaps this is because, as Judith Butler has suggested, the ideal essence of gender and sexuality is maintained at all only through a continual, repeated performance. The gendered self, she argues in *Gender Trouble*, is "structured by repeated acts that seek to approximate the ideal of a substantial ground of identity, but which, in their occasional *discontinuity*, reveal the temporal and contingent groundlessness of this 'ground'" [emphasis added].[28] People seek to consistently perform cohesive, accepted narratives of identities — gay male, masculine male, feminine female, and so forth — yet perennially fail to follow the cultural prescription completely. In this way, the constructed character of such cultural narratives is revealed. Consequently, then, the potential for the actors to undermine what are accepted as gender and sexual norms is made greater by the fact that the star system invests its representation of norms and desires within actual bodies and persons.

Performative cracks in the heteronormative narrative of self are numerous in Jake Gyllenhaal's case. The presence of such openings coincides with the general audience and media conclusion that Gyllenhaal is the less conventionally masculine, more sexually ambiguous actor of the pair, and that his character, Jack Twist, is more comfortable with his sexuality than is Ennis. In this regard, Stephen Holden conveys the typical portrait of Gyllenhaal and his role in the *New York Times*, remarking that "[t]he pain and disappointment felt by Jack, who is softer, more self-aware and self-accepting, continually registers in Mr. Gyllenhaal's sad, expectant silver-dollar eyes."[29] A particularly compelling instance of Gyllenhaal's conflicted performance of sexuality lies in his widely reported claim that "it's flattering when there's a rumor that says I'm bisexual. It means I can play more kinds of roles ... I've never really been attracted to men sexually, but I don't think I would be afraid of it if it happened."[30] While Gyllenhaal lists interesting movie roles as his primary reason to be flattered, thus reinforcing the above argument that the actors tend to couch their identification with their gay roles within the discourse of acting, there is also a more complex performance at work. In subtly qualifying his disavowal of gay desire by saying he has "never *really* been attracted," Gyllenhaal discursively renders his sexuality as ambiguous. This is the kind of performative move analyzed by De Angelis with regard to Keanu Reeves, whom he argues "actively participates in the construction of his persona in ways that suggest that the appeal to both gay and straight audiences is quite strategic."[31] In this light, we can read Gyllenhaal's equivocal statement on bisexuality as a descendent of Keanu Reeves's response to the question of whether he is gay: "No ... But ya never know."[32] Herein, Gyllenhaal also becomes the type of star that Marjorie Garber asserts places himself in a "heightened performative state, this state of being simultaneously all-desiring and all-desired,"[33] which she claims is an intrinsic feature of all great stars. Indeed, many of his other actions in the media surrounding the film testify to his comfort with appealing to both sexes. Appearing in the October 2005 issue of *Out* magazine in a range of alluring poses, for instance, constitutes a direct performative challenge to heteronormative gender and sexual ideals: here is a self-declared straight man who has no qualms about appearing sexy to men. Further, there are instances in which Gyllenhaal plays with the boundaries between filmic fiction and private life that some have felt the need to police, as previously noted. For instance, he quips that "I fooled around with Heath Ledger and Michelle Williams got pregnant,"[34] thereby campily insisting that performance is inextricable from life. As Susan Sontag asserts in her classic 1964 definition of camp, here Gyllenhaal seems to "understand Being-as-Playing-a-Role. It is the farthest extension, in sensibility, of the metaphor of life as theatre."[35]

Ledger, on the other hand, who has been characterized in the media as the more butch of the pair, nevertheless caused controversy at the 12th Annual Screen Actors Guild Awards by placing his hand on his hip in a manner considered fey by some present, while onstage presenting the vignette of *Brokeback Mountain*. Consequently, he defended himself against accusations that he was making fun of the film by claiming that he has actually had such mannerisms since childhood, saying "I've stood like that since I was a kid. You can ask me mum. It's nerves I guess. I'm a very fidgety person, always moving, never able to sit or stand still."[35] Clearly, whether or not he is aware of it, Ledger is mounting a performative challenge to heteronormativity similar to Gyllenhaal's. Not only does he assert the gestures as constitutive of his identity over time, but he also attempts to overturn, or at least expand upon, traditional expectations of which actions an ostensibly straight male body can perform.

The paradoxical nature of the celebrity persona coupled with its inherent performativity undoubtedly raises more questions than it answers, but ultimately carries productive potential. What does it mean that Jake can also be Jack, that Ennis is so clearly a part of Heath? Indeed, by examining the fraught site of stardom, we gain a clearer sense of the fact that such difficulty can propel new understandings of the workings of identity in the realm of cultural politics. Specifically, by locating the discourse of queer representation at the site of contingent flux that is the celebrity body, our culture perhaps unwittingly prevents the calcification of gay identity politics, and certainly opens up queerness to renewed interrogation. In these ways, perhaps Jack Twist and Ennis del Mar finally realize a certain mode of liberation, albeit outside of the strictures of the movie's narrative.

Notes

1. Richard Dyer, *Stars* (London: British Film Institute, 1998); Marshall, David P., *Celebrity and Power* (Minneapolis: University of Minnesota Press, 1997).

2. Marshall, 16.

3. David L. Lipsky, "Heath Ledger's Lonesome Trail," *Rolling Stone*, Mar. 23, 2006, 49.

4. "Brokeback Mountain — Oprah," *YouTube*, Jan. 27, 2006, <http://www.youtube.com/ w/Brokeback-Mountain — Oprah?v=iquvcFgFKok& search= oprah> (accessed Feb. 12, 2006. Video removed from site due to terms of use violation).

5. Michael De Angelis, *Gay Fandom and Crossover Stardom: James Dean, Mel Gibson, and Keanu Reeves* (Durham, N.C.: Duke University Press, 2001), 4–5.

6. "Jake Gyllenhaal Fix — Not dial up friendly...," *Ohnotheydidnt*, Apr. 7, 2006, <http:// community. livejournal.com/ohnotheydidnt/6272866.html #cutidl> (accessed Apr. 7, 2006).

7. "A Crash on Brokeback Mountain," *Sex and the Second City*, Mar. 6, 2006, <http:// www.sexandthe2ndcity.com/2006/03/a_crash_on_brok.html> (accessed Apr. 6, 2006).

8. Dave Cullen, "Watching Brokeback Mountain — Just About Perfect," *Conclusive Evidence: of Dave Cullen Having Existed*, Nov. 20, 2005, <http://blogs.salon.com/0001137/ categories/brokebackMountainBest/> (accessed Aug. 10, 2006).

9. "Jake Gyllenhaal Fix."

10. Quoted in Dyer, 24.

11. "Brokeback Mountain — Oprah."

12. Quoted in Marshall, *Celebrity and Power*, 17.

13. Richard deCordova, "The Emergence of the Star System in America," in *Stardom: Industry of Desire*, ed. C. Gledhill (New York: Routledge, 1991), 27–28.

14. "'Brokeback' Producers Reaffirm Heath Ledger's Heterosexuality," *Defamer*, November 21, 2005, <http://www.defamer.com/hollywood/heath-ledger/index.php?refId=147760> (accessed Aug. 10, 2006).

15. Charles Karel Bouley II, "It's Very Brave of Them," *Advocate.com*, Dec. 13, 2005, <http://www.advocate.com/exclusive_detail.asp ?id=23334> (accessed Feb. 12, 2006).

16. Dyer, 21.

17. Focus Features, *Official Site Brokeback Mountain*, 2005, <http://www.brokebackmoun tain.com/ home.html> (accessed Aug. 10, 2006).

18. See Bouley in "Brokeback Mountain — Oprah"; "Brokeback Mountain Making of— Logo Movie Special," *YouTube*, <http://youtube.com/watch?v=zHCR7dSYBEQ&search=broke back%20mountain%20logo> (accessed Aug. 10, 2006).

19. Marshall, *Celebrity and Power*, 21.

20. ""Magazine Scans G-O," *IHeartJakeMedia.com*, <http://www.iheartjakemedia.com/index.php?cat=41&page=3> (accessed Aug. 10, 2006).

21. "Brokeback Mountain — Oprah." See also Lipsky; Alexa Moses, "It's Kissing Another Human Being. So What?," *smh.com.au: Sydney Morning Herald*, Jan. 14, 2006, <http://www.smh.com.au/ news/film/its-kissing-another-human-being-so-what/2006/01/13/1137118969951.html> (accessed Apr. 5, 2006); Stephen Galloway, "Heath Ledger, Actor," *The Hollywood Reporter.com*, Dec. 8, 2005, <http://www.hollywoodreporter.com/thr/interviews/ article_display.jsp?vnu_content_id= 1001658528> (accessed Apr. 6, 2006).

22. "Magazine Scans A-F," *IHeartJakeMedia.com*, <http://www.iheartjakemedia.com/displayimage.php?album=58&pos=3> (accessed Aug. 10, 2006).

23. "Brokeback Mountain Making of."

24. Ibid.

25. Lipsky, 49.

26. "Brokeback Mountain Making of."

27. "Brokeback Mountain — Oprah."

28. Judith Butler, *Gender Trouble: Feminism and the Subversion of Identity* (New York: Routledge, 1990), 179.

29. Stephen Holden, "Riding the High Country, Finding and Losing Love," *New York Times*, Dec. 9, 2005, <http://movies2.nytimes.com/2005/12 /09/movies/09brok.html?ex= 1144814400&en=c639beb71a508ec4&ei=5070> (accessed Apr. 6, 2006).

30. "Bisexual Rumours Flatter Gyllenhaal," *News for Brokeback Mountain: IMDb*, Nov. 22, 2005, <http://www.imdb.com/title/tt0388795/news> (accessed Aug. 10, 2006).

31. De Angelis, 181.

32. Quoted in De Angelis, 180.

33. Marjorie Garber, "Bisexuality and Celebrity," in *The Seductions of Biography*, ed. Mary Rhiel and David Suchoff (New York: Routledge, 1996), 18.

34. "Biography for Jake Gyllenhaal," *IMDb*, <http://www.imdb.com/ name/nm0350453/bio> (accessed Apr. 6, 2006)

35. Susan Sontag, "Notes on 'Camp,'" in *Camp: Queer Aesthetics and the Performing Subject*, ed. Fabio Cleto (Ann Arbor: University of Michigan Press, 1999), 56.

36. Elizabeth Snead, "Heath Explains his SAG Giggles," *Los Angeles Times: The Envelope*, Feb. 3, 2006, <http://stylescenes.latimes.com/fashion/2006/ 02/heath_explains_.html> (accessed Apr. 6, 2006).

14

Lessons Learned on Brokeback Mountain: Expanding the Possibilities of American Manhood

by John Ibson

In today's parlance, it is what it is. Part of the beauty of Annie Proulx's short story and Ang Lee's rendering of it is the utter lack of didactic tone; neither work seems essentially an effort to use art to address social problems. Not that Brokeback Mountain *doesn't address contemporary cultural concerns, but Proulx's and Lee's works both have the quality of an epic, transcending issues of the day; each is likely to still be appreciated long after those current concerns, and all of us, have disappeared.*

It is a particular hazard in cultural studies to view every form of artistic expression, indeed every experience one has, as some sort of lesson. Is this film, painting, novel, or comedian's routine perhaps something to be dealt with in a class, as an assignment or at least an aside, or else used in research, to be analyzed in depth or at least to enliven a footnote? I think I sometimes have trouble convincing students of the importance of Socrates' insistence that the unexamined life isn't worth living because for me rigorous examination, rather than simple experience or enjoyment, can at times seem a burden, an impediment to feeling.

The above is hardly a fresh insight, but it seemed a necessary introduction to considering how extraordinarily valuable a teaching tool and research topic Brokeback Mountain *might be. For me, a gay man who was also nineteen in 1963, as were Ennis and Jack when they met that year, the story has a significance quite apart from any meaning I discern when I put on my teacher's or scholar's hat. That said, I can imagine the movie and the short story's being part of several courses of mine: highly useful in my Sexual Orientations in American Culture, in my Prejudice and American Culture, and in my Literature and Culture, to be sure, but also in my courses on The American Male and on 1960s America. And those are just courses that I myself offer. I could imagine* Brokeback Mountain*'s being valuable in several other courses and certainly in fields beyond my own. Additionally, though I didn't have the good sense to refer to Proulx's story in my recent book on American male relationships,* Picturing Men, *I might profitably have done so; as discussed below, I believe that some of that book's findings may enrich one's understanding of* Brokeback Mountain.[1]

ະເ ະເ ະເ

History's fundamental lesson warns those comfortable with contemporary social arrangements, as it reassures those oppressed by current practices: It hasn't always been like this, and isn't likely to stay this way forever. This lesson is certainly true when it comes to the way that American men today are inclined and allowed to express their affection for each other — whether that affection involves romance, sexual longing, or just profound fondness. *Brokeback Mountain* is a tragedy of thwarted same-sex love, yet may also be instructively seen as a movie that raises disturbing issues about how all American men must navigate appropriate ways to express fondness for each other, whether or not that fondness is accompanied by sexual desire. Our culture still so scorns sexual desire between two men that there is a common fear that such desire might accompany any fondness, as well as a fear that other people might jump to conclusions about the implications of two men's mutual attraction. Countless American males might recognize bits of themselves in Ennis del Mar and Jack Twist, and that may account for the film's tremendous appeal to some as well as the utter disinterest that others claim, some disingenuously.

Homophobia afflicts all males in our society, those who genuinely are sexually attracted to each other, like Ennis and Jack, as well as those whose love or simple affection has no sexual dimension. The countless adolescent boys who feel the need to leave an empty theater seat between themselves, and the even-younger American boys who learn to stop kissing their fathers, putting their arms around or holding hands with their male friends, and having sleepovers with their buddies — all are victims of their society's extraordinary discomfort with male-to-male affection. For one man to tell another he loves him, some joking around often trivializes the expression, with all the depth of a commercial for Bud Light; if two men embrace, a reassuring punch is often part of the action. Simply because they are men, gay males may often be no less free of inhibition in expressing affection than their straight brothers.[2] One of the many pleasures of *Brokeback Mountain* — and perhaps one reason for its considerable popularity — is that it presents us with scenes with which we are so unfamiliar in real life, and hence for which many understandably yearn: men being genuinely tender and lovingly playful with each other. Except for that passionate reunion witnessed by Ennis's wife Alma and one furtive stay in a motel, Ennis and Jack must, of course, flee to their Edenic retreats for such rare scenes to occur, but when they're there, the playfulness and the passion — whether marked by joy or anger, by an embrace or a fight — are vivid.

In the campsite scene witnessed from afar through binoculars by a disgusted Joe Aguirre (Ennis and Jack's boss during their initial time together herding sheep on Brokeback Mountain) the film's screenplay has it like this: "Two men pulling off their clothes, out in the middle of nowhere, they play, running, joking" (SP 21). The need to escape to their Edens defines the problem; the comparative unfamiliarity of such scenes in actual everyday life makes the believable tenderness and profound attachment between Ennis and Jack all the more remarkable, a profound tribute to the artistry of Proulx and Lee, of screenwriters Larry McMurtry and Diana Ossana, and certainly also that of Heath Ledger and Jake Gyllenhaal.

The tenderness and attachment portrayed so compellingly in *Brokeback Mountain* are rather more than a matter of two guys kissing, though one might not discern that from press coverage of the movie. In the printed and televised interviews whose remarkably large numbers reflected the widespread interest that the *Brokeback* story aroused, the frequency with which Ledger and Gyllenhaal were asked about the challenge of kissing another man was culturally revealing. It was the one completely predictable question, whether an interview was with the likes of Charlie Rose, Oprah Winfrey, or *Entertainment Tonight,* and the query had about it the sophistication of tittering children. Was a passionate male embrace really *so* strange, so utterly unfamiliar, to contemplate? Clearly for many it was.

It is critical to recognize that Ennis and Jack were nineteen in 1963, the year they met. They were thus shaped by the culture of 1950s America, an environment unusually hostile to male intimacy.[3] When most American boys learned to fear and despise any suggestion of queerness in themselves, Ennis received a peculiarly graphic lesson: His father made it a point to show his nine-year-old son the sexually mutilated corpse of a rancher whose relationship with the man with whom he shared a home had bothered his neighbors. "My daddy, he made sure me and my brother seen it. Hell, for all I know, he done the job," Ennis recalled (SP 53). That was a scene to haunt a man for a lifetime; it was no wonder that Ennis kept his feelings for Jack, powerful as they were, so severely controlled.

Jack's dream for himself and Ennis — simply to live together in peace —

was a modest one, in contrast to the dreams of men today who want to marry each other. Yet, living when they did, Ennis could only warn Jack that if their feelings were ever to "grab on to us again in the wrong place, wrong time, we'll be dead" (SP 52). Their intimacy had to remain in the shadows, making *Brokeback Mountain* a tale of unrealized potential. In "I Don't Want to Say Goodbye," one of Gustavo Santaolalla's several evocative compositions for the movie's soundtrack, is expressed a seemingly simple desire that echoes lyrically Jack's dream of living together. For two American males of Jack's and Ennis's era and upbringing, it was difficult enough even to bring that desire to consciousness, let alone realize it.[4]

Picturing Men shows a different world: men clearly comfortable with each other, feeling free to physically express mutual affection for all to witness — not hidden away on a Brokeback Mountain, but in front of a camera, wholly without the coldness or the reassuringly exaggerated gestures that would come to mark photographs from a later time. That lost world was — assuredly — not in every way better than the world of men today, but that earlier world was dramatically different from ours, and our understanding it and the reasons for its demise might improve men's relationships nowadays, with each other and with the women in their lives.

The notion that a male world of comfortable intimacy has been lost can be derived from a systematic scrutiny of thousands of everyday photographs of two or more American men together, from the dawn of photography before the Civil War until the early 1950s — both studio portraits as well as the snapshots that became common after the invention of roll film in 1888 — men indoors and out, in homes, dorm rooms, and bunkhouses, at the beach and in the work place, soldiers, sailors, and civilians, camping, hunting, and posing for athletic team portraits. The ways men posed with each other changed markedly over the period surveyed, and those changes in posing for the camera document drastic changes in the quality of men's various relationships with each other over a century of men's emotional history.

As cultural evidence, photographs record certain things, yet are wholly silent about others. In looking at Figure 1, a photograph taken around 1915, we see something as common then as it is rare today: not simply the men's pose, but the fact that they had their portrait taken in a photographer's studio. Many observers may confidently think they see evidence of romance and a likely sexual relationship in this photograph, but that judgment reveals something only about the observer, not the subjects. Without an inscription, we can actually discern nothing from this image regarding a matter that has come to obsess us about relationships: whether the parties are having sex with each other.

What we do observe in this photograph — and in countless others from the same period and earlier — is male intimacy, two men who were so comfortable with each other that they felt no need to clown around, to reassure themselves and anyone who would see their photograph that nothing culturally scorned was being displayed. Another of history's critical lessons is that change always brings both gain and loss. Certain losses that American men have experienced in their relationships with each other have been severe. It is not just men sexually drawn to each other whose lives today are full of unrealized potential. Some of the appeal of *Brokeback Mountain* can surely be explained by noting the space between men that is so much the rule offscreen in everyday life today, a space that could briefly be bridged by seeing the film and reading the story, as it was bridged by Ennis and Jack in their infrequent getaways.

Figure 1. This photograph, taken in a photographer's studio around 1915, was typical of many "friend" photos taken in the late nineteenth and early twentieth century. Such poses were common for pals who simply wanted to have a picture taken with each other. This pose of intimacy is likely to be misunderstood by many people today.

Brokeback Mountain *and Cultural Change*

After a year that brought us Heath Ledger's Ennis del Mar and Philip Seymour Hoffman's Truman Capote, a year in which both of those performances were so prominently and justly celebrated, it might be time to consider how well we are all served by categorizing people based on the sex of their desired sexual partners. What in the world could possibly be thought to meaningfully unite Ennis and Truman? To say this is certainly not to suggest that whether one desires a man or a woman is inconsequential, but it is to wonder whether desire's direction alone should define a person. And to wonder about that is assuredly not to question the necessity of laws protecting people against prejudice, against the still-widespread bigotry of those who definitely do believe that categories of sexual identity are meaningful, and that those in the "gay" category are evil-doers. Though Wyoming is hardly the sole site where violent homophobia remains, Matthew Shepard was murdered in the very state where much of *Brokeback Mountain* is set — slain in 1998, not 45 years earlier when young Ennis del Mar's neighbor was killed.

Neither Americans nor anybody else in the world have always believed that sexuality is oriented, as if by some sort of erotic compass. For the past century or so, however, the idea that persons should be divided into the identity categories of "heterosexual" and "homosexual" (words that are themselves just a century and a half old) has held great sway. Gore Vidal's idea that there are no homosexuals, only homosexual acts, has, like many of his notions, been often quoted but little accepted.[5] It's not just the tabloids that seem obsessed with questions of who is and who isn't; it's been a question that has greatly interested most of us, beginning with decisions we made about ourselves. So powerful is the assumption that sexual orientation exists in an essential, uniform way that some serious scientists nowadays even search for a "gay gene."[6]

Recognition of the extraordinary diversity among persons in our society who yearn sexually for people of their own sex, an inescapable insight in the face of Ennis del Mar and Truman Capote, is overdue — among countless persons who think of themselves as straight as well as many of those who call themselves gay. Fully recognizing that diversity would, of course, challenge stereotypes, and might also lessen the significance given the notion of sexual orientation itself and its attendant categories. What if the test of a relationship's worth had more to do with commitment than the sex of the parties? What if we managed to care more about whether two people loved each other profoundly, as Ennis and Jack surely did, or (again, like those two men) just brought each other great pleasure, than about whether they were of the same sex? In such a society, not only could Ennis del Mar and Jack Twist have come down from Brokeback Mountain and realized their modest dream of living together in peace, but if "gay marriage" disappeared as such a powerful distraction, might not many Americans pay more attention to more significant issues? Talk about having a stake in certain beliefs! There's more than the happiness of two fictional ranch hands at issue here.

It seems plausible that the attention showered on the film about those two ranch hands resulted from — and perhaps even contributed to — the growing acceptance, or at least toleration, of same-sex attraction in contemporary America. *Brokeback Mountain* has clearly done a remarkable amount of "cultural work," as a not insignificant element of a wide-ranging change in American values, a cultural change which appalls some with its seemingly fast pace as it annoys others who find its pace way too slow.[7] Only a later generation of historians can judge whether *Brokeback Mountain* simply played a part in a lessening of homophobia in America — no small accomplishment for a movie based on a 28-page story — or was involved in a much more substantial cultural process: a move away from a dichotomized sexuality and the related notion that our sexuality is best viewed as being "oriented." When Ennis and Jack insisted to each other, in the aftermath of their first sexual experience, that they were not gay, it was for them clearly a ritual of reassurance, one that many American men in analogous situations over the past century have undoubtedly duplicated. But questioning the dichotomizing of sexuality, and the consequent grounding of the identities of very different people solely in the sex of their desired sexual partners, is not necessarily a surrender to homophobia. It can instead represent a wholly fresh way to view sexual expression.

The Brokeback *Phenomenon*

Though Annie Proulx's short story was published to some acclaim in the *New Yorker* in 1997, and attracted appreciative readers in the years following, the story's reception hardly presaged the flurry of interest that Ang Lee's 2005 film would arouse. It is no exaggeration to speak of a *"Brokeback* phenomenon" — so intense and widespread was the attention paid to *Brokeback Mountain.* Attention began well before the movie's debut, when it was simply announced that the film had been cast, increased exponentially through the buildup to the Academy Awards in 2006, and has continued to the present — with, for instance, the publication of the anthology in which this essay appears. Gauging the dimensions of the *Brokeback* phenomenon and then scrutinizing certain facets of it — magazine and newspaper articles, interviews in print and on television, websites, cartoons, even linguistic innovations — reveals much more than how effective were Proulx, Lee, McMurtry, Ossana, Ledger, Gyllenhaal, and others involved in the film. Assaying the *Brokeback* phenomenon takes us well beyond the movie itself, into the areas already touched upon in this essay: American men's relationships with each other and American notions of sexual identity. The phenomenon is perhaps best explained by considering the likelihood that *Brokeback Mountain* powerfully tapped into some central cultural concerns of this moment in American history.

With an astonishing amount of coverage in blogs such as Andy Towle's elaborate Towleroad, numerous articles in magazines such as *The Advocate* and the *Gay and Lesbian Review*, and special programs on the cable channel Logo, various forms of gay media staked a claim to *Brokeback Mountain* as a breakthrough film with gay content and appeal. In such diverse films as *My Beautiful Laundrette, Gods and Monsters, Latter Days, Trick, Longtime Companion, Jeffrey, Chuck and Buck, Maurice, Love! Valour! Compassion!, Edge of Seventeen, The Sum of Us,* and *Philadelphia,* the previous two decades or so had, of course, witnessed an utterly unprecedented number of movies centering on the experiences of gay men of all ages in the United States and elsewhere. Some of these films were lighthearted and celebratory, some ponderous and self-pitying, others subtle, poignant, and provocative, all reflecting and contributing to the dramatic shift in the cultural coding of homosexuality that had begun late in the twentieth century, particularly in the United States, Canada, and much of Europe.

But in its coverage in gay media, *Brokeback Mountain* was seemingly something else again, greeted as if it were somehow the first film of its kind. When Logo nominated 181 movies as contenders for its "Click List" of the 50 best LGBT (lesbian, gay, bisexual, and transgender) films ever made, the winner was *Brokeback Mountain*.[8] The new edition of Proulx's short story published to coincide with the film's debut topped the amazon.com list of the 100 best selling "Gay and Lesbian" books for months, and InsightOut, an LGBT book club, gave the book elaborate attention. Lesbian comedian Kate Clinton joked that seeing the film was required for homosexuals: "We get our gay card punched on the way out."[9] GLAAD, the influential Gay and Lesbian Alliance Against Defamation, posted an extraordinary "Brokeback Mountain Resource Guide" on its website: a list of the film's many reviews and awards, along with a list of articles about the movie, links to clips of television coverage, and a *Brokeback* bibliography of relevant books. Printed, GLAAD's Resource Guide ran to nine pages. The film was twice a cover story in the nation's principal gay and lesbian magazine, *The Advocate*, with each article treating *Brokeback* as a movie and a phenomenon without precedent and as a work of art in which the gay community had a singular stake.[10]

With Ang Lee as its director and with actors of the stature and mainstream appeal of Heath Ledger and Jake Gyllenhaal as its stars, the film did seem to represent something fresh as a representation of American men sexually involved. It powerfully challenged stereotypes prevalent in popular culture and the larger society, both conventional notions of how such men look and comport themselves as well as beliefs about where they are likely to live and work. Even serious scholarship had slowly recognized the extent of same-sex involvements in "nonmetropolitan settings." Interestingly enough, in the *Chronicle of Higher Education*, in his valuable assessment of an increasing focus on "rural space" by those studying gender and sexuality, historian Colin R. Johnson began not with a review of books but with a discussion of *Brokeback Mountain*.[11]

Americans of various sorts had grown accustomed to, and increasingly comfortable with, gay men who resembled the stereotype, who remained in the place to which the culture had consigned them. Broadening the culture's notion of what gay men might be like and where they might live and work would truly be culturally subversive. That is to say, in the flowering of gay fiction of the past few decades — some of novelists David Leavitt's and Michael Cunningham's characters, for instance, like gay suburbanites Danny and Walter in Leavitt's *Equal Affections* or pansexual Bobby in Cunningham's *A Home at the End of the World*—has threatened mainstream cultural assumptions much more than have the artfully drawn but nonetheless conventional gay males in the works of revered (and older) gay novelists such as Edmund White and Andrew Holleran.[12] As created by Proulx and recreated by McMurtry, Ossana, Lee, Ledger, and Gyllenhaal, characters Ennis del Mar and Jack Twist were more challenging to convention, powerfully confronting assumptions common within the gay community itself as well as outside it. The story's head-on challenge to convention surely explains much of the fuss the movie created. Acting awards, like other judgments by critics, are never mere assessments of skill. *Brokeback Mountain's* presentation of men who so dramatically defy widespread stereotypes of gay males may have been at least partially responsible for an Academy Award's going to Philip Seymour Hoffman for his impersonation of Truman Capote, just the sort of gay man with whom many Americans have grown comfortable, instead of to Heath Ledger, whose majestic performance relied on no existing models of what gay men are supposedly like.

It doesn't take a doctrinaire Freudian to realize that people commonly resort to humor's alleged lack of seriousness to deal with what are actually their most substantial concerns.[13] Though it has its mirthful moments, virtually all of them occurring when Ennis and Jack are in one of their wilderness hideaways, *Brokeback Mountain* is a thoroughly sober tale, yet it invaded American humor to a revealing extent. Indeed, though more than simple jokes were often involved in American humor's embrace of the movie, it is surely no exaggeration to speak of what folklorists would term a *"Brokeback* joke cycle."[14]

Around the time of the movie's appearance, Jay Leno's and David Letterman's *Brokeback Mountain* jokes pervaded their monologues; especially (and hardly surprisingly) with Leno, the jokes were usually juvenile. "The president said we must continue to find new sources of oil," Leno joked. "The only place he doesn't want any drilling, *Brokeback Mountain.*" Letterman devoted one of his famous "Top Ten" lists to "Signs You're a Gay Cowboy," with such entries as "You enjoy ridin', ropin', and redecoratin'." There seemed to be a national obsession with men in love unleashed by the film. It was no surprise that "Saturday Night Live" came up with a *Brokeback* parody of its own, but there were countless other humorous takes on the film, and some were less predictable. *Brokeback to the Future,* a bogus movie trailer loosely based on *Back to the Future,* and a similar parody called *Brokeback Squadron,* based on Tom Cruise's *Top Gun,* became popular on the internet.

The film even became a frequent theme in another visual medium, comic strips and the cartoons. The *New Yorker* cover of February 27, 2006, had caricatures of Bush and Cheney posed as were Ledger and Gyllenhall in the most common poster and ads for the movie, an amusing drawing that could only work if there were widespread familiarity with that poster. In the magazine's January 2, 2006, issue, *New Yorker* cartoonist Bill Haefeli, who often draws gay characters, had a male couple in their bedroom, with one offering the other a cowboy hat, to which the other replies, "And what if I don't want to be Jack *or* Ennis?" More conceptually provocative was George Booth's cartoon in the *New Yorker* issue of January 23 and 30, 2006: Two elderly men rock on the porch of a rural house that looks older than they do, as one asks the other, "Were we gay?" Young males were the subject of a late–2005 cartoon by Larry Wright of the Detroit *News:* Walking past a theater showing *Brokeback Mountain*, one little boy tells the other, "My mom and dad went to the movie last night and today they threw away my cowboy hat and toy six-guns." Even Dagwood Bumstead couldn't escape the *Brokeback* phenomenon: In Dean Young's May 15, 2006, strip, Blondie asks her husband what he's watching on television. "It's an old-fashioned movie," Dagwood reports, "when the cowboy only kissed his horse."

No cartoonist devoted more attention to the film than Aaron McGruder in his smart and edgy strip about middle-class African Americans, "Boondocks." In a story consuming an entire week in December 2005, Robert Jebediah Freeman, a man of the old school who is raising his grandsons Huey and Riley in the suburbs and who is often either perplexed or dismayed by modern life, yearns for a traditional "manly" movie and, unaware of its exact theme, decides to see *Brokeback Mountain* with his friend Tom. After Tom and Robert are mistaken for a gay couple by other moviegoers, the old man is appalled by what he sees on screen and returns home to report his angry confusion to his bemused grandsons.[15]

Irony attended the *Brokeback* phenomenon as well. "Brokeback" quickly became an adjective connoting ambiguous masculinity or definite homosexuality. Usually employed kiddingly, even affectionately, but by no means without significance, the linguistic innovation may have emerged in yet another visit to the film by "Boondocks": On January 22, 2006, Robert was told my his grandson that the "man-bag" he was carrying looked "pretty Brokeback." "Dude, please tell me you're not wearing perfume," one joke in the emerging *Brokeback* cycle had a guy say to his friend. When the other insists, "What? No ... it's cologne, I swear," the first one says, "Well, it smells pretty brokeback to me." Hip-hop humor wasn't to be left out: "Yo son, me and my homeboys went skinny dipping yesterday," says one male, to which another replies, "Yo that is straigh brokeback."[16] High fashion weighed in: At designer

Garavani Valentino's January, 2006, show in Milan, male models in cowboy hats and jeans that cost as much as a month's wages for Twist and del Mar, walked down the runway hand-in-hand.[17] Finally, the movie's linguistic impact was further demonstrated by the popularity, for joking around, of Jack Twist's anything-but-funny lament to Ennis, "I wish I knew how to quit you." Screenwriter and humorist Andy Borowitz hoped that line from the film might become the new "Show me the money," the famous admonition of Cuba Gooding, Jr.'s Rod Tidwell in another film about contemporary masculinity's pressures, 1996's *Jerry Maguire*.[18]

Mainstream media attention to *Brokeback Mountain* was assuredly not confined to humor, suggestive as that humorous attention might be. *Time* and *Newsweek* both had articles on the film, each with a tone of astonished respect, pieces much longer than conventional movie reviews, exploring the film's larger cultural significance and treating it as clearly a landmark, both in film history and in the evolution of American sexual attitudes.[19] Newspapers also dealt with *Brokeback Mountain* as an event, much more than as a mere movie, frequently monitoring the film's considerable popularity in areas apart from big cities on either coast. Even George W. Bush, on a rare occasion when a citizen's question appeared not to have been screened by the president's handlers, was asked whether, as a rancher, he planned to see the movie. (He said that he did not.)[20]

Though the story is mostly set in Wyoming, where the fictional Brokeback Mountain is supposedly located, the gorgeous landscapes in the film were shot hundreds of miles north in Alberta. Nevertheless, and despite the state's being the actual location of Matthew Shepard's 1998 murder, Wyoming travel promoters reported a dramatic increase of interest in their state because of the film. "We've got beautiful country out here," said Mike Willard of the Chamber of Commerce in the tiny towns of Worland and Ten Sleep, "and a lot of great people, and we're very open to everybody and anybody." Such an assessment of small-town Wyoming's easygoing tolerance surely would have surprised Ennis del Mar, but of course he had no tourist dollars to spread around.[21]

With little dissent, film critics showered *Brokeback Mountain* with acclaim. The movie itself won virtually every award in sight, except the Best Picture Oscar, and though Ledger and Gyllenhaal lost some of the awards for which they were nominated, their performances were widely celebrated. Peter Travers of *Rolling Stone* declared the film "unmissable and unforgettable," and that assessment was shared by many. In a morning-after-the-Oscars judgment that seemed marked more by insight than sour grapes, Kenneth Turan of the *Los Angeles Times* decided that *Brokeback Mountain's* genuinely subversive quality and its lasting value was shown more conclusively in its *not* winning the Best Picture Oscar than would have been shown by a victory in that category. "Sometimes you win by losing," Turan decided.[22] It did seem likely that the winner, *Crash*, with its comparatively unchallenging point that racial prejudice is harmful and complicated, would prove the much less memorable movie. Annie Proulx was considerably more embittered over the outcome than Turan, declaring "*Trash*—excuse me—*Crash*" to be "a safe pick of 'controversial film' for the heffalumps."[23]

Considering what a sure thing *Brokeback* had seemed to be up until the moment the Best Picture winner was announced, its loss of that prize deserves some scrutiny; Turan's column provides a clue to why it might have lost. "More than any other of the nominated films," he would recall, "'Brokeback Mountain' was the one people told me they really didn't feel like seeing, didn't really get, didn't understand the fuss over." Was it maybe the "unconscious fears and unconscious prejudices" of Academy voters, Turan wondered, that ultimately denied *Brokeback Mountain* its seemingly assured distinction as Best Picture of the Year?[24] Perhaps that win was too much to expect; Academy voters are assuredly a more conventional lot than the members of the foreign press who decide the Golden Globes. Who would have ever predicted, just two decades ago, that gay marriage would even be debated in so short a time? It is almost as unlikely that anyone in Ronald Reagan's America could have predicted that a movie like *Brokeback Mountain* would be made at all in just a few years, let alone be nominated for Best Picture, let alone win.

Conflicts over sexual orientation are often but a distraction from a more fundamental matter: what sort of men and women do we want our society to encourage and reward? Stigmatizing gay men and lesbians, and the resulting propagation of certain negative stereotypes about them as failed men and failed women, function as a way of reminding everyone, regardless of their sexual yearnings, of the culture's gender ideals. *Brokeback Mountain* explored a radically different sort of manhood, not just an alternative way for men to express affection for each other. It may have been its offering all men such a different way to be that made the film so appealing to some and so troubling to some others, making even the prospect of seeing it, as Turan reported, distasteful to some Academy members.

No other reviewer's comments aroused as much anger as did those of Gene Shalit of the *Today* show in misreading Jack Twist as a "predator" simply because he initiated sexual activity with Ennis del Mar—a perspective, some say, taken from a notably obtuse angle. Shalit, who has a gay son for whose sexuality he has publicly voiced support, found the film "wildly overpraised" and saw the relationship between Twist and del Mar as nothing more than the result of the fact that Jack "tracks Ennis down and coaxes him into sporadic trysts."[25] But some other reviewers also read the relationship with a defensive superficiality and, like Shalit, characterized Twist in a way that may have inadvertently revealed how much the film challenged conventional notions of manhood. In some reviews, there appeared a seemingly minor, but perhaps quite revealing, point about Jake Gyllenhaal's Jack Twist, a subtle performance that many reviewers probably did not notice enough, with Heath Ledger's Ennis del Mar obviously such a triumph. Instead of seeing Gyllenhaal's Twist as a man desperately in love as well as sexually aroused, a man better able than his partner to express his feelings, some saw Twist's emotional openness and vulnerability merely as whining.[26] That characterization mirrored the way male vulnerability of various sorts is stigmatized in American everyday life: witness the common admonition that "big boys don't cry" and the common belief, disdainfully expressed by many a woman, that "men are such babies when they're sick."

Ennis, Jack, and American Male Emotions

Though they shared the same variety of sexual desire (a desire that both refused to define as "queer") and similar hardscrabble upbringings, Ennis del Mar and Jack Twist might be seen as representing two different styles of American male emotionality. Taciturn Ennis was the sort of man his culture encouraged, especially during the 1950s, although his emotional reserve was extreme even by American standards. Jack weeps over one parting with Ennis, but after an earlier good-by, Ennis hits a wall until his knuckles bleed. Jack's plaintive cry, "I wish I knew how to quit you," became a laugh line outside the theater; Ennis's "If you can't fix it, you've got to stand it," in contrast, was no laughing matter, but simply a motto of American masculinity.

It would be a mistake to stress the differences between Ennis and Jack, however. Only in contrast to Ennis does Jack seem emotionally open, if that openness is to be measured by words. Neither man ever actually speaks to the other of his love, though about it there should not be a moment's doubt. In their screenplay, as did Proulx in her story, McMurtry and Ossana comprehend the workings of American masculinity well, realizing the ways in which some American men learn to navigate obstacles their culture places in the way of their being close, to use ways other than words to express affection. Though Ennis's difficulty with words, the essence of Ledger's performance, surely should not be made into a virtue, talk nonetheless can be cheap — and by no means always a sign of emotional health. A touch, a glance, and sharing an activity can speak profusely and profoundly, as can silence itself. Very little is said, after all, when Jack and Ennis are reunited for the first time, and not one word is spoken when Ennis fervently embraces not Jack but Jack's shirt near the end of the film. Coming down from Brokeback at the end of the summer that forged their bond, "the boys ride together," according to the screenplay, "side by side, each too full of feeling to speak" (SP 26).

Many American men know what such scenes of males quietly together feel like. Was it a concern that some scenes in the film and the feelings they conveyed would not seem altogether queer, and hence comfortably distant, but on the contrary would be quite familiar that kept some men out of the theater or else guardedly enthusiastic when there? In addition to recalling how often he was asked about what it was like to kiss Heath Ledger, Jake Gyllenhaal reported the tiresome frequency of male reporters' remarks when interviewing him about the film: "They come in and they're all, like, 'I just want you to know I'm straight.'" Ledger shrewdly suggested that the discomfort with which some men approached the film might actually be linked to "a fear that they are going to enjoy it."[27] In "Cowboys Are My Weakness," an amusing *New York Times* Op-Ed piece, Larry David, with his typically disarming directness, assumed and parodied the persona of just such a guy: "If two cowboys," David worried, "male icons who are 100 percent all-man, can succumb [to lust for another man], what chance do I have, half- to a quarter of a man, depending on whom I'm with at the time." No way would he see *that* movie, David insisted. "In fact cowboys would have to lasso me, drag me into the theater and tie me to the seat, and even then I would make every effort to close my eyes and cover my ears."[28] Heath Ledger's and Kenneth Turan's (and Larry David's) explanations of some men's discomfort with *Brokeback Mountain* seem utterly plausible, so well did the film capture the tensions within contemporary American manhood.

"What might have been," in the well known the lines of Whittier's poem, are said to be the saddest words a person can write or speak. When Ennis is left with only his memories of Jack and with the shirts they wore on Brokeback Mountain, the sense of unrealized potential is overwhelming — for Ennis and for us as we see their story come to an end. The film and short story surely have one of the more unrelentingly sad conclusions in American writing, but there is a lesson in Ennis's, and our own, sadness. It is not simply austere religious upbringings like those of both Ennis and Jack that can induce lasting fears about the implications of male affection. Though Rufus Wainwright's gorgeously haunting soundtrack song, "The Maker Makes," seems to indict religion as what makes the chain to keep a person from "bustin' through," it was American mainstream culture itself, not simply much of American religion, that came to inhibit male emotionality.

Inducing anxiety about men's closeness, putting space between American men, became in the twentieth century an integral part of becoming a man. How many American males today, like Ennis, are left with only a saddening memory of a relationship that had to fall short of what it might have been?[29] The American rite of passage into male adolescence commonly demands a toughening up and a leaving behind of the less guarded emotions sometimes allowed to boys, including boys with each other. The critical point here is the fundamental historical lesson mentioned earlier in this essay: it was not always the way it is now, and hence does not have to remain this way.

When it comes to male closeness, of all varieties, it is not simply that it might have been different — it clearly once was, and not just in boyhood or in Eden or on Brokeback Mountain, but in everyday life for many American males of all ages. Chains made can be broken. Sad as is the story of Ennis and Jack, their love story's very appearance, and the enormous interest it has aroused, may have reflected, may even have promoted, some weakening of the chains that have kept American men apart. Despite the worries of some and the hopes of others, books and films all by themselves do not change lives, but so widespread has been the *Brokeback* phenomenon that it may not be extravagant to think that the remarkable work of Proulx, McMurtry, Ossana, Lee, Ledger, and Gyllenhaal may have brought American men, if only ever so slightly, closer together.

Notes

1. John Ibson, *Picturing Men: A Century of Male Relationships in Everyday American Photography* (Chicago: University of Chicago Press, 2006).

2. One analysis of male emotionality on its own terms is Neil Chethik, *Fatherloss: How Sons of All Ages Come to Terms with the Deaths of Their Dads* (New York: Hyperion, 2001). See also Susan Faludi, *Stiffed: The Betrayal of the American Man* (New York: William Morrow, 1999); Sam Keen, *Fire in the Belly: On Being a Man* (New York: Bantam, 1992); Michael Kimmel, *Manhood in America: A Cultural History* (New York: Free Press, 1996); Sally Robinson, *Marked Men: White Masculinity in Crisis* (New York: Columbia University Press, 2000). Arguing that American gay men enjoy less emotionally repressed relationships than straight men is Peter M. Nardi, *Gay Men's Friendships: Invincible Communities* (Chicago: University of Chicago Press, 1999.) Of the many books bemoaning the troubled situation of American boys, one of the most insightful is still William Pollack, *Real Boys: Rescuing Our Sons from the Myths of Boyhood* (New York: Henry Holt, 1998).

3. On the sexual repressiveness of the 1950s, especially regarding homosexuality, see Robert J. Corber, *Homosexuality in Cold War America: Resistance and the Crisis of Masculinity* (Durham, N.C.: Duke University Press, 1997); John Gerassi, *The Boys of Boise: Furor, Vice, and Folly in an American City* (Seattle: University of Washington Press, 2001); David K. Johnson, *The Lavender Scare: The Cold War Persecution of Gays and Lesbians in the Federal Government* (Chicago: University of Chicago Press, 2004); Neil Miller, *Sex-Crime Panic: A Journey to the Paranoid Heart of the 1950s* (Los Angeles: Alyson, 2002).

4. On sexual identity based on the sex of the object of one's desire, see John D'Emilio and Estelle Freedman, *Intimate Matters: A History of Sexuality in America* (New York: Harper & Row, 1988), 226–229; Jonathan Ned Katz, *The Invention of Heterosexuality* (New York: Dutton, 1995). For a consideration of whether *Brokeback Mountain* may meaningfully be seen as a gay film, see David Leavitt's *Slate* review, "Men in Love: Is *Brokeback Mountain* a Gay Film?" Dec. 8, 2005, <http://www.slate.com/id/2131865/> (accessed June 15, 2006).

5. Vidal, *At Home: Essays 19820–1988* (New York: Random House, 1988), 48.

6. On the current search for a "gay gene," see Dean Hamer, *Science of Desire: The Gay Gene and the Biology of Behavior* (New York: Touchstone, 1995); Simon LeVay, *Queer Science: The Use and Abuse of Research into Homosexuality* (Cambridge, Mass.: MIT Press, 1997).

7. The valuable idea that literature performs "cultural work" is developed in Jane Tompkins, *Sensational Designs: The Cultural Work of American Fiction, 1790–1860* (New York: Oxford University Press, 1985).

8. *Logo*, <http://www.logoonline.com/shows/events/50_greatest_films/nom_az.jhtml> (accessed Sept. 13, 2006).

9. "Film Spurs Culture of Gay Cowboy Jokes," *USA Today* online, <http://www.usato day.com/life/movies/news/2006–01–25-brokeback-humor-cover_x.htm> (accessed Sept. 13, 2006).

10. Alonso Duralde, "Hot Hot Heath," *The Advocate* (Jan. 17, 2006), 48–57; Adam B. Vary, "The *Brokeback Mountain* Effect," *The Advocate* (Feb. 28, 2006), 36–41. See also, on Jake Gyllenhall in the gay press, Bruce Shenitz, "Kissin' Cowboy," *Out* (October 2005), 92–99, 124. The GLAAD Resource Guide was at <http://www.glaad.org/eye/brokeback_mountain.php? PHPSESSID=f723dd> (accessed Sept. 13, 2006). A poignant assessment of the film by a gay writer is Andrew Holleran's "The Magic Mountain," in *Gay and Lesbian Review* (March-April 2006): 12–15.

11. Colin R. Johnson, "Rural Space: Queer America's Final Frontier," *Chronicle of Higher Education* (Jan. 13, 2006): B15.

12. David Leavitt, *Equal Affections* (New York: Weldenfeld and Nicolson, 1989); Michael Cunningham, *A Home at the End of the World* (New York: Farrar, Straus, and Giroux, 1990).

13. Recognizing this serious side of humor without resorting to a psychoanalytic approach is John Moreall, *Taking Laughter Seriously* (Albany: SUNY Press, 1982).

14. Alan Dundes's work has been particularly helpful in exploring the cultural significance of everyday joking. See Dundes and Carl R. Pagter, *Why Don't Sheep Shrink in the Rain: A Further Collection of Photocopier Folklore* (Syracuse, N.Y.: Syracuse University Press, 2000).

15. McGruder returned to the topic two months later, showing Robert's shock when he hears Willie Nelson, a favorite of his, singing on the radio his remarkable song about cowboy love (released on Valentine's Day, 2006), "Cowboys Are Frequently, Secretly (Fond of Each Other)." Robert's shock eventually wears off, and when his grandson is surprised to find the old man watching Nelson's video of the song on television, Robert replies, "I'm practicing tolerance, boy. Now move.... The pansies are line-dancing." In the next day's strip, realizing that listening to that music, like seeing *Brokeback Mountain,* wouldn't make him gay, and that "maybe all this gay cowboy stuff is saying that it's manly to be in touch with your feminine side," Robert sets off to make lattes for himself and his grandson.

16. The internet is still the best source for measuring *Brokeback Mountain*'s linguistic impact. See "Urban Dictionary," <http://www.urbandictionary.com/define.php?term=broke-back>(accessed Sept. 13, 2006); "Language Log" <http://itre.cis.upenn.edu/~myl?languagelog/archives/002913.html (accessed Sept. 13, 2006).

17. Cynthia H. Cho, "The 'Brokeback' Effect," *Los Angeles Times*, Mar. 1, 2003, E3.

18. On Borowitz's remark, see "Flood of 'Brokeback' Jokes Gets Mixed Reaction from Gays," http://www.seattlepi.nwsource.com/movies/258640_ brokebackhumor 08.html (accessed June 18, 2006).

19. Sean Smith, "Forbidden Territory," *Newsweek*, Nov. 21, 2005, 68–70; Richard Corliss, "How the West Was Won Over," *Time,* Jan. 20, 2006, 60–63.

20. Peter Wallsten, "Unscripted Moment Over 'Brokeback,' "*Los Angeles Times*, Jan. 24, 2006, A10. On mainstream press coverage, see also Robert W. Welkos and Elaine Dutka, "Can 'Brokeback Mountain' Move the Heartland?" *Los Angeles Times,* Dec. 14, 2005, A1, A34.

21. On tourists' recently increased interest in Wyoming, see Alan Solomon, "Seeking 'Brokeback's' Backdrop," *Los Angeles Times,* Feb. 5, 2006, L3.

22. Kenneth Turan, "When the Chance Came to Make a Statement, the Academy Played It Safe," *Los Angeles Times,* Mar. 6, 2006, E1, E7.

23. Annie Proulx, "Blood on the Red Carpet," *The Guardian,* Mar. 11, 2006,

<http://books.guardian.co.uk/comment/story/0,,1727309,00.html> (accessed Sept. 13, 2006).
    24. Turan.
    25. On the controversy over Shalit's review, see "Gene Shalit Is a Bigot," <http://rightrainbow.com/archives/2006/01/gene_shalit_is.html>(accessed Sept. 13, 2006), and "'Today' Show trashes 'Brokeback,'" <http://www.washblade.com/blog/index.cfm?blog_id=4381> (accessed Sept. 13, 2006).
    26. See, for example, the review by Michael Barnes in the *Austin American-Statesman,* "'Brokeback Mountain' Keeps Viewers Thinking," http://www.austin360.com/movies/content/shared/movies.B/brokebackmountain/aas.html (accessed June 15, 2006).
    27. Smith, "Forbidden Territory," 70.
    28. Larry David, "Cowboys Are My Weakness," *New York Times,* Jan. 1, 2006, <http://nytimes.com/2006/01/01/opinion/01david.html> (accessed Sept. 13, 2006).
    29. Some answers to this question were provided by the many messages submitted to the movie's website, in response to the invitation to "Share Your Story." Countless ones recall memories of a thwarted relationship. See the official *Brokeback Mountain* website, <http://www.brokebackmountain.com/>.

whether Ennis and Jack should be labeled heterosexual, bisexual, homosexual, gay, queer, or unlabeled. Before deciding, keep this in mind: Being labeled by others is largely a function of perceptual constancy — their need to minimize variation or ignore anomaly and to stick with terms already known so that they can comprehend more readily and maintain control. By their reductive nature, labels discount authentic reality. Self-labeling implies both *identifying* and *owning*; such naming brings both security and risk. James Valentine writes, "In a name there is definition and evaluation, comparison and contrast, limitation and containment.... Names have the power to contain and deny being. They can confine it within definitional limitations that make it difficult to conceive of an identity outside the container. Where bound up with contemptuous connotations, containment is especially damaging."[2] Ennis del Mar and Jack Twist indulge in homosexual acts two or three times a year for nearly twenty years. Neither denies the physical act; both acknowledge that it brings an intensity unmatched by heterosexuality. Physically, then, they communicate emphatically well with one another; the visceral pleasure of their sex needs no label. If the reasoning Apollo escapes them, the preverbal Dionysus does not.[3]

In trying to find the words for what they enjoy — in the context of their personal biographies and their nation's cultural history — language either frightens or fails them. Although they are seventy years away from Lord Douglas's poem and much closer in years to Stonewall, gay pride, and queer studies, they are much more in tune with the nineteenth-century attitude of an unspeakable (and shameful) love — as are the majority of those around them. But even our own era is not all that far from silence as a coping mechanism: "Don't ask, don't tell" (with its implied "be it, do it, just keep shut up about it"). The vocabulary of the 1960s gave Ennis and Jack such words as "queer," "homo," "fairy," and "faggot" to name certain types of people with whom Ennis consciously sees no similarity. He denies that he is "queer," but his double negative interestingly straddles identity categories: "I'm not no queer" (SS 7). In the reunion scene in the motel bed, Ennis says, "You know, I was sittin' up here all that time trying to figure out if I was —? I know I ain't" (SS 13). For Ennis there is no confusion about the word his mind has thought: "queer." He knows that they are not queer because "I mean here we both got wives and kids, right?" Limited knowledge, limited conclusion, limited language. Based on what he knows, Ennis cannot identify what happens between Jack and him when they are together or why the feeling lingers and intensifies when they are apart. As Paul Ricouer observes, "The nonidentifiable becomes the unnamable."[4] The men may be comfortable swapping occupational labels, camp tender and herder, but not swapping labels of sexual orientation. David Leavitt observes, "In the end, Brokeback Mountain is less the story of a love that dares not speak its name than of one that doesn't know how to speak its name, and is somehow more eloquent for its lack of vocabulary."[5] Their continued silence after that summer is perhaps explained in part by Norman K. Swazo's observation that silence is "that preserve which safeguards the innocence of the future from the transgressions of the past?"[6] With a past of Brokeback memories and a present of return trips to the mountains, Ennis may see his innocence only in the future, only in his silence. If he doesn't say it, it's not real; no one hears it, no one knows it — like a kid who closes his eyes so no one can see him.

In *Brokeback Mountain*, language consistently fails Ennis and Jack. They lack a vocabulary acceptable to them to talk about their "friend"-ship as they have both named it. Often they are silent. When they first see each other outside Aguirre's trailer, not a word is said. No "howdy" or "hello"; no "you here for the job?" Only awkward stares and stolen glances. Ennis is taciturn by nature — a man who introduces himself with only his first name. The more open Jack displays his gregariousness in the bar and later around the campfires of many summer nights. He even gets Ennis to relax and open up. After hearing Ennis speak six sentences in a row one evening, Jack observes, "Friend, that's more words than you've spoke in the past two weeks." Ennis confesses, "Hell, it's the most I've spoke in a year" (SS 15).[7] As their friendship grows and the whiskey flows, they develop an ease in conversation, mostly small talk, nothing intellectually stimulating or therapeutically revealing. The characteristic silence — or a few words at best — of the mythic cowboy continues to shape both men. Neither the story nor the film depicts moments when Ennis and Jack discover significant mutual philosophies or values that bond their love in a nonsexual way; in terms of discourse, they are relatively dull. In her short story Proulx clearly points to the silence that surrounds the nineteen-year-old that first summer: "They never talked about the sex, let it happen, at first only in the tent at night, then in the full daylight with the hot sun striking down, and at evening in the fire glow, quick, rough, laughing and snorting, no lack of noises, but saying not a goddamn word..." (SS 7). Silence is the necessary ambiance of their liminal license.

When that first summer ends and their separate normalized worlds call them back, neither man can talk about what has been going on all summer. They ride down the mountain "too full of feeling to speak" (SS 26). The departing conversation is typically Western macho, two tough guys verbally pretending nothing had happened that summer. It is easy to deny or ignore because they lack the language necessary to discuss their relationship and the ramifications of departure. Awkward body language conveys some clues, but verbally here's all they can muster:

JACK (squints, nervous): You gonna do this again next summer?
ENNIS: Maybe not. (pause) Like I said, Alma and me's getting' married in November. Be tryin' to get somethin' on a ranch I guess. (pause) You?

JACK: Might go up to my daddy's place, give him a hand through the winter. (shrug) Or I might come back ... (tries for a weak smile) ... if the army don't get me.
ENNIS : Well, see you around, I guess.
JACK: Right [SP 27–28].

Thus locked in their prescribed stereotypes, Jack drives off as Ennis walks in the same direction — no offer of a ride. While Ennis's conscious mind cannot process the departure, his body buckles and his gut tries to heave his despair. Only a threatening growl at a passerby and his own frustrated grunts break his silent misery. Ironically this scene about the inadequacy of language and the cost of inarticulateness is followed immediately by a church full of people reciting in unison some of the most frequently spoken words in the history of the English language, the Lord's Prayer. When the script is available and his community around him, Ennis knows what to say: "I do." Even without the script and the witnesses, at that point in time, he still is not likely to find his way to the truth: "I don't."

A Love Unspoken

In neither the short story nor the movie does Ennis or Jack speak of their relationship in terms of love. For Ennis their passion is "this thing that grabs us," this uncontrollable thing that could get them killed, like Earl, the old rancher who was murdered when Ennis was nine because he lived with Rich, another man — two men don't live together in Wyoming in the fifties or the sixties without running a big risk. Conventional wisdom had it that two men live together for only one thing: sex, homo style. What do queers and fags know about love? When *Shuffle Along*, an historic black musical revue by Eubie Blake and Noble Sissle, both African Americans, was in rehearsal prior to opening in New York City in 1921, its creators were very nervous about including a serious romantic ballad, "Love Will Find a Way," because white audiences believed that "Negroes don't have romance; they don't fall in love."[8] How many people feel that way even today about gay people: obsessed with sex, incapable of love?

Ennis sees people on the street and wonders if this indecent urge happens to other people, meaning of course, other men; meaning of course, sex. Ennis knows that men and women *love* each other; certainly he and Alma had exchanged declarations of love. Is love then rooted only in a relationship between a man and a woman who have sex together, raise a family together, and work together to provide economic necessities? In 1963 and for many years thereafter, like most others, Ennis would have answered yes to that question.

If so, no wonder he has so much trouble explaining why as Jack and he decamped, he felt "furious and despairing all at once, more emotions stirring in him than he can handle"—Jack's bruised cheek a testament to his turmoil. Or why as they descended the slopes of Brokeback Mountain to bring the sheep home, he felt "he was in a slow-motion, but headlong, irreversible fall." Or why, as Ennis left Jack, did he begin to feel "like someone was pulling his guts out hand over hand a yard at a time." Or why he dropped to his knees to puke but nothing came out. Or why he then punched the wall, "bloodying both his knuckles." Or why he ferociously barks at a passerby, "What the fuck you lookin' at!" as he knelt in a shaded alley overpowered by "pain, longing, loneliness, ... emotions stronger than he's ever felt for another person..."(SS 8–9). These emotions do not conform to what he thought he was allowing himself: "a one-shot thing," recreational sex to pass the summertime. Ennis knew he wasn't queer; Jack said he wasn't either. They are not like "those guys you see around some time" (SS 14), presumably gays identifiable by stereotypical body language, voice, or dress. They were not like them. So what's going on here?

That summer before sex enters the picture, just talking with Jack for hours around the campfire makes Ennis feel so good that "he could paw the white out of the moon" as he rides back to the sheep (SS 6). He even finds his smile and his laugh again. Then comes the full-mooned night when Jack calls a shivering Ennis into the tent and under the blanket. Jack makes a bold first move, taking Ennis's hand and placing it on his erection. What follows are frenetic actions physicalizing fear, anger, and lust, cascading into raw and rapid sex. Yet as it begins, Ennis and Jack briefly touch forehead to forehead, their faces like a two-piece jigsaw puzzle snapped into place, forecasting the tenderness of tomorrows. Once the sexual appetites are fed, a time will come to satisfy a greater hunger. The second night in the tent allows the men to explore more than the sexual act itself: touching, kissing, holding; a tenderness, an intimacy, a surrender that speak of love. Gently stroking his face, Jack almost inaudibly breathes his reassurances to the fearful Ennis, "It's all right.... It's all right," the phrase inviting the literal meaning as well as the colloquial. Is it a sexual high the rest of that summer that has the "two of them on the mountain flying in the euphoric, bitter air, looking down on the hawk's back and the crawling lights of vehicles on the plain below" (SS 7)? Or something more?

When their reunion brings them to a motel-room bed four years later, the intimacy is still there: "Ennis pulled Jack's hand to his mouth, took a hit from the cigarette, exhales" (SS 13). He tells Jack, "I like doin it with women, yeah, but Jesus H., ain't nothing like this. I never had no thoughts a doin it with another guy except I sure wrang it out a hundred times thinking about you" (SS 13). We have seen Ennis thinking about Jack. In a duplication of the "silent embrace" pose, Alma is seen kneeling on the bed behind Ennis, draping her arms around him, resting her chin on his left shoulder, and nuzzling his head. Poignantly, his eyes are shut; his face — and what lies behind the face — betrays that he is not there with her but in a tent on Brokeback Mountain. Ennis tells Jack about his stomach cramps and dry-heaving after they parted and shares with him what he concluded after a year of puzzling it out: "I shouldn't a let you out a my sight." But now back in society, he fears their lack of control: "No reins on this one" (SS 13). Vivid evidence was given to that assessment when earlier the two men outside Ennis's apartment hugged fiercely "and easily as the right key turns the lock tumblers, their mouths came together" (SS 10) in kisses ricocheting from wall to wall, their bodies shaking in passion. When they did separate for breath, Ennis called Jack "little darlin," the term he used for his horses and his daughters. So again, what's going on here? Ennis surely must know somewhere that it is more than sex but never fully *owns* the answer until Jack is forever gone.

Unlike Ennis, Jack does have sex with other men, as Proulx reveals in her story: he "had been riding more than bulls, not rolling his own." Years later when Jack's marriage and job have finally put money into his pocket, Proulx tells us that he "found ways to spend it on his buying trips" (SS 18). In the movie we see how Jack spent some of his money in Juarez: on a tall masculine street hustler with whom he disappears into a black hole of purchased sex. When Jack is between his "fishing trips" with Ennis, he has found a way to satisfy his carnal appetite, nothing more. We see no evidence that Jack goes to gay bars in search of a gay relationship as that term was evolving in the 1970s, post–"hippie free love" and pre–AIDS. Nor is it easy to picture Jack at a Gay Pride parade or hooting at the bitchy humor of Emory in the Dallas Little Theatre's production of *Boys in the Band*, or going to a leather bar in New Orleans with black chaps and a bare behind. Neither Jack nor Ennis is comfortable with urban gay stereotypes, even in a decade when stereotypes still provided gays with a measure of community. Neither is likely any time soon, if ever, to take part in some sociopolitical liberation movement. It's only about them, two people. And both, Proulx tells us, are homophobic, especially Ennis,[9] who *needs* to think he isn't queer, and Jack better not be.

Throughout the story it is Jack who wants to redefine who he is, and Ennis is the core of that redefinition: "What if you and me had a little ranch together somewhere, little cow-and-calf operation, it'd be a sweet life." Jack is willing to try to make it work, however impractical it might prove to be. On their first return trip to Brokeback Mountain, they seem to be at home there as they relax by the dying campfire and gaze at the stars. Jack makes his pitch, "You know, it could be this way. Just like this, always," but Ennis resists, reminding him of their family obligations and the dangers of two men living together. And who knows? Who knows whether a life together would have stayed sweet? Who knows whether both might have met the brutality of a tire iron? Or perhaps, their relationship would have continued to enrich each partner as they grew eventually to find no shame in their love. And perhaps some day — "fairy tales do come true," the song tells us — their society would accept them as they are. Who knows? It is not until Randall, the new ranch foreman in town, enters the picture that Jack is given an alternative to Ennis: another strong, seemingly sensitive person who might be very happy living on a quiet ranch in Wyoming with another man. We know that Randall is not Jack's first choice.

"The Silent Embrace"

On their final trip together we see men who have grown old, their desperation and bitterness masked in deference to the full enjoyment of their short time together. Even after years of "fishing trips," Jack has not adjusted to life away from Ennis: "Tell you what ... truth is, sometimes I miss you so bad I can hardly stand it" (SS 80). (Jack has heard Ennis's advice: if you can't fix it you've got to stand it. Is Jack coming to realize that the inverse is also true?) Ennis's news about not being able to make the planned trip in August uncaps Jack's frustration and confirms his resignation to Ennis's unwillingness to change. "Cutting fence now, trespassing in the shoot-em zone," Ennis threatens to kill him if he learns the truth he has long suspected (SS 21). If Jack is having sex with women, that's okay; it means that he — and by extension, Ennis — is a Man. But if Jack is having sex with other men, it means that he — and by extension, Ennis — is queer. Ennis the Man threatens to murder that truth. But the heart-felt honesty of Jack's response unmasks the Man, leaving the vulnerable and frightened Human Being who is also Ennis.

Jack's angry desperation at realizing how much time they have lost and how little they have to show for their years together brings Ennis to his knees again, collapsing into anguish in response to Jack's kicker, "I wish I knew how to quit you" (SS 83):

> Why don't you then? Why don't you let me be? It's because of you, Jack, that I'm like this. I'm nothing. I'm nowhere.

Jack goes to comfort Ennis, who finally gives into his embrace, "a fierce, desperate embrace — managing to torque things almost to where they had been" (SS 21). But Ennis *is* nowhere; Proulx had cruelly predicted it at the end of the hiring scene outside Aguirre's trailer: "Two deuces going nowhere" (3).

Ennis had unconsciously set the stage for where they are now: "We can get together once in a while way the hell out in the back of nowhere..." (SS 53). He is nothing because he has not owned who he is.[10] He is nowhere because he has still not named the "friend"-ship for what it is. Not in the short story or the screenplay, but in the film itself, Ennis adds one more sentence following "I'm nowhere": "I can't stand this any more." Does this mean that Ennis too may be ready to consider the inverse of his watchcry: If you can't stand it, you've got to fix it. What would he do to fix it? Begin by dropping Cassie and heterosex? Then what? Did he have some news for Jack in November?— too late.

Unable to live with any conventional label and unable to find an unconventional one that suits them, Ennis will return to his home that is no home. He will try to be a good supporter of his girls, who will never know Jack as a person or a step-parent; he will avoid Alma because she's got his number. He has lived the lie because he thinks it cannot be fixed. In Gaelic, the name *Ennis* has two translations: "island"— better than nowhere but still just one — or "only choice." An only choice is no choice; it's a given. Did Ennis choose to love another man, or was it a given? Is Jack Ennis's only choice, or Ennis, Jack's? Unwilling to stay nowhere or on his own island, Jack will return to his other option, Randall, with a decision to make.

It is after this emotion-filled scene, the last minutes they will ever be together, that Jack indulges his memory of that "single moment of artless, charmed happiness in their separate and difficult lives"— the moment that first summer on Brokeback when Ennis had embraced him from behind, wrapping his right arm around Jack's shoulder and chest and leaning his chin on Jack's left shoulder. They stood like this, "the silent embrace satisfying some shared and sexless hunger." Some of the impact of the flashback lies in seeing how innocent and peaceful Ennis and Jack looked eighteen years earlier — not desperate, not confused, not stuck in a lie, and not crumpled to the ground. Back then after weeks of sharing memories and dreams, of horseplay, of sex, of flying together, they had found an unguarded intimacy where touch easily and sweetly — and wordlessly — spoke their love.

The short story and the film deal with this embrace in different ways, but in both it is a magical moment of silent, love-bound peace. In the film the embrace lasts less than a minute and occurs in the day time, giving this moment a verdant setting and letting Jack and Ennis be seen in the bright vitality of their youth. In the short story the embrace occurs over "a long time," many minutes as the ashes of the campfire settle into coals. It is nighttime and stars can be seen "through the wavy heat layers above the fire," giving the scene a starlit romantic and mysterious aura. The bodies of Ennis and Jack cast a shadow like "a single column against the rock." Ennis hums and rocks in the "sparklight" as Jack leans into his steady heart beat, "the vibrations of the humming like faint electricity," and Jack falls into a trance-like, drowsy state. Ennis finally awakes him with words he recalls from his childhood, "Time to hit the hay, cowboy. I got a go. Come on, you're sleepin on your feet like a horse." Jack stares after Ennis as he departs on his horse to return to the sheep. Jack's face glows with love; he knows what he knows. But sadly he knows that Ennis is not there yet: "Nothing marred it, even the knowledge that Ennis would not then embrace him face to face because he did not want to see nor feel that it was Jack he held. And maybe, he thought, they'd never got much farther than that. Let be, let be" (SS 22).

"*Jack, I Swear...*"

Cold and accusing in his look, John Twist nonetheless gladdens Ennis when he tells him that Jack used to mention Ennis del Mar and their plans to move up to the Twist ranch, build a small cabin, and live there. The smallest bit of a smile can be seen on Ennis's face when he hears this, for in announcing it to his parents, Jack had given evident validation of just how sincere he had been all those years about their living together. But then John Twist earns his name and delivers heart-stopping news: "Then, this spring he's got another fella's goin a' come up here with him and build a place and help run the ranch, some ranch neighbor a his from down in Texas." Ennis betrays no trace of a reaction, but a stomach which cannot handle a piece of cherry cake will certainly have difficulty with this news.

When Ennis discovers Jack's shirt over his shirt — Jack embracing Ennis, "the pair like two skins, one inside the other, two in one" — he gets the message: Jack loved him. Love? Ennis has always known it somewhere, just never fully owned it. He breathes the fabric of Jack's shirt, desperate to find his smell, "the faintest smoke and mountain sage and salty sweet stink of Jack" (SS 26) but the only scent is the imagined scent of long-ago Brokeback memories, the summer when Jack washed these shirts by hand, intimately, in the stream. With Jack's body in ashes, his shirt is now the closest to his skin Ennis will ever get. In a touching act of unintended courage Ennis takes the shirts, bundles them up, and silently lets Mrs. Twist know that they are his to take. He does not care what John Twist thinks. Acquiescing to something that resembles understanding, she provides a sack for the shirts. He mumbles an awkward thanks to Mrs. Twist as he walks into the yard of that "lonely house," where the shape of Jack's loneliness began.

Later the doubts. When was the last time Jack had looked at their shirts? Were they just a forgotten trophy, "stiff with long suspension from a nail" (SS 26). Again and again Ennis feels the blow of John Twist's surprise punch:

"...another fella's goin a' come up here with him...." But there were no other shirts secreted away, only his and Jack's, not part of a collection. Even if he had never found the shirts, in so many ways over the years Jack had been sending him that unspoken message: "I love you." Lureen had told Ennis that Brokeback Mountain was Jack's favorite place; it was the place where they once flew together higher than the hawks. It was the place to which Jack wanted the ashes of his body to be welcomed back. It was their *home*— it was *their* home. He doubted that Jack had brought that "ranch neighbor a his from down in Texas" up to Brokeback. No music in those words, no way. Yet he was long suspicious about Jack's "uncharted territory" with other men in many Mexicos. But year after year it was to Ennis that Jack offered to leave his Texas family and begin a "sweet life" together, away from the rest of the world. Didn't that say "I love you"? Ennis knew in his heart that he was loved.

In spite of their ongoing physical passion ("the brilliant charge of their infrequent couplings"— SS 20) and in spite of the ease of their intimacy and the profound sense of peace they found when they were together, Ennis had steadfastly denied Jack his dream of a place of their own for he could muster neither the courage nor the vision to step out of his "loop" onto a new plane of being. Worse yet, Ennis had never verbalized his love to Jack. In his timidity, he had cheated Jack of that knowledge. But didn't Jack know that he was loved? He had a right to know. Ennis could not endure the thought that Jack had died *hungry* to be loved. To be loved.

When Alma Junior tells her father of her plans to marry, Ennis does not choose the clichéd "Do you love him?" but goes to the heart of the matter: "This Kurt fella ... does he love you?" The ellipsis allows Ennis a beat to find the voice of his new wisdom. Alma Junior is "startled — and touched by the question." To her too it must seem so much wiser than the anticipated cliché. Her blushing answer: "Yes, Daddy. He loves me" (SS 95)

When we again see the shirts in Ennis's closet, it is his shirt now that enfolds Jack's. The shirts match the pose of the silent embrace, Ennis behind and wrapping himself around Jack, "two in one." The totem is his declaration of love — but too late to be seen or heard. A message unperceived is not a communication. Still Ennis knows what he knows. Yet, as Proulx (28) writes:

> There was some open space between what he knew and what he tried to believe, but nothing could be done about it, and if you can't fix it you've got to stand it.

What he knew was that he *loved* Jack and Jack had *loved* him. What he tried to believe, with varying degrees of success (the "open space"), was that Jack died *still* loving him. What he tried to believe, with varying degrees of success, was that Jack's new relationship with this rancher friend was, if anything, but a foothill beneath the mountain. What he tried to believe harder than anything else, sometimes across a vast and grieving prairie of space, was that Jack died knowing that Ennis loved him too. But, though he knows now, still he doesn't dare to speak the name: "Jack, I swear...." Much of the sadness of this story lies in Ennis's unfixable loneliness and in this message undelivered, a silence that burns for the word. But another sadness weighs in for Ennis as well.[11]

The Sadness of Impossibility

What did McMurtry and Ossana achieve by adding the scene in which Junior visits her father with news of her wedding. In part, it is a chance for Ennis to demonstrate that he has learned two important lessons in his life: 1. the significance of being loved ("This Kurt fella, does he love you?") and 2. the precedence of family over work ("I reckon they can find themselves another cowboy. My little girl ... is gettin' married"). It has also been suggested that this final scene in the movie and a line in the prologue of the short story ("he might have to stay with his married daughter until he picks up another job") place Ennis in a new home with his daughter so he will not be alone. If he decides to stay with her, he reestablishes his paternal position, waiting for the grandkids-to-be to climb on his lap. Maybe Junior will even give him a grandson. However, this view has been challenged as an interpretation which merely takes the traditional view that heteronormativity is the true and final home of happiness, that Ennis could never have found a home with Jack, and that Jack had to die before Ennis could get on with his life — an all too familiar narrative for gay fiction: one dies, the other lives, no happy endings for deviants. That perspective has great validity when viewed from 2006.

At the end of this scene the screenplay gives a revealing stage direction after he toasts his daughter: "ENNIS smiles back at his luminous daughter. But his smile can't hide his regret and longing, for the one thing that he can't have. That he will never have" (SS 96). Certainly Ennis will never again have Jack nor the opportunity to take Jack up on his offer to live together — to "marry" Jack. However, in the context of Ennis's likely adherence to the dominant, engrained sociocultural predilection that marriage exists to serve procreation, another impossibility may sadden the stale air of Ennis's trailer after Junior departs. By its very nature, homosexuality carries with it an inescapable reality: no progeny — or partial progeny at best. Of course, no good Darwinian — or creationist, for that matter — will underestimate the compelling necessity for species to breed.

From a less scientific perspective, in looking back to the ancient Greeks, we find tragic dramatic tales, originally presented as funereal dithyrambs, which served to demonstrate many civic lessons but only one universal and primary lesson: We will all die. Death will claim Oedipus, Antigone, the messenger, the shepherd, the sheep, you, and me. High-born, low-born; high die, low die. Tragedy is somber because it wears the mantle of our mortal truth, and rail as much as we or the fictional protagonists like, we will all lose. But Greek drama did not stop with that truth because humans have a weapon which the gods cannot deny us on a wholesale basis. That weapon is reflected in the other dramatic mask, born of the phallic songs: comedy — the Dionysian dance of fertility. The Greeks, the Elizabethans, and other great comic dramatists knew that comedy was written and performed to fly in the face of the death-wielding gods. And they knew how comedy should end: in marriage with the implied opportunity for procreation. If our god(s)-given tragic truth is everyone's mortality, then by putting on the mask of comedy, humanity can laugh in the face of the gods because through procreation, the progenitors will not die completely. Their genes and their DNA or whatever regenerative microscopic speck of biological matter is discovered in the future will extend their mortality, sometimes even mirroring their looks and their personalities and continuing into a future that could be as long as humankind's continued existence.

According to that perspective, the homosexual couple is denied this "escape" from death (as are childless couples and singles). Certainly gays can lead individual lives of joy, prosperity, philanthropy, achievement, and creativity, but they will not literally procreate. Today we know that those gays and lesbians without progeny in their lives may find their energies more focused on the here and now, and even more importantly, may be more willing to restructure how they spend their allotted time on earth. Judith Halbestam has written with great clarity about alternative narratives: "Queer subcultures produce alternative temporalities by allowing their participants to believe that their futures can be imagined according to logics that lie outside of the conventional forward-moving narratives of birth, marriage, reproduction, and death."[12] Indeed, as Jennifer Vanasco writes, "[I]t's refreshing to think about children as a true choice instead of a biological or social necessity."[13] Another view in support of alternative life patterns is expressed by Anthony Storr, who notes that "there is always an element of uncertainty in interpersonal relationships in the West that causes marriage, supposedly the most intimate tie, to be so unstable. If we did not look to marriage as the principal source of happiness, fewer marriages would end in tears."[14]

Of course, same-sex partners can have children as Ennis and Jack did but not by each other; for that they turned to Alma and Lureen. They and we could never know what a union of Ennis and Jack might have turned out to be. Though Jack might call their ejaculations "gun's going off," he and Ennis have to face the truth that they are firing blanks at indifferent targets. Gays can adopt children and so serve society, but while the nurture may be richly shared, the nature cannot be. Gays may leave behind them indelible memories for their friends and families but after the passing of a generation or two or three, those memories will likely prove to be delible after all. They may create lasting works of art — paintings, sculptures, stories, plays, poems, music, or buildings — but while these products may in/spire (give metaphoric breath to) many generations to come, they cannot produce a brand-new breather whose lungs share the DNA of the creators. This unavoidable biological truth denies gays the primal comic opportunity, the chance to laugh in the face of death — assuming, of course, that the "gods" are watching or caring. (God knows, those Olympians have long since made their last trip across the River Styx.) To Ennis del Mar, God is still watching, and Ennis knows nothing of narratives (alternative or otherwise) beyond a few good hunting stories. Like the serfs of medieval history who were told by their priests not to complain about their meager lives for heaven would reward them after death, Ennis lacked the ability to step back from his life long enough to see it for that it was and to realize that he could *change* it — to realize his duty to self as well as to species.[15] Accordingly, *Brokeback* may be viewed as the tragedy of a blind, mute prisoner who cannot fully own his feelings nor envision alternatives for his salvation nor realize that the cell door is not locked.

Without the choice to procreate with their partners, gays are faced with two primal choices: 1. how do I live? (authentically or inauthentically, creatively or stereotypically, giving or taking, loving or frozen, reaching out or crumbling in) and 2. how do I prepare for my death?— the end of my line. Jack got careless and died sooner than he wanted to. Ever careful, Ennis is left alive and alone, basking in the pain of his unfixable personal loss. With the news of Alma Junior's wedding plans delivered, he must sense anew the fruitlessness of his homosexual love. Alma Junior may be half him but she is also half Alma Senior — and not a trace of Jack. No Jack. No Jack Junior. The only trace: Jack's shirt and the random dander a microscope might detect. So from his perspective as an individual human being, if Ennis is indeed drawn into grandpa's hetero-rocking chair, it is only because, with Jack gone, he sees no other choice except for a long, lonely, mournful wait, buttoning and unbuttoning the bloodied shirt of the love who had no eggs.

The Penguins Speak

Ennis is thousands of miles away from the penguins of Antarctica, but they may still offer lessons of possibility. *March of the Penguins*, the award-winning National Geographic documentary from Warner Bros., shows a life cycle of incredible endurance, one that has well served the emperor penguins of Antarctica for thousands of years.[16] A testament to the validity of evolution, their existence revolves around procreation. They spend the few warm months gorging themselves for the species-imposed famine that lies ahead as they prepare for their rituals of courtship, insemination, and birth. In early fall the penguins from the coastal areas migrate inland to the exact breeding ground where they all were born, as were millions of their ancestors. They congregate in tightly formed, circular masses because a newborn penguin, depending on only its own body warmth and that of its parents to survive the world's cruelest winters, would freeze to death. The herding instinct is salvation each and every winter, as the shared warmth of hundreds of birds allows most to survive — and more significantly for the species, to copulate and to hatch chicks. Once the long, hungry winter begins to depart, they return to the sea for a few warmer months and a daily feast of fish. Occasionally during this process one couple may get negligent and allow an egg to fall away too long from the warmth of its parents and freeze to death. The documentary shows one couple who experiences such a loss. They stare at the cracked egg as if in mourning and find sound for their despair. Then with no progeny to worry about, they both return to the sea and its food. That winter others will serve the continuation of the species.

In 2004 the *New York Times* carried an interesting story about Roy and Silo, two chinstrap penguins who made their home in the Central Park Zoo — two "gay" penguins. An inseparable couple for six years, "[t]hey exhibit what in penguin parlance is called 'ecstatic behaviors': That is, they entwine their necks, they vocalize to each other, they have sex."[17] Neither is interested in females, nor are they in them. While unsuccessful in their attempts to hatch a rock they put in their nest, they did succeed when their keeper gave them a fertilized egg to hatch." Hatch it did, and for two and a half months they nurtured a healthy chick, Tango, to independence. Roy, Silo, Tango, and the other Central Park Zoo penguins are spared the harsh reality of Antarctic winters. They are kept — fed and sheltered. They need not commit to months of starvation and chill, thus escaping the Darwinian idea that only the fittest survive to procreate — or at least redefining it.

Most of us humans are kept as well: employment that sustains us well enough, school, churches, television, internet, cellphones, DVDs, cars, grocery palaces, shopping malls, sports fields, toys. Periodically we are reminded that the world can be a dangerous place: cancer, AIDS, crime, Katrina, Osama. But from most angles, there is no compelling necessity for each person to feel an obligation to breed. Anthony Storr suggests that "our present preoccupation with, and anxiety about, human relationships has replaced former anxieties about the unpredictability and precariousness of the natural world.... As [Ernest] Gellner puts it, 'Our environment is now made up basically of relationships with others.'"[18] Perhaps lowering the expectations of universal "compulsory heterosexuality"[19] will become not only desirable for some individuals but welcomed by society in an overpopulated, over-fumed, overheated world.

As with the penguins, some of the laws of nature may have been rewritten and even repealed in the last hundred years. There may be a new reason to laugh at the primal level; maybe the absurdists got it right: Laugh now! Will we arrive at a day when the future is less important than the present, when breeding matters less than love?

Notes

1. See Merlin Holland, *The Real Trial of Oscar Wilde* (New York: Estate/HarperCollins, 2005); Michael S. Foldy, *The Trials of Oscar Wilde: Deviance, Morality, and Late-Victorian Society* (New Haven: Yale University Press, 1997).

2. Valentine, "Naming the Other: Power, Politeness and the Inflation of Euphemism," *SociologicalResearch Online* 3, no. 4 (Dec. 31, 1998): 10.1, <http://www.socresonline.org.uk/3/4/7.html> (accessed Mar.15, 2006).

3. Friedrich Nietzsche, *The Birth of Tragedy and Other Writings*, ed. *Raymond Geuss* and Ronald Speirs (Cambridge: Cambridge University Press, 1999).

4. Ricouer, *Oneself as Another*, trans. K Blamey (Chicago: Chicago University Press, 1992), p. 149.

5. Leavitt, "Men in Love: Is *Brokeback Mountain* a Gay Film?" *Slate Magazine*, 8 Dec. 2005, <http://www.slate.com/id/2131865/> (accessed Sept. 15, 2006).

6. Swazo, "A Preface to Silence: On the Duty of Vigilant Critique," *Janus Head*, <http://www.janushead.org/2-2/nswazo.cfm> (accessed Sept. 15, 2006).

7. The short story does not paint Ennis as taciturn — painfully so at first — as the screenplay does. Perhaps McMurtry and Ossana wanted to shape Ennis more clearly into the mold of the strong, silent cowboy type.

8. For live testimony to this outmoded, now-flagrant perception — blacks are incapable of romantic love — see PBS's *Broadway: The American Musical*, "Episode Two: Syncopated City," in the section on the black musical revue, *Shuffle Along*, written in 1927 by Noble Sissle and Eubie Blake. The latter appears with singer Alberta Hunter on the DVD (Paramount) and recalls his fear that his love song, "Love Will Find a Way" for two African Americans would not be well received because "Negroes don't have romance." One story has it that on opening night of *Shuffle Along* Blake was on stage playing for the show while his collaborators were stationed at the stage door, ready to make a getaway in case the audience got violent during "Love Will Find a Way"—see http://www.slashdoc.com/documents/58365 or http://www.umich.edu/~musausa/blake.htm (accessed Sept. 15, 2006).

9. Proulx, "Getting Movied," *Story to Screenplay*, 130.

10. "Owning" is a term Martin Heidegger uses as another way to express authenticity. See Joseph P. Fell, *Heidegger and Sartre: An Essay on Being and Place* (New York: Columbia University Press, 1979), 39.

11. In analyzing why Brokeback might not win the Best Picture Oscar a month before the awards, Eric Boehler suggested that the "profound sadness" of the film would cost it support among gays. See Boehler, "Cowboy Controversy," *Rolling Stone*, Feb. 10, 2006, <http://www.rollingstone.com/news/story/9257407/cowboy_controversy> (accessed April 19,2006).

12. Halberstam, "What's That Smell?: Queer Temporality and Subcultural Lives," *Scholar & Feminist Online, Public Sentiments* 2, no. 1 (summer 2003). <http://www.barnard.columbia.edu/sfonline/ps/halberst.htm> (accessed May 15, 2006). See also Halberstam, *A Queer Time And Place: Transgender Bodies, Subcultural Lives* (New York University Press, 2005).

13. Jennifer Vanasco, "Can Baby Time and Queer Time Co-Exist?" *Gay City News* 2, no. 5 (Jan. 31-Feb. 6, 2003), http://www.gaycitynews.com/gcn205/canbabytime.html (accessed May 15, 2006).

14. Anthony Storr, *Solitude: A Return to Self* (New York: Free Press, 1988), xiii.

15. Deciding to give priority to self over social role is what makes Ibsen's Nora a proto-

type for modern protagonists — and what makes *A Doll's House* thematically akin to *Brokeback Mountain*, although Nora has the courage and insight that Ennis lacks.

16. *March of the Penguins*, National Geographic Film, Warner Pictures, 2005, DVD; also see http://wip.warnerbros.com/marchofthepenguins/> (accessed Sept. 10, 2006).

17. Dinitia Smith, "Central Park Zoo's Gay Penguins Ignite Debate," Feb. 7, 2004.

18. Storr, Solitude, 1–2.

19. Adrienne Rich, "Compulsory Heterosexuality and Lesbian Existence," in *The Lesbian and Gay Studies Reader*, ed. Henry Abelove, Michele Aina Barale, and David Halperin (New York: Routledge, 1993), 227–254.

Select Bibliography

All references to the primary texts are taken from the combined collection *Brokeback Mountain: Story to Screenplay* by Annie Proulx, Larry McMurtry, and Diana Ossana (New York: Scribner, 2005).

The short story (SS) in this collection is Proulx, Annie. "Brokeback Mountain,"1–28.

The screenplay (SP) in this collection is McMurtry, Larry, and Diana Ossana. *Brokeback Mountain*, 1–97.

The movie version is available on DVD, *Brokeback Mountain*, directed by Ang Lee, Universal/Focus Films, 2005.

Abelove, Henry. "Freud, Male Homosexuality, and the Americans." In *The Lesbian and Gay Studies Reader*, ed. Henry Abelove, Michele Aina Barale, and David Halperin, 381–393. New York: Routledge, 1993.

Alley, Henry. *The Quest for Anonymity: The Novels of George Eliot*. Newark: University of Delaware Press, 1997.

Alpers, Paul. *What is Pastoral?* Chicago: University of Chicago Press, 1996.

Appadurai, Arjun. *Modernity at Large: Cultural Dimensions of Globalization*. Minneapolis: University of Minnesota Press, 1996.

Babuscio, Jack. "Camp and Gay Sensibility." In *Gays and Film*, ed. Richard Dyer, 40–57. New York: Zoetrope, 1984.

Bourdieu, Pierre. *Distinction: A Social Critique of the Judgement of Taste*. Cambridge, MA: Harvard University Press, 1984.

_____. *The Logic of Practice*. Cambridge, UK: Polity Press, 1990.

Butler, Judith. *Gender Trouble: Feminism and the Subversion of Identity*. New York: Routledge, 1990.

_____. *The Psychic Life of Power: Theories in Subjection*. Stanford: Stanford University Press, 1997.

Carr, David. "Los Angeles Retains Custody of Oscar," *New York Times*, Mar. 7, 2006.

Cohen, Derek, and Richard Dyer. "The Politics of Gay Culture." In *Homosexuality: Power and Politics*, ed. Gay Left Collective. London/New York: Allison & Busby, 1980.

Crompton, Louis. "Virgil." In *The Gay and Lesbian Literary Heritage*, ed. Claude J. Summers. New York: Henry Holt, 1995.

Dargis, Manohla. "Masculinity and Its Discontents in Marlboro Country. *New York Times,* Dec. 18, 2005, sec. 2: 3.

Daum, Meghan. "A Breakthrough Called *Brokeback.*" *Los Angeles Times,* Jan. 7, 2006: B17.

David, Larry. "Cowboys Are My Weakness." *New York Times,* Jan. 1, 2006, <http://nytimes.com/2006/01/01/opinion/01david.html> (accessed Sept. 13, 2006).

De Angelis, Michael. *Gay Fandom and Crossover Stardom: James Dean, Mel Gibson, and Keanu Reeves.* Durham: Duke University Press, 2001.

de Cordova, Richard. "The Emergence of the Star System in America." In *Stardom: Industry of Desire,* ed. C. Gledhill, 17–29. New York: Routledge, 1991.

De León, Arnoldo. *Racial Frontiers: Africans, Chinese, and Mexicans in Western America, 1848–1890.* Albuquerque: University of New Mexico Press, 2002

DeLuca, Kevin Michael, and Anne Teresa Demo, "Imaging Nature: Watkins, Yosemite, and the Birth of Environmentalism." *Critical Studies in Media Communication* 17, no. 3 (Sept. 2000): 241–261.

Dyer, Richard. *Stars.* London: British Film Institute, 1998.

Ebert, Roger. "The Fury of *Crash*-lash," *Chicago Sun-Times,* Mar. 6, 2006, http://rogerebert.suntimes.com (accessed Sept. 17, 2006).

_____. Review of *Crash, Chicago Sun-Times,* May 5, 2005

_____. Review of *Brokeback Mountain, Chicago Sun-Times,* Dec. 16, 2005

Edelman, Lee. *No Future: Queer Theory and the Death Drive.* Durham, N.C.: Duke University Press, 2004.

Fauconnier, Gilles. *Mappings in Thought and Language.* Cambridge, UK: Cambridge University Press, 1997.

Fell, Joseph P. *Heidegger and Sartre: An Essay on Being and Place.* New York: Columbia University Press, 1979.

Fiedler, Leslie. "Come Back to the Raft Ag'in, Huck Honey!" In Adventures of Huckleberry Finn: *A Case Study in Critical Controversy* (2d ed.), ed. Gerald Graff and James Phelan, 519–525. Boston: Bedford/St. Martin's, 2004.

_____. *Love and Death in the American Novel* (rev. ed.). New York: Stein and Day, 1975.

Fone, Byrne R. S. "The Other Eden: Arcadia and the Homosexual Imagination." In *Essays on Gay Literature,* ed. Stuart Kellogg. Binghamton, NY: Harrington Park, 1985.

Foucault, Michel. *The History of Sexuality, Volume I: An Introduction.* New York: Vintage Books, 1978/1990.

Franklin, Garth. "Interview: Ang Lee, 'Brokeback Mountain.'" *Dark Horizons,* Dec. 7, 2005, http://www.darkhorizons.com/news05/brokeback2.php.

French, Philip. *Westerns: Aspects of a Movie Genre.* Manchester, UK: Carcanet, 1973

_____. *Westerns Revisited.* Manchester, UK: Carcanet, 2005.

Frontain, Raymond-Jean. "Theocritus." In *The Gay and Lesbian Literary Heritage,* ed. Claude J. Summers. New York: Henry Holt, 1995.

Freud, Sigmund. *Introductory Lectures on Psycho-Analysis.* Tarns. and ed. James Strahey. New York: W. W. Norton, 1920/1966.

_____. *New Introductory Lectures in Psycho-Analysis.* Trans. and ed. James Strachey. New York: W.W. Norton, 1933/1965.

Frye, Northrup. *Anatomy of Criticism: Four Essays.* Princeton, NJ: Princeton University Press, 1957.

Garber, Marjorie. "Bisexuality and Celebrity." In *The Seductions of Biography,* ed. Mary Rhiel and David Suchoff. New York: Routledge, 1996, 13–30.

Goffman, Erving. *Asylums: Essays in the Social Situations of Mental Patients and Other Inmates.* Garden City, NY: Anchor Books/Doubleday,1961.

Gorton, Dan. "The Hate Crime." *Gay and Lesbian Review Worldwide* 13, no. 2 (Mar. 2006): 13–14.

Gross, Larry. "Out of the Mainstream: Sexual Minorities and the Mass Media." In *Gay People, Sex and the Media,* ed. Michelle A. Wolf and Alfred P. Kielwasser, 19–46. New York: Harrington Park Press, 1991.

_____. *Up from Invisibility: Lesbians, Gay Men, and the Media in America.* New York: Columbia University Press, 2001.

Grundmann, Roy. Review of *Brokeback Mountain. Cineaste* 31, no. 2 (Spring 2006).

Gundlach, Jim, and Steven Stack. "The Effect of Country Music on Suicide." *Social Forces* 71, no. 1 (Sept. 1992): 211–218.

Gur-Ze'ev, Ilan. "Martin Heidegger, Transcendence, and the Possibility of Counter-Education." In *Heidegger, Education, and Modernity,* ed. Michael A. Peters, 65–80. Lanham, MD: Rowman & Littlefield, 2002.

Gutzwiller, Kathryn J. *Theocritus' Pastoral Analogies: The Formation of a Genre.* Madison: University of Wisconsin Press, 1991.

Guy-Bray, Stephen. *Homoerotic Space: the Poetics of Loss in Renaissance Literature.* Toronto: University of Toronto Press, 2002.

Halberstam, Judith. *In a Queer Time and Place: Transgender Bodies, Subcultural Lives.* New York: New York University Press, 2005.

_____. "What's That Smell?: Queer Temporality and Subcultural Lives," *Scholar & Feminist Online, Public Sentiments* 2, no. 1 (summer 2003). <http://www.barnard.columbia.edu/sfonline/ps/halberst.htm> (accessed May 15, 2006).

Halperin, David M. *Before Pastoral: Theocritus and the Ancient Tradition of Bucolic Poetry.* New Haven, CT: Yale University Press, 1983.

_____. *Saint Foucault: Toward a Gay Hagiography.* New York: Oxford University Press, 1995.

Hammond, Paul. *Figuring Sex Between Men from Shakespeare to Rochester.* Oxford: Oxford University Press, 2002.

Harris, Lee. "Misunderstanding *Brokeback Mountain.*" *TCS Daily.* Jan. 17, 2006. <http://www.tcsdaily.com/article.aspx?id=011606D.> (accessed Sept. 19, 2006).

Harry, Joseph. "Parasuicide, Gender, and Gender Deviance." *Journal of Health and Social Behavior* 124 (December 1983): 350–361.

Heidegger, Martin. *Basic Writings.* London: Routledge, 1996.

_____. *Being and Time.* Trans. John Macquarrie and Edward Robinson. New York: Harper & Row, 1962.

Hill, Jane H. "Language, Race, and White Public Space." *Contemporary Issues Forum: American Anthropologist* 100, no. 3 (1998): 680–689.

Holden, Stephen. "Riding the High Country, Finding and Losing Love." *New York Times.* Dec. 9, 2005. Online. Apr. 6 2006. http://movies2.nytimes.com/2005/12rok.html?ex=1144814400&en=c639beb71a508ec4&ei=5070 (accessed April 15, 2006).

Holleran, Andrew. "The Magic Mountain." *Gay and Lesbian Review Worldwide* 13, no. 2 (Mar. 2006): 12–15.

Hunter, Stephen. "A Picture of Two Americas in 'Brokeback Mountain.'" *WashingtonPost.Com,* Feb. 2, 2006,<http://www.washingtonpost.com/wp-dyn//content/article/2006/02/01/AR2006020102477.html> (accessed Mar. 9, 2006).

Ibson, John. *Picturing Men: A Century of Male Relationships in Everyday American Photography.* Chicago: University of Chicago Press, 2006.

Jacobson, Matthew Frye. *Whiteness of a Different Color: European Immigrants and the Alchemy of Race.* Cambridge, MA: Harvard University Press, 1998.

Jensen, Michael. "The *Brokeback Mountain* Oscar Snub," *AfterElton*, Mar. 7, 2006, <http://www.afterelton.com/movies/2006/3/snub.html> (accessed Sept. 19, 2006).

Johnson, Colin R. "Rural Space: Queer America's Final Frontier." *Chronicle of Higher Education* (Jan. 13, 2006): B15.

Lacan, Jacques. *The Seminar of Jacques Lacan.* "Book I: Freud's Papers on Technique." Ed. Jacques-Alain Miller, trans. John Forrester. New York: W.W. Norton, 1991.

Laclau. Ernesto. *Emancipation(s).* London/New York: Verso, 1996.

Leavitt, David. *Equal Affections.* New York: Weldenfeld and Nicolson, 1989.

_____. "Men in Love: Is *Brokeback Mountain* a Gay Film?" Slate. Dec.8, 2005, <http://www.slate.com/id/2131865/> (accessed Sept. 19, 2006).

Lee, Nathan. "*Brokeback Mountain.*" *Film Comment* 42. no.1 (Jan./Feb. 2006): 42.

Lim, Shirley Geok-lin. "Gender Transformation in Asian/American Representations." In *Gender and Culture in Literature and Film East and West: Issues of Perception and Interpretation,* ed. Nitaya Masavisut, George Simson, and Larry E. Smith, 95–112. Honolulu: University of Hawaii Press, 1994.

Lipsitz, George. *The Possessive Investment in Whiteness: How White People Profit from Identity Politics.* Philadelphia: Temple University Press, 1989.

Looby, Christopher. "'Innocent Homosexuality': The Fiedler Thesis in Retrospect." In Adventures of Huckleberry Finn: *A Case Study in Critical Controversy* (2d ed.), ed. Gerald Graff and James Phelan, 526–541. Boston: Bedford/St. Martin's, 2004.

Loy, R. Philip. *Westerns and American Culture, 1930–1955.* Jefferson, N.C.: McFarland, 2001.

Mars-Jones, Adam. "Out Takes." *The Observer*, Dec.18, 2005: 1.

Marshall, P. David. *Celebrity and Power.* Mineapolis: University of Minnesota Press, 1997.

Marx, Leo. *The Machine in the Garden: Technology and the Pastoral Ideal in America.* Oxford: Oxford University Press, 1964

McMurtry, Larry. "Adapting Brokeback Mountain." In *Brokeback Mountain: Story to Screenplay,* 139–142. New York: Scribner, 2005.

_____. *Walter Benjamin at the Dairy Queen: Reflections at Sixty and Beyond.* New York: Simon and Schuster, 1999.

Mendelsohn, Daniel. "An Affair to Remember." Review of *Brokeback Mountain. New York Review of Books* 53.3 (Feb. 23, 2006): 12–13.

Moos, Dan. *Outside America: Race, Ethnicity, and the Role of the American West in National Belonging.* Hanover, N.H.: Dartmouth College Press, 2005.

Morton, Donald. "Pataphysics of the Closet." In *Marxism, Queer Theory, Gender,* ed. M. Zavarzadeh, Theresa L. Ebert, and Donald Morton, 1–70. New York: Red Factory, 2001.

Mulvey, Laura. "Visual Pleasure and Narrative Cinema." *Screen* 16, no.3 (1975): 6–18.

Nietzsche, Friedrich *Nietzsche: The Birth of Tragedy and Other Writings.* Ed. Raymond Geuss and Ronald Speirs. Cambridge: Cambridge University Press, 1999.

Omi, Michael, and Howard Winant. *Racial Formation in the United States: From the 1960s to the 1980s.* New York: Routledge, 1994.

Ordona, Robert. "'Brokeback Mountain'—As Gay as It Gets: An Interview with Ang Lee." *Gay.Com.* <http://www.gay.com/entertainment/interview.html?coll=pno_entertainment&sernum=1139> (accessed Sept. 19, 2006).

Ossana, Diana. "Climbing Brokeback Mountain." In *Brokeback Mountain: Story to*

Screenplay by Annie Proulx, Larry McMurtry, and Diana Ossana, 143–151. New York: Scribner, 2005.

Packard, Chris. *Queer Cowboys: And Other Erotic Male Friendships in Nineteenth Century American Literature.* New York: Palgrave/Macmillan, 2005.

Perez, Gilberto. "Saying 'Ain't' and Playing 'Dixie': Rhetoric and Comedy in *Judge Priest.*" *Raritan* 23, no. 4 (2004): 34–54.

_____. "Toward a Rhetoric of Film." *Sense of Cinema* 5 (April 2000). <http://www. sensesofcinema.com/contents/00/5/> (accessed Sept. 19, 2006).

Proulx, Annie. "Getting Movied." In *Brokeback Mountain: Story to Screenplay*, by Annie Proulx, Larry McMurtry, and Diana Ossana, 129–138. New York: Scribner, 2005.

Rich, Adrienne. "Compulsory Heterosexuality and Lesbian Existence." In *The Lesbian and Gay Studies Reader*, ed. Henry Abelove, Michele Aina Barale, and David Halperin (New York: Routledge, 1993), 227–254.

Ricouer, Paul. *Oneself as Another.* Trans. Kathleen Blamey. Chicago: University of Chicago Press, 1992.

Roediger, David R. *The Wages of Whiteness: Race and the Making of the American Working Class.* New York: Verso, 1991.

Rood, Karen L. *Understanding Annie Proulx.* Columbia: University of South Carolina Press, 2001.

Rorke, Robert. "Quitting Brokeback." *Publishers Weekly* 8 (May 2006): 29–33.

Rowell, Michael. "Mountain High." *Out Smart Magazine* (December 2005): 28–36.

Russo, Vito. *The Celluloid Closet* (rev. ed.) New York: Harper & Row, 1981/1987.

Salamon, Mark. "A Harrowing Affair: Commentary from a *Brokeback Mountain* Fan," Mar.13, 2006, <http://www.afterelton.com/movies/2006/3/affair.html> (accessed Aug. 10, 2006).

Saxton, Alexander. "The Racial Trajectory of the Western Hero." *Amerasia Journal.* 11, no. 2 (Fall-Winter 1984): 67–79.

Schamus, James. Letter to the editor. "'Brokeback Mountain': An Exchange." James Schamus, Joel Conarroe, reply by Daniel Mendelsohn. *New York Review of Books* 53, no. 6 (Apr. 6, 2006), <http://www.nybooks.com/articles/18846> (accessed Aug. 18, 2006).

Schneider, Richard, Jr. "Not Quitting *Brokeback.*" *Gay and Lesbian Review Worldwide* 13, no. 2 (Mar. 2006): 10.

Sedgwick, Eve Kosofsky. *Between Men: English Literature and Male Homosocial Desire.* New York: Columbia University Press, 1985.

_____. *Epistemology of the Closet.* Berkeley: University of California Press, 1990.

_____. *Tendencies.* Durham, N.C.: Duke University Press, 1993.

Shapiro, Gregg. "Interview with *Brokeback Mountain* Director Ang Lee." AfterElton.Com, Dec. 9, 2005. <http://www.afterelton.com/movies/2005/12/anglee/html> (accessed June 16, 2006).

Shepherd, Paul. *Man in the Landscape: A Historic View of the Esthetics of Nature*, 2d. ed. Athens: University of Georgia Press, 2002.

Simmon, Scott. *The Invention of the Western Film: A Cultural History of the Genre's First Half-Century.* Cambridge, UK/New York: Cambridge University Press, 2003.

Slatta, Richard W. *Cowboys of the Americas.* New Haven, CT: Yale University Press, 1990.

Slotkin, Richard. *Gunfighter Nation: The Myth of the Frontier in Twentieth-Century America.* New York: Harper-Collins, 1992.

Smith, Andrew Brodie. *Shooting Cowboys and Indians: Silent Western Films, American Culture, and the Birth of Hollywood.* Boulder: University Press of Colorado, 2003.

Snell, Bruno. *The Discovery of the Mind in Greek Philosophy and Literature.* Trans. T. G. Rosenmeyer. New York: Dover Publications, 1982.

Sontag, Susan. "Notes on 'Camp.'" In *Camp: Queer Aesthetics and the Performing Subject*, ed. Fabio Cleto, 56. Ann Arbor: University of Michigan Press, 1999.

Steinberg, Sybil. "E. Annie Proulx: An American Odyssey." *Publishers Weekly* (June 3, 1996): 57–58.

Storr, Anthony. *Solitude: A Return to Self.* New York: Free Press, 1988.

Sullivan, Nikki. *A Critical Introduction to Queer Theory.* New York: New York University Press, 2003.

Swaab, Peter. "Homo on the Range." *New Statesman* (Dec. 12, 2005): 40–42.

Swazo, "A Preface to Silence: On the Duty of Vigilant Critique" <http://www.janushead.org/2–2/nswazo.cfm> (accessed Sept. 15, 2006).

Takaki, Ronald T. *A Different Mirror: A History of Multicultural America.* Boston: Little, Brown, 1993.

Theocritus. *The Idylls of Theocritus.* Trans. Thelma Sargent. New York: W.W. Norton & Co., 1982.

Traub, Valerie. *The Renaissance of Lesbianism in Renaissance England.* Cambridge: Cambridge University Press, 2002.

Trebay, Guy. "Cowboys, Just Like in the Movies." *New York Times*, Dec. 18, 2005, sec. 9: 1.

Tuan, Yi-Fu. *Space and Place: The Perspective of Experience.* Minneapolis: University of Minnesota Press, 1977.

Turan, Kenneth. "Breaking No Ground: Why 'Crash' won, why 'Brokeback' lost and how the Academy chose to play it safe." *Los Angeles Times.* Mar. 5, 2006.

Turner, Mark. "Compression and Representation." *Language and Literature* 15, no.1 (2006): 17–27.

_____, and Gilles Fauconnier. *The Way We Think: Conceptual Blending and the Mind's Hidden Complexities.* New York: Basic Books, 2002.

Valentine, James. "Naming the Other: Power, Politeness and the Inflation of Euphemism," *SociologicalResearch Online* 3, no. 4 (Dec. 31, 1998): 10.1, <http://www.socresonline.org.uk/3/4/7.html> (accessed Mar.15, 2006).

Vidal, Gore. *At Home: Essays 1982–1988.* New York: Random House, 1988.

Virgil. *The Eclogues and Georgics of Virgil.* Trans. C. Day Lewis. Garden City, NY: Anchor Books, 1964.

Wagner, James. "Cowboy — Origin and Early Use of the Term." *West Texas Historical Association Yearbook* 63 (1987): 91–100.

Warner, Michael. *Publics and Counterpublics.* New York: Zone Books, 2002.

Weiss, Joanna. "Considering the Source: *Brokeback Mountain* Turns a Short Story into a Hollywood First." *Boston Globe*, Dec. 11, 2005, N13.

Wirt, John. "*Brokeback Mountain* Tells an Unconventional Love Story." *The Advocate* 13 (January 2006):17.

Woods, Gregory. *A History of Gay Literature: The Male Tradition.* New Haven, CT: Yale University Press, 1998.

Zimmerman, Jens. "Quo: Vadis?: Literary Theory Beyond Postmodernism." *Christianity and Literature* 53, no. 4 (summer 2004): 495.

Žižek, Slavoj. *The Ticklish Subject: the Absent Centre of Political Ontolog.* London/New York: Verso, 1999.

About the Contributors

Henry Alley is a professor emeritus of literature in the Honors College at the University of Oregon. He has three published novels, *Through Glass* (1979) *The Lattice* (1986), and *Umbrella of Glass* (1988). Recently his *Leonardo and I* won the Gertrude Press 2006 Fiction Chapbook Award. His stories, over the past thirty years, have appeared in such journals as *Seattle Review, Virginia Quarterly Review*, and *Harrington Gay Men's Quarterly Fiction*. His articles have been published in *The Journal of Narrative Technique, Studies in the Novel, Twentieth Century Literature*, and *Kenyon Review*. His essay on versions of *Mrs. Dalloway*, including the film *The Hours*, is forthcoming from *Paper on Language and Literature*. The University of Delaware Press published his book-length study, *The Quest for Anonymity: The Novels of George Eliot*, in 1997.

Lisa Arellano is an assistant professor jointly appointed in American Studies and Women's, Gender, and Sexuality Studies at Colby College. She received her Ph.D. in modern thought and literature from Stanford University in 2004. She is currently working on a book entitled *Identity and Historiography: American's Lynching Past*. Her research and teaching interests include critical historiography and narrative analysis, comparative ethnic studies, and gender and sexuality studies.

Jen E. Boyle is an assistant professor of English and an affiliate of the graduate program in Screenwriting and Film Studies at Hollins University . She completed her M.A. in comparative literature and Ph.D. in English at the University of California, Irvine. In 2006–2007 she was a Pembroke Fellow at Brown University. Along with her principal scholarly work in cultural studies and early modern studies, she also publishes on embodiment and queer theory and culture.

Long T. Bui is currently pursuing a Ph.D. at the University of California, San Diego in the Ethnic Studies Department. Long received his B.A. in Asian American studies and political science from the University of California at Irvine. He is currently completing a project on identity politics in AIDS advocacy work in the San Diego area. His research interest focuses on the areas of public health, race, and sexuality. Also, he is also pursuing an alternative career in standup comedy ... fearfully.

Jessica L.W. Carey is a Ph.D. candidate in English at McMaster University in Hamilton, Ontario. Her research is primarily in ethics, and she will be seeking in her dissertation to tie together current understandings of animality, queer theory, and vegetarian subjectivity in the cultural framework of carnophallogocentrism. Her essay in this volume grew out of a graduate course in celebrity culture, which allowed her to

coalesce her personal interest in the film *Brokeback Mountain* with her critical investment in popular queer representations.

W. C. Harris is associate professor of English at Shippensburg University, where
he specializes in early and nineteenth-century American literature as well as gay and
lesbian studies. He is the author of *E Pluribus Unum: Nineteenth-Century American
Literature and the Constitutional Paradox* (2005), and his essays have appeared in journals such as *The Journal of American Culture, American Literary History, Arizona Quarterly*, and *The Walt Whitman Quarterly Review*, as well as in a previous McFarland
anthology, *The New Queer Aesthetic on Television* (2006).

John Ibson, a specialist in visual culture and in the cultural history of gender
and sexuality, is professor of American studies at California State University, Fuller-
ton. The author of *Will the World Break Your Heart? Dimensions and Consequences of
Irish-American Assimilation* (Garland, 1990) and *Picturing Men: A Century of Male
Relationships in Everyday American Photography* (University of Chicago Press, 2006),
he is currently working on a book about American manhood in the 1950s. A mere
two days after his first viewing of *Brokeback Mountain*, he happened to (literally)
bump into Heath Ledger at an L.A. photography show, an Ennis encounter that he
thinks surely informed his essay in some way or another.

Ginger Jones was a 2006–2007 Fulbright Scholar in American literature at the
University of Montenegro, and currently professor of English and Huie-Dellmon
Endowed Professor at Louisiana State University at Alexandria. Jones has written
book chapters and journal articles about ethnic and other minorities in Louisiana
("From Bella to Belle: The Southern/Italian Woman" and "Whose South Is It Anyway: The Impact of Ethnicity on Creativity"), and presented papers at conferences
in the United States and Europe. Her research interests include the impact of place
and socialization upon literature, and the poetry of exile. Jones' work has been published in *Cyclopedia of Literary Places, Critical Survey of Poetry, The Southern Humanities Review, The Sheridan Edwards Review, The Atlanta Review* and is forthcoming in
American Dreams: Comparative Dialogues in U.S. Studies and in *Science and Literature*.

John Kitterman teaches American literature and film courses at Ferrum Col-
lege. Most of his research has been in contemporary American culture and in African
American culture. His most recent publications have been "Home(land) Invasion:
Poe, Panic Rooms, and 9/11" in *The Journal of American Culture*; "The College
Dropout Speaks on Campuses" in *The Chronicle Review*; and "Identity Theft: Sim-
ulating Nirvana in Postmodern America" in the anthology *Finding the Ox: Essays on
Buddhism in America*, forthcoming from SUNY Press. He received both his under-
graduate degree and his Ph.D. in English from the University of Virginia. He has
also taught at Longwood University, Old Dominion University, and Norfolk State
University.

Dean Kostos is the author of *Last Supper of the Senses* (which was submitted for
a Pulitzer Prize), *The Sentence That Ends with a Comma* (which was taught at Duke
University), and the chapbook *Celestial Rust*. He co-edited the anthology *Mama's Boy:
Gay Men Write About Their Mothers*, a Lambda Book Award finalist. His poems have
appeared in *Barrow Street, Bloom, Boulevard, Chelsea*, the *Cimarron Review, The James
White Review*, Oprah Winfrey's website *Oxygen, Rattapallax*, the *Southwest Review*,
the *Western Humanities Review*, and elsewhere. He has taught poetry writing at the

Gallatin School of NYU, The Columbia Scholastic Press Association, Gotham Writers' Workshop, The Great Lakes Colleges Association, Pratt University, and Teachers & Writers Collaborative.

Xinghua Li is a Ph.D. candidate in the Department of Communication Studies at the University of Iowa. She received her B.A. in advertising from Fudan University in Shanghai , China in 2003 and her M.A. in media studies from the University of Iowa in 2005. She is interested in cultural/political theory informed by poststructuralism and psychoanalysis, and she hopes to use them to explain contemporary cultural phenomena and seek redemptive values in popular culture. To contact her, please send email to: xinghli81@yahoo.com.

Charles Eliot Mehler decided in the fall of 2002 to return to school to study theatre, after nearly twenty years of teaching mathematics. In May 2004, Mehler earned his MA in Speech/Theatre from Kansas State University, and is currently a Ph.D. candidate in theatre at Louisiana State University. As a playwright, Mehler has served as librettist and composer for the musical plays *Wealth, and How Not to Avoid It* (a musical adaptation of Shaw's *Major Barbara*) and *Poster Children*. He wrote the lyrics for *Hard Road* (book by Jane Boyd Wendling) and *Downtown* (book by Barbara Georgans). He is also the author of the non-musical plays *Flip-Flop* and *Jack from Will and Grace,* as well as a verse translation of Alfred Jarry's *Ubu Roi.* Mehler is currently at work on verse translations of Moliere's *Critique of the School for Wives* and *Impromptu at Versailles.*

Hiram Perez is an assistant professor of English at William Paterson University. He also teaches Women's Studies and African American Studies. Research interests include African American literature, critical race theory, immigration, popular culture, the psychoanalysis of race, and queer theory. His work has appeared in *Transformations: The Journal of Inclusive Scholarship and Pedagogy, Social Text, Cineaste,* and in the collection *East Main Street: Asian American Popular Culture.* Currently, he is completing a book on the relationship between shame and racial embodiment. His next project investigates racialized desire as it is constructed and articulated through formations of gay cosmopolitanism. Both his scholarship and his teaching seek to recuperate identity politics.

Jim Stacy holds a Ph.D. in performance studies from New York University where he served as a Shubert Fellow. He has been published in the *Journal of American Drama and Theatre, Theatre Journal, Theatre Studies, Theatre Symposium,* and *Southern Theatre* and has presented papers at the Southeastern Theatre Conference, the Southwest Theatre and Film Association Conference, the Southern States Communication Association, and the William Inge Festival. He has taught theatre and communication courses at Northwestern State University of Louisiana, Northern Kentucky University, Loyola University of Chicago, DePaul University, and LSU-Alexandria where he is currently an associate professor of theatre/communication studies. Other experience includes serving as editor-in-chief for Thinkwell (an online educational publisher) and as a copyeditor for the former Holt, Rinehart and Winston.

Noah Tsika is currently a graduate student in cinema studies at New York University, Tisch School of the Arts. He earned his undergraduate degree in Film and Television Studies from Dartmouth College, where he received the Maurice Rapf

Award. His research interests include queer reception practice, stardom, and Hollywood cinema, and he has written on film for a variety of publications including *Cineaste*. He is currently completing a book-length popular biography of the actress Anne Revere, as well as a novel. He lives in New York.

Index

LIVERPOOL JOHN MOORES UNIVERSITY
Aldham Robarts L.R.C.
TEL 0151 231 3701/3634